ADVANCED MICROSOFT® WORD®

ADVANCED MICROSOFT® WORD®

Mark Brownstein

Osborne **McGraw-Hill**
Berkeley, California

Osborne **McGraw-Hill**
2600 Tenth Streeet
Berkeley, California 94710
U.S.A.

For information on translations and book distributors outside of the U.S.A.,
please write to Osborne **McGraw-Hill** at the above address.

A complete list of trademarks appears on page 323.

ADVANCED MICROSOFT® WORD®

234567890 **DODO** 8987

ISBN 0-07-881010-8

To Barbara and Charles, two great kids, and to Vonnie, who helped make them so special.

CONTENTS

ACKNOWLEDGMENTS

Writing a book takes a lot more than just sitting in front of a typewriter, word processor, notepad, or whatever tool an author uses. A book of this type takes effort from many different people.

I would like to thank the good people at the Waggener Group, Microsoft's public relations firm, for their willing assistance in providing me the copies of Word 3.0 and the mouse I needed to write this book. I would like to thank Microsoft for supporting a "competing" book. Microsoft's technical support staff was excellent; they indicated areas where special attention was needed and helped me to make this book even more relevant to new and experienced readers.

The folks at Osborne/McGraw-Hill were also great. I want to thank Jean Stein for suggesting the book and riding herd on me as I wrote it. Thanks to Liz Fisher for all of her many questions about the figures. And thanks to the technical reviewer whose very few comments were on target. I'd like to thank the copy desk for cleaning up my drafts and not bothering me with silly questions.

I'm also grateful to NCR and NEC for the use of their systems and am especially grateful to Cordata for the use of their laser printer.

I'd like to thank my kids, Charles and Barbara, for forfeiting part of their short summer vacation so that Daddy could write the book. I'd like to thank my wife, Vonnie, for her support and for putting up with the long hours and deadline pressure.

Finally, I'd like to thank you, the reader, for buying this book and proving that all the effort was worthwhile.

INTRODUCTION

Many authors look forward to writing the introductions to their books. This is true for me also. Contrary to what you may expect, and somewhat contrary to logic, the introduction is usually one of the last parts of a book to be written. This is because an author may not really know, going into a book, how it will develop: what explanations are needed, what conventions are used for text, instructions, and so on. The goal of the introduction is to put the book that follows into perspective for the reader.

When I was approached to write a book on Microsoft Word, I was not overly enthusiastic about the project. I had just finishing writing *Advanced Guide to MultiMate and MultiMate Advantage* and really liked the program. Word was a package somewhat foreign to my experience with many different word processors: it worked best with a mouse, didn't give you character or line numbers, and had odd menus and strange terminology.

But I looked at Word again. Version 3.0 had been released and boasted dozens of improvements over Version 2.0. Microsoft provided me with a copy of Word 3.0 (thanks, Microsoft), and I loaded it onto my system. The first good thing I noticed was that copy protection had been removed — I didn't have to worry about losing Word if the system somehow ate it. The second thing I noticed was that this version was considerably faster than 2.0.

So I began a crash course in Word 3.0. I wrote letters, made forms, designed columns — did the things that are a real headache using most word processing programs.

A call to Microsoft's excellent technical support staff gave me the perspective I needed to really appreciate Word: Microsoft Word is not a word processing program. Although I address this point near the close of this book, it's also worth discussing here. It's a point that any dyed-in-the-wool, traditional word processor user (like me) should stop and consider.

Microsoft Word is a page processing program. It isn't designed just to put words onto paper. The real value of Microsoft Word is the flexibility it gives you in allowing you to mix type sizes, styles, and characteristics easily and with a fairly good approximation of what the actual print will look like. If you have a dot matrix printer (including laser printers, which, when you boil it all down, are just fancy, high-performance dot matrix printers) that allows you to use different-sized fonts, you will quickly appreciate the benefits a page processor provides.

For example, if you are producing an in-house newsletter, you can set the heading in an 18- or 24-point typeface and drop into a readable 8-, 10-, or 12-point body style. Headlines can be in another type size, or merely a bold version of your body text. But no matter which type styles you use, the system can automatically adjust the vertical spacing to make your printed page look good. This is beyond the capabilities of most word processors.

As I continued to use Word, I was sometimes frustrated by the user interface. When I wanted to save a file, I wanted to tell the system to do just that, not to have to select Transfer Save and then type in a name. Using a mouse, this took three steps. I was used to hitting a single key combination and having the save performed for me.

Many of Word's menus are two or more levels deep. If you use a mouse, you have to click the buttons a lot. I'm not a mouse person. I like to keep my hands on a keyboard. Taking my hands off the keys, finding a mouse, and then carefully moving it around my cluttered desk was a chore I preferred to avoid. Although my mouse was hooked to the system, I barely used it at all; I found it faster to press the keys to select a command, and almost as fast to use the function keys to highlight text.

I found that for the basic things—text input and editing—Word was not unusual. Deletions, insertions, moves, copies, and searches were all fairly easy to do. Using the scrap takes some getting used to, but is an efficient way to move or copy text from one area to another.

When I got beyond basics, however, I saw how Word really shines. Style sheets, for example, became an extremely useful part of my writing regimen. I quickly developed a specific style that I applied to my section headings, a different style for body text, a third style for my page headers, and yet another for my tips and notes. I made use of the system's hidden characters to set up an index of illustrations and of section headings for each chapter.

The system's gallery was a tremendous help. Words and phrases I used frequently were saved into the gallery (actually a macro facility) where they could be called up with a few keystrokes. For example, every time I wanted to type Microsoft Word, I just typed mw and then pressed F3. The system automatically replaced my two letters with two words. My computer-generated letterhead and a date line were automatically inserted after I had typed just two letters.

When used to its fullest, Microsoft Word is a great time-saver. It gives you tremendous flexibility in your document preparation and provides you with a great deal of power. All but the first chapter of this book was written using Microsoft Word exclusively. The writing was done on an NCR PC4 computer. A second computer, an NEC APC-III, was used to test all the examples. This system was also used to capture the graphics used in this book. All the figures and illustrations were captured using a program called Inset. The graphics were printed on a Cordata Laser 300 printer.

As I wrote the book, I began appreciating more and more the great features of Word. It takes quite a bit for this jaded word processing skeptic to say that he really likes a word processing program, but it is now easy to say—I really do like Microsoft Word.

I've been doing word processing almost continuously since the first wave of semi-affordable word processing equipment became available in the late seventies. I started with a system that had a 31 character display, moved up to one with 16 lines, and finally got into CP/M and **PCDOS** word processing. For quite some time, I resisted the move from dedicated word processors to word processing programs for personal computers primarily because they didn't have the power of the dedicated systems. This is no longer true.

After using (or at least trying) dozens of word processing programs, I realized that a few actually surpassed the dedicated machines I was used to. Microsoft Word certainly does. It makes many of the difficult jobs simple. I assume that many word processor operators who will be the eventual users of this book have had the same experience and developed the same basic biases. Microsoft Word is an excellent word processing package; don't feel apprehensive about leaving a dedicated system, because Word *will* work for you.

My goal when I took on this writing project was to write a book that was of value to the reader. I wanted to explain how to use the special features that have made Word so valuable to me. I wanted to address the areas of confusion that Microsoft's technical support staff indicated were frequent problems. My goal was to make this book, and Microsoft Word, of maximum value to you. I hope I succeeded.

So that you can get the most out of Microsoft Word, I am making available a range of products that enhance the use of this package. These include instructions and printer definition tables for additional laser printers, basic merge documents and glossary listings for quick and easy preparation of form letters, input devices to speed the entry of text and commands, and other utilities.

For a catalog or further information, send $2.50 to cover postage and handling to:

Mark Brownstein
P.O. Box 3904
Northridge, CA 91323

INSTALLATION AND SETUP

If you have just gotten your copy of Microsoft Word, you're probably eager to load it on your computer. Resist the temptation for now. If you are already using Word, feel free to skip this section, although you may possibly miss some options that may make start-up easier for you. This chapter demonstrates some of the choices you can make to tailor your version of Word to best fit your needs, so that Word can work almost as an extension of yourself.

BACKING UP YOUR DISKS
(VERSION 3.0 ONLY)

Before you do anything, you must back up your disks. Versions 1.0 and 2.0 of Microsoft Word don't allow you to set up your system using backups, but Microsoft has wisely removed copy protection from version 3.0 of Word. This helps prevent you from recording over the supplied programs. You should always make a copy of all your programs and then run the programs from your backup disks.

The reason for this concern is simple: floppy disks are extremely vulnerable to magnetic fields (such as the field created by a fluorescent light or magnet, for example), and they can also wear out. Many things can make a floppy disk fail. It doesn't happen very often, but you can be sure that it will happen when you can least afford it. Although Microsoft will replace defective disks, you probably will not want to wait for them to send you a replacement disk.

TIP: Be sure to keep your originals in a safe place, away from your backup copies. This protects your originals from whatever might damage your backup disks. Putting your eggs in many baskets is the best way to protect yourself from data loss. ■

If you are using Word on a hard disk system, you can install the program without using a backup. For versions 2.1 and earlier, you must use your original to install the program. The few minutes it takes to back up version 3.0 can be extremely valuable if anything ever goes wrong with your hard disk drive or your original disks. To make backup copies, follow the directions in your computer's manual.

INSTALLING WORD

A number of choices can be made to make the start-up of Word fit your needs. If you have a floppy disk system, do you want to bring up Word on a system disk and automatically load the program every time you turn on the computer? If you use a hard disk, do you want the system to load Word automatically every time you turn on the computer? Do you want to see your formatting marks as you edit a document, or is a "clean" screen preferable?

Before you make these choices, you must make another choice. Will you run Word on a floppy disk system or a hard disk system? Word is a fairly large program. Including the dictionary and utilities, it takes up more than one disk. You may be able to get by with only the word processing features, but if you want to use the spelling checking or hyphenation features, the disk swapping involved can become quite a nuisance.

Putting the entire program, including dictionary and utilities, onto a single hard drive provides the computer with very fast access to all the programs and data it needs to perform any function you might select. On this basis alone a hard disk is a tremendous help. Another advantage of having a hard disk is your system's ability to boot automatically from the hard disk. To start your computer using a hard disk system, you only have to turn on the power, make sure that your floppy drive door is open, and wait until the system comes up. In addition, you can store thousands of pages of documents on a hard disk drive. It makes sense to back up all the documents onto floppy disks, but as a readily available, rapidly accessed file system, a hard disk drive is hard to beat.

Finally, the cost of hard disks may be less than you expect. At the time of this writing, a 10 MB (10 million byte) drive is available for as little as $350, and a 20 MB drive costs only about $100 more. The added convenience and time savings of using a hard disk drive should quickly make this your third most important computer purchase. (The first most important is the computer itself; the second is Word.) This book assumes that most users operate a hard disk system.

Installing on a Floppy Disk System

If you want to start your computer with Word, you should first make a formatted system disk on which to copy the Word program. To do this, put your DOS startup disk in the A: drive, and a blank disk in the B: drive. Boot DOS in the A: drive, making sure both drive doors are closed.

Type: **Format B: \s**

Depending upon your system and which version of DOS you use, the system prompts you to place a blank disk in the B: drive and press a key to begin formatting. Once this is done, the disk in the B: drive spins, and after a short time the system reports that formatting is complete, tells you how many bytes are available, and asks if you want to format another disk. Tell the system you don't want to make another formatted system disk by pressing N.

Next, insert the copy of your Word utility disk into the A: drive, and

Type: **setup** RETURN

to begin installation of your copy of Word. If you use Word 2.0, the screen looks like the one at the top of the following page.

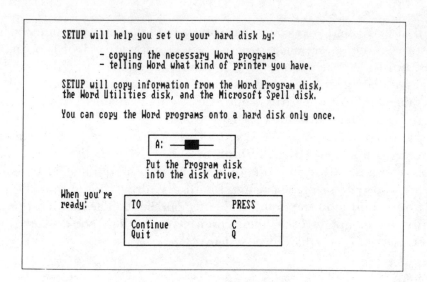

If you use Word 3.0, the screen looks like this:

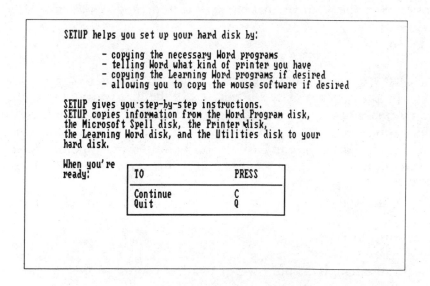

Follow the system's prompts to install the program onto your system.

Installing on a Hard Disk System

Once your system is up and running, insert the Word utility disk into the A: drive and

Type: **setup a:** RETURN

The system checks that you have a hard disk and produces one of the screens illustrated previously (depending upon which version of Word you are installing).

If you are upgrading from version 2.0 to version 3.0, the system gives you the option of removing version 2.0 from a hard disk to a floppy disk or deleting it completely. Because Word 2.0 is a copy-protected program, the disk used to load it onto the system has a built-in counter, allowing you to install the program only once. If you wish to reuse version 2.0, you must remove the program from the hard disk, increasing the counter on the installation disk by 1 and enabling the install disk to put the program onto this (or another) system. However, it should be noted that version 3.0 is fully compatible with all features and functions recorded in documents prepared with version 2.0, so there should be little or no need to use version 2.0 again. If for some reason you want to remove version 2.0, do so now, following the system prompts.

Follow the additional system prompts to install Word and the associated files on your hard disk system. If you are installing Word onto your system for the first time, you should follow the items in the Setup Menu, as shown in Figure 1-1.

NOTE: You don't need to copy the Learning Word program onto your hard disk. The system allows you to run the program from the floppy disk in A: drive — this may save some space on the hard disk drive. However, the first time you request help from the system, the system loads the contents of this disk onto the hard disk. ∎

As you copy the Word and Spell programs onto your hard disk, the system asks you for the name of a directory to which to load the programs. In most cases the most logical choice for subdirectory names is Word. If you haven't already made a subdirectory called Word, the system will make one for you.

```
                        SETUP MENU

   TO                                              PRESS
  ┌─────────────────────────────────────────────────────┐
  │ Copy the Word and Spell programs onto the hard disk.   W │
  │                                                       │
  │ Copy the Learning Word program onto the hard disk.     L │
  │                                                       │
  │ Copy printer information onto the hard disk.           P │
  │                                                       │
  │ Copy mouse information onto the hard disk.             M │
  │                                                       │
  │ Quit SETUP                                             Q │
  └─────────────────────────────────────────────────────┘

   If you're using SETUP for the first time, do these in order.
```

Figure 1-1.   The Setup Menu for version 3.0

Loading Word Automatically at Power On

If you do mostly word processing, it may be worthwhile to save a step and automatically load Word when you power up the system. In order to do this, you must update the AUTOEXEC.BAT file on your boot disk or on your hard drive's boot directory.

   If you have a floppy disk system, first copy the AUTOEXEC.BAT file from your original boot disk onto the Word boot disk. To do this, insert your original boot disk in the A: drive and the Word boot disk in the B: drive and

Type: **copy a:autoexec.bat b:** RETURN

The system prompts, "1 File(s) copied." If you use a hard disk system, copy your AUTOEXEC.BAT file from your boot directory to the Word directory.

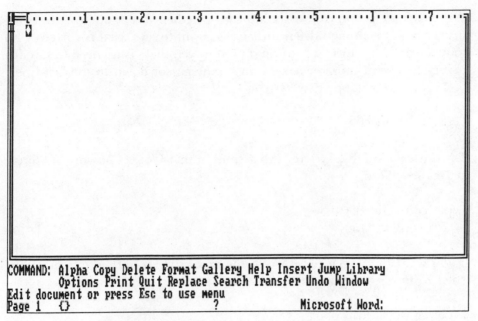

```
COMMAND: Alpha Copy Delete Format Gallery Help Insert Jump Library
         Options Print Quit Replace Search Transfer Undo Window
Edit document or press Esc to use menu
Page 1   {}                        ?              Microsoft Word:
```

Figure 1-2.   The Edit screen

Assuming you are loading Word from the word subdirectory,

Type: **copy c: \autoexec.bat c: \word**

After following the appropriate steps for your system, insert the Word boot disk into the A: drive or change directories to get to the Word directory. To start Word,

Type: **word** RETURN

The Word Title screen appears, followed soon after by the Word Edit screen, as shown in Figure 1-2.

Next, load your AUTOEXEC.BAT file into Word so that it can be edited. For the purposes of this editing session, you won't be using the mouse or any advanced features. To load the file,

Type: ESC **t l autoexec.bat** RETURN

If the system prompts you to indicate whether you want to lose edits, answer *n*. (This prompt determines if you want to save what is currently on your screen; since there's nothing on screen yet, there is no need to save it.) Using the cursor movement keys, move the cursor down to the last line.

If you use a floppy disk system,

Type: **word** RETURN

If you use a hard disk system, and assuming that Word is on your subdirectory called Word,

Type: **cd \word** RETURN
     word RETURN

If you want the system to return to the main subdirectory after you've finished running Word, add the following line:

Type: **cd **RETURN

Next, review your input to make sure you have made no errors and

Type: **ts autoexec.bat**

Don't press RETURN yet. Once AUTOEXEC.BAT has been typed in as the name of the file to save, you must tell the system that you don't want to save the file as a formatted file. (A *formatted file* contains special information about the appearance of this document, and these codes may make this file nonexecutable.) Press TAB to move to the Formatted field and

Type: **n** RETURN

The file is now saved as an executable file that can automatically load Word every time you start the computer.

The last step is to exit Word and, if you have a hard disk system, to move the file to the main subdirectory. To exit Word,

Type: ESC **q** RETURN

The system returns you to DOS. Finally, if you have a hard disk system,

Type: **copy autoexec.bat c:** \RETURN

To test the operation of this file, you may wish to turn off the system and then restart it, or you can use the CTRL-ALT-DEL key combination to cause the system to warm boot. (A *key combination,* in which the relevant keys are pressed simultaneously, is always indicated by hyphens between keys.)

START-UP OPTIONS

At first glance, it appears that Word doesn't give you much choice in your start-up parameters. However, this isn't so. Word automatically loads the system with the configuration you used the last time you used Word. In addition, the system can determine what type of graphics card is installed in your computer.

   If you have a color card, you may start the system configured for color. To do this,

Type: **word s/c** RETURN

If you use a Hercules or Hercules-compatible monochrome card, you can get more characters on a line by typing word /h RETURN when you load the program. These formats can, of course, be recorded into your AUTO-EXEC.BAT file.

Ruler and Window Options

In addition to establishing the initial start-up menus, you can also have the system start Word configured to other particular needs. Normally, when Word begins, the screen displays a text area with a box border. The line, or ruler, at the top can be set to show the format for page width and tabs if you set this default. In order to do so, start the Word program. Next,

Type: ESC **w o**

This brings you to the Window options at the bottom of the screen, as shown in Figure 1-3. You can tab to the "ruler: Yes No" prompt, or you can quickly get to it by pressing SHIFT-TAB. To change your default to

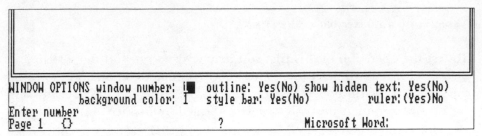

```
WINDOW OPTIONS window number: 1█  outline: Yes(No) show hidden text: Yes(No)
               background color: 1   style bar: Yes(No)          ruler: (Yes)No
Enter number
Page 1   {}                          ?               Microsoft Word:
```

Figure 1-3.   The Window options

show the ruler, answer *y* to the prompt. The ruler at the top of the screen looks like this:

```
║═[·········1·········2·········3·········4·········5·········]·········7·····⌐
  ░
  □
```

The Style Bar option, which indicates which style you have attached to your document, the Show Hidden Text option, and the Outline option are beyond the scope of this chapter and are treated in more detail in Chapters 11 and 12. The Background Color option can be saved for window 1 only if you have a color graphics card and have loaded Word using the WORD/C command. To change this setting, tab to this field and then press the RIGHT ARROW key to list the available background colors. Once you've made your selection, type in the number of your choice.

Once you've made all desired changes,

Type: RETURN

to save them. Unless you change these options before you quit the current session, these options will be in effect the next time you start Word.

Other Options

A variety of other options are available when using Word. To get to some basic options,

Type: ESC o

The bottom of the screen looks like this:

```
┌──────────────────────────────────────────────────────────────┐
│                                                                │
│                                                                │
│OPTIONS visible: None Partial Complete  printer display:(Yes)No  menu:(Yes)No │
│     default tab width: 0.5"    measure:(In)Cm P10 P12 Pt             mute: Yes(No)│
│Select option                                                   │
│Page 1    ◇                      ?              Microsoft Word:  │
└──────────────────────────────────────────────────────────────┘
```

The Visible option allows you to specify the types of formatting characters visible on your screen during an edit. If you select None, only text is displayed on the screen — paragraph marks and other symbols within a document are not displayed. If you select Partial, some, but not all, formatting symbols are displayed: tabs, paragraph marks, and limited formatting codes. This may be useful if you are setting up tables or columns, since you can more easily tell where to place your characters or formatting commands. Finally, Complete shows all formatting and text marks.

The Printer Display option allows you to view the document as it will appear when printed. Microsoft recommends that this default be set to No, since the character alignment is not accurate in other than 10 pitch (10 characters per inch) mode.

The Menu option allows you to choose to display the menu at the bottom of the screen. If you tell the system that you don't want the menu, you will have three extra lines visible for editing. When you need to see the menu, you can call it up by pressing ESC or by moving the mouse into the menu area and touching the left mouse button. Once you're comfortable with Word, you will probably prefer to set this default to No.

The Default Tab Width option sets the distance between the preset tabs. Word automatically sets up your documents with such tabs — setting the default (in inches) tells the system the desired width of each tab.

The Measure option allows you to tell the system which unit you want to use when setting tabs and ruler. The default is In (inches), and Word computes your settings based on inches. If you are most comfortable with the metric measurements, you may prefer to change your measure to Cm (centimeters). P10 represents 10 pitch characters, while P12 represents 12 pitch. Pt uses a *point* measure. This may be a new term to many WORD users. The term is most often used in the printing and typesetting industries and is a measure of character size. Seventy-two points make an inch;

thus, if you were to set up your measure in terms of points, you would be able to use these fine divisions to produce very well spaced characters (if your printer supports the fine divisions).

Finally, the Mute option indicates whether you want the system to beep when you have entered a command that it doesn't understand. You should probably use this feature.

Although other options can be set here, they are discussed later in the appropriate chapters. You should remember, however, that whatever settings you have made when you finish your current editing session will be in effect the next time you start Word. You can continually customize your system as you go along to most closely meet your exact needs.

THE KEYBOARD AND THE MOUSE

If the title of this chapter sounds something like that for a children's story, it's not by accident. "The Tortoise and the Hare" might be a good analogy for the distinction between the keyboard and the mouse. The tortoise is something like the keyboard: large, slow, but consistent, and capable of reaching the goal. The hare and the mouse, besides being zoologically related, both have their similarities: they're fast, efficient, and many times not quite the right tool for the job.

Two basic functions are performed by the mouse used for Microsoft Word. First, the mouse acts as a pointer: it points at functions or commands you wish to select or points at the beginning and end of text blocks you wish to highlight, identifying an area on which you want to act. Second, the mouse functions as a selection device. Microsoft Word recognizes two buttons, left and right, on a compatible mouse. (Note that many mice from other manufacturers have three buttons; when this is the case, Word doesn't recognize the middle button.) In addition to recognizing either left or right, the system also assigns a particular meaning to the combination of the two.

In many ways, the mouse can be thought of as an enhancement of the keyboard. Where you may normally have to press special function keys or key combinations to accomplish a particular task, the mouse may be able to accomplish the same task when you move it to a selection menu or screen area and press the appropriate button.

SELECTING TEXT

Any text that can be selected using the keyboard can be selected using the mouse. Of the basic keyboard commands, the function keys, F6 through F10, select most of the text you want to highlight. Using these keys, you can select anywhere from a single word to an entire document. The various keystrokes and their effect are shown in Table 2-1. Thus, to select a single word to the right of the cursor, you would press F8; to select a word to the left of the cursor, you would press F7, and so on.

Each keystroke highlights only the amount of text you have selected. Whenever you make a new selection, any highlights from other areas are removed. If you wanted to highlight two sentences, for example, you couldn't do so simply by pressing F9 twice. If you wanted to highlight two characters, you couldn't do so by pressing the RIGHT ARROW key twice.

In order to highlight more than one section of text at a time, you must be able to extend a highlight. F6 invokes the Extend function. Extend is a toggle. When you press F6 to turn on (toggle on) the feature, all the areas you indicate are highlighted. Once you process the highlighted text (copy, move, delete, and so on), the Extend feature is toggled off. When you are in Extend mode, the letters *EX* appear at the bottom of the screen, as shown at the top of the next page.

To Highlight	Press
Character left	LEFT ARROW
Character right	RIGHT ARROW
Word left	F7
Word right	F8
Sentence	F9
Next sentence	SHIFT-F8
Previous sentence	SHIFT-F7
Current line	SHIFT-F9
Line above	UP ARROW
Line below	DOWN ARROW
Next paragraph	F10
Whole document	SHIFT-F10

Table 2-1.   Selecting Text Using Keyboard Commands

```
Page 1  {}                    ?        EX Microsoft Word: WORD.DOC
```

Thus, to highlight any amount of text, first press F6 and then press the appropriate function or cursor movement key to select text. (Note: If you want to highlight large sections of text, you can use the UP ARROW or DOWN ARROW key in combination with F6.)

Using a Mouse

You can also use a mouse to select any amount of text you desire. At the left side of the screen are three distinct areas, although there is no obvious visible difference between them until you need to take advantage of the features. When you use a mouse, the location of the mouse on the screen is represented by an arrow or a blinking box, depending upon whether you are using Word in a text or color (character) mode.

Figure 2-1 shows what the mouse pointer looks like on a blank screen.

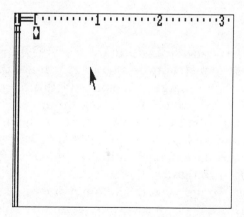

Figure 2-1. The mouse pointer on the screen

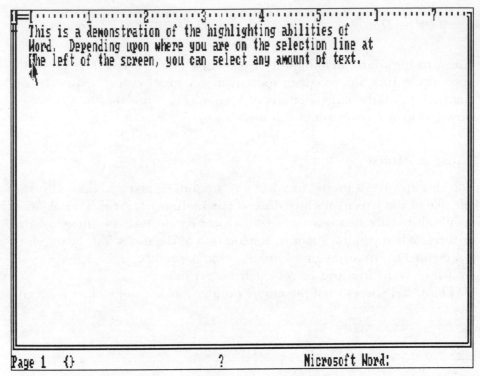

Figure 2-2. Selected area after left mouse button has been pressed

Figure 2-2 shows the arrow, still within the text area, plus the area selected by touching the left mouse button. Figure 2-3 shows the mouse pointer further to the left in the margin. A mouse in this area is used to select larger sections of text. You should note that the arrow is now pointing to the right. Careful attention to the arrow's direction helps you to assess the amount of text you are selecting. Figure 2-4 shows the arrow when it is moved to the left margin. At this position, the mouse is used to give commands for scrolling through text.

Figure 2-5 demonstrates what the mouse pointer looks like in the color (character) mode. Instead of an arrow, a rectangular block indicates the position of the mouse. This block increases in size as you enter each margin area — that is, when the mouse location is on the far left margin, the cursor is full height; when it is in the selection area, it is about two-thirds height; and when it is in the regular text area, it drops to about one-third height.

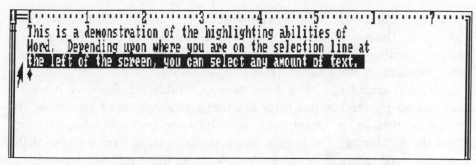

Figure 2-3.   Position of pointer for selecting larger areas of text

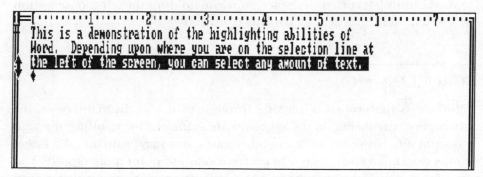

Figure 2-4.   Position of pointer for scrolling through text

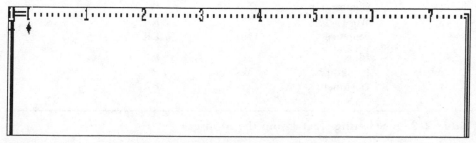

Figure 2-5.   Mouse pointer in color (character) mode

The area between the left margin and the text area is called the *selection bar*. Again, the mouse pointer changes its direction or size to indicate that it is now pointing into the selection bar. Table 2-2 lists the basic mouse controls required to make a variety of text selections.

To select areas larger than those shown in Table 2-2, you need not press F6. In order to select as much (or as little) text as you need, just move the mouse pointer to the beginning (or end) of the text you want to select. Press the left button and hold it down while moving over the rest of the text you wish to highlight. As you do this, the highlight expands to include all text between the point you first marked and the present location of the cursor. Finally, release the button when you have reached the end (or beginning) of the highlighted text. The next time you press a mouse button, the selection is cancelled, and you must start all over again.

To select more than a screen at a time, you can move the mouse pointer to the bottom left corner of the screen while holding the left mouse button down. The screen begins to scroll text upward.

SCROLLING

Scrolling is the process of moving through your text. In many cases, the cursor movement keys on the keyboard are sufficient for scrolling through a document. However, in many other cases you may want to take larger jumps through a document or to get from point to point more rapidly. You may, for example, be near the end of a long document and want to return to the beginning. Using the UP ARROW key to move the cursor to the top of

Selection Desired	Selection Bar	Button(s)
Character	No	L
Word	No	R
Sentence	No	LR
Line	Yes	L
Paragraph	Yes	R
Document	Yes	LR

Table 2-2.   Selecting Text Using the Mouse

Scroll Desired	Keystrokes Needed
Up in document	PGUP
Down in document	PGDN
Start of document	CTRL-PGUP
End of document	CTRL-PGDN
Left side of line	CTRL-CURSOR LEFT
Right side of line	CTRL-CURSOR RIGHT
Up one line	CURSOR UP (scroll lock on)
Down one line	CURSOR DOWN (scroll lock on)
Left 1/3 of window	CURSOR LEFT (scroll lock on)
Right 1/3 of window	CURSOR RIGHT (scroll lock on)

Table 2-3.   Scrolling Text Using Keyboard Commands

the screen and holding the key down to keep it there can get the job done, but there's an easier way: pressing CTRL-PGUP. A list of the key combinations for rapid scrolling is shown in Table 2-3.

The key combinations that require the scroll lock on only work if there is more than a full screen of text. For example, if you were working on a document 100 characters wide, putting the scroll lock on and pressing CTRL-RT ARROW would move the the contents of the screen to the right. Similarly, if you had more than 24 lines of text, you could use the UP ARROW and DOWN ARROW to move the contents of the window rather than simply to move the cursor up or down in text. In other words, this option moves the page of text on the screen; it doesn't just move the cursor over stationary text.

Using the Mouse

The mouse does an excellent job of scrolling through a document. The mouse pointer is used in conjunction with the scroll bars at the left and bottom corners of the screen. These bars indicate the borders of the window you are editing.

Scrolling Horizontally   If you look closely at the scroll bar on the left side of your screen, you will see a small line, as shown in the following illustration.

This scroll line shows you where in your document your current window is. If you had a long document, for example, and were near the end of the document, the scroll line would be near the bottom of the window.

There are two basic ways to make use of the scroll line. You can scroll text one window (or less) at a time. To do this, move the mouse pointer to the scroll bar. To tell the system how many lines you want to scroll, move the arrow so that it points at the distance you want to move. For example, if you moved the arrow to the bottom of the scroll bar, you could scroll a screen at a time. Moving it to the middle of the scroll bar scrolls the screen about one-half the length of the window at a time.

Pressing the right button moves your text up. Pressing the left button moves your text down on the page. This may not be an intuitive choice. However, if you visualize the arrows as being a continuation of the arrows that run across the bottom of the screen, it will become clear that a right arrow points down and a left arrow points up.

If you prefer to move through large sections of a document, you can move the pointer to the approximate portion of the document you are trying to find (that is, if you want to move to the middle of a document, you position the pointer at the middle of the scroll bar). Next, press the left and right mouse buttons at the same time, and you are moved to the desired section of the document. You may have to use the left and right mouse buttons to fine tune your selection and bring you to the exact position you desire.

Scrolling Vertically   If you had a document wider than your screen, you would probably want to scroll from side to side to be able to see the parts that weren't displayed on your screen. To do this, you would make use of the bottom scroll bar. As with the horizontal scrolls, the further you move from a starting position, the more area you scroll. For example, if you placed the mouse cursor at the bottom right margin, you would scroll roughly a screen width each time you pressed the mouse button. Moving the cursor to the middle of the scroll bar would scroll about one-half screen at a time. Pressing the left button moves the screen to the left. Similarly, the right button scrolls the screen to the right. Unlike the horizontal scroll, the vertical scroll selections can't be used to move quickly to the beginning or end of a document.

ADDITIONAL MOUSE FUNCTIONS

The mouse is capable of many functions besides scrolling and highlighting text. In Microsoft Word, for example, it can perform some functions that can't be performed using the keyboard. For example, you may wish to copy a particular format or lettering style from one area of text to another. Using the mouse, you can quickly copy a format. There is no equivalent method on the keyboard. The mouse is also useful for entering commands and for moving and copying text. Once you get used to using a mouse, you may become very comfortable doing pointing, moving, editing, selecting, and formatting with the mouse.

However, if you are a "keyboard person," you may find the mouse something of a nuisance, since you have to take your hands off the keyboard to enter simple commands. Microsoft Word has relatively many menus. For example, to save a document, you can't just type in a simple SAVE command. You must first press ESC, press T for "transfer," press S for "save," and then type in a name for the document or press RETURN to keep the name already assigned to the document. In effect, you're following many steps to accomplish something that should be simple.

Using a mouse, you have to go through roughly the same routine. At first, it may seem simpler to aim and select with the mouse. However, in most cases Microsoft allows you to enter the first letter of each command to select an option from each menu or to select text by using a simple key sequence (for example, ALT-B selects bold print and bypasses two menus).

You can function very well without a mouse, although if you do have a mouse, you have rapid access to most functions and can perform some more easily than you can with the keyboard. Ultimately, however, you will probably find that the mouse works best for special functions and the keyboard "shortcuts" are best for much of your command entry. In many cases, both mouse and keyboard are appropriate tools for the functions discussed in this book. It will be up to you to determine which method most closely suits your needs. That's the real goal of this book: to tailor Microsoft Word to your particular needs and style.

EDITING

Editing text with Microsoft Word is quite different from editing with most other word processors. Although in both cases you type in text and perform functions in a similar manner, the process of creating and adjusting text using Word differs from most other word processing programs. If you are accustomed to using other word processing software, you may have a more difficult time learning and adjusting to Word than someone who hasn't used a word processor before. You should therefore read the next section before turning to the subsequent sections.

LINE CREATION VERSUS
PAGE CREATION

With most other word processors, you are dealing in discrete, distinct characters. In most cases you are primarily concerned with typing 65 characters per line and about 54 lines per page. Most word processors provide information on the screen that tells you exactly where your cursor is. You can tell at a glance what page you are on and where in the page you are.

When you begin typing your first document with Microsoft Word, you may be disconcerted to find that very little of this information is provided. Note that the top of the screen has a ruler line. This was selected as a default setting when the system was last used. It is an easy way to tell how far into a page your text is, but may not be particularly useful to you.

At the left of the screen, a line (referred to in Microsoft documentation as a *thumb*) tells you approximately how much of a page you've filled up. At the bottom (and usually until you have the system paginate your text), a message indicates you are currently on page 1. At the middle of the screen is a question mark (this appears only if you are using a mouse), and at the right is the name of your current document (if you've given it a name). Two command lines may also be shown at the bottom of the screen. These lines usually come up when you start the system. However, as with the ruler, the system was set to show the command line only when needed.

Where other word processors are designed strictly as text editors, Word can be thought of as a graphics editor that works with text. This is an important distinction. Word is designed something like a low-end type composition program. Instead of allowing you to type documents using a mixture of similar-sized type styles, Word allows you to mix many different type styles and sizes on a single page. With the right printer, you can do a very acceptable job of typesetting. Although laser printers haven't yet matched the clarity and resolution of commercial phototypesetting equipment, they've come close and thus can provide text suitable for most in-house documents.

These features aren't only of value to people with laser printers. Word's support of dot matrix, ink jet, daisy wheel, and thimble printers is also good. Although Word's capabilities depend to a large extent on the capabilities of your printer, in most cases you can mix a variety of print attributes: typefaces, type sizes, italics, boldface, single and double underline, small caps, and so on.

Since Word allows you to mix various type sizes, you may find that a page of large type can hold fewer printed lines. Thus, the line count continually supplied by most word processing programs loses relevance when you use Word. A popular strategy when using Word is to type a document with little concern for the number of pages. Once the document is typed, you can assign spacing and type attributes to the various sections and just before printing have the system automatically repaginate the document.

Although this approach may be new to many users, it is probably the most satisfactory one when working with Word. And although you may end up with too few (or too many) pages, Word provides you with a wide range of options for adjusting the overall length of a document (such as varying margins, line spacing, header space, and characters per inch [pitch]).

It may seem a bit backward (and also a bit awkward) to type in text and then go back and assign such attributes as format, font, and so on, but Word makes the process quite simple. A number of approaches to assigning formatting and print attributes are discussed in more detail later. You can format a single paragraph or page and all subsequent paragraphs will carry the same formatting information; you can use pre-developed "style sheets" to assign specific formatting settings to selected text areas; you can copy character and paragraph formats using the mouse; or you can make changes as you go along. Once you have learned how to use style sheets and the other optional methods for defining text format, you should be quite comfortable with typing now and formatting later.

STARTING THE PROGRAM

Microsoft Word provides you with a variety of options for starting your word processing session. You can, for example, start the program and tell it to take you to the document you were working on when you ended your last editing session. In this case the system looks up the information stored in the last session, brings you back to the point where you last edited your text, restores the formatting information you used when you last edited your document, and enables you to continue right where you left off.

If you've used other word processors that require you to remember the name of the document you last worked on and to search for the place you left off, you'll quickly appreciate this capability of Word. Since you are producing your first document in this chapter, you do not need this feature immediately. However, the proper command syntax is important, since you can enter the program using the same set of commands. Since, with this particular option, you are returning to the last document you edited, you can type the name of the program (Word) followed by a space, a slash, and the letter for the option (/l).

To start Word and return to the last edited document,

Type: **word /l**

The Graphics Mode

Microsoft Word supports a few different modes for on-screen display. The graphics mode normally comes up when you type word RETURN. This mode sends information to your computer's video processor, which represents each of the dots that make up the symbols or characters you type. In most cases the screen is painted with a resolution of 640-by-200 dots. Thus, instead of sending the code for the letter *a* to the video processor, Word sends the instructions to print the dots that make up the letter *a*.

Because few video cards are capable of producing color output in this so-called high-resolution mode, you aren't able to produce color characters on a color screen while you are in this mode. If you are using an EGA card and a color monitor, you may be able to produce color characters in this high-resolution mode. In this mode Word can cause your monitor to display special character attributes, such as italics and underlines, and in some cases different-sized characters. In addition, the mouse pointer is an arrow shape and somewhat easier to work with than the pointer in the character mode.

The Character Mode

The character mode works somewhat differently from the graphics mode. Instead of sending instructions to display each individual dot for each character, it sends the code for the standard character. As a result, the system is unable to display special character attributes (such as italics or underlines) as they would look when printed. Instead, if you use a color monitor and color video card, these special characters are displayed in color.

If you use an EGA card and EGA monitor, it may be better to use the standard graphics mode, since you will probably be able to display the special characters both in color and in the new form in which they will be printed. To start up Word in the character mode,

Type: **word** /c RETURN

The use of color is of value in a number of cases. While in this mode you can assign different background colors to the text windows. For example, if you were editing a document, you might wish to have the original document in one window and the copy being edited in a second window. By putting a background color in your original window, you could quickly tell which version of the document you were working on. Similarly, the ability to assign colors to any of multiple windows can reduce the confusion you might otherwise experience when moving text from window to window. In addition using a colored background may make it easier to find the cursor than it is when using a black background.

The Hercules (High-Resolution) Mode

One of the problems some users have with Microsoft Word is that the on-screen text area is rather small. Although you can set the system to allow three extra lines at the bottom of the screen, the maximum number of lines you can normally produce is 22.

If you have a Hercules or compatible monochrome card and a high-resolution monochrome monitor, you can instruct the system to produce smaller characters, allowing you to display 43 rows of up to 90 characters. To start the system in Hercules mode,

Type: **word /h** RETURN

Starting With a Document

When you first start Word, you are able to tell the system to load a desired document or to begin a document. To do this, type word followed by the name of the document. For example, if you wanted to start Word and immediately load a document called DOC1.DOC, you would type word DOC1.DOC RETURN. The system would then search for the document you named and display it in the system's document window. If the system could not find the document, it would prompt you to indicate whether you wanted to create a file. If so, typing the letter *y* would instruct the system to begin a document named DOC1.DOC.

This system is somewhat limited, since it only looks for the document on the drive and directory you use to start Word. Thus, if you run Word from the hard disk but prefer to do your editing on a floppy, you will be unable to start the system and load the document on the other drive simultaneously. (If this document was the last one you edited, the /l command would load from whichever drive or directory you last edited.)

Of course, Word doesn't require you to give a name to a document when you first start working with it. You can simply type the basic **WORD** command, which results in an empty text screen, and then begin typing your text. You are asked to give the document a name when it is time to save it.

The codes presented previously are useful for starting up the system. There may be times when you wish to use color mode and go back into the document you last worked on. To enter multiple commands, type word, press SPACE and type the codes you wish to use. For example,

Type: **word /c/l** RETURN

If you want to start Word in Hercules mode and load in the document called DOC1.DOC,

Type: **word /h doc1.doc** RETURN

STARTING A DOCUMENT

You can now prepare a document using Word. This first document is called DOC1.DOC. To start Word, type the appropriate command to match your system's configuration, following the command with the name of the document. In the case of a standard system in graphics mode,

Type: **word doc1.doc** RETURN

Your screen should look like the one on the following page.

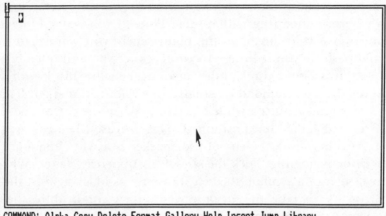

```
COMMAND: Alpha Copy Delete Format Gallery Help Insert Jump Library
         Options Print Quit Replace Search Transfer Undo Window
Edit document or press Esc to use menu
Page 1   {}                        ?            Microsoft Word: DOC1.DOC
```

This screen provides you with a fair amount of information. At the top left corner is the number of the window. Along the left margin is the scroll line, or thumb line. At the top of the line is a small horizontal line, the thumb. This tells you which part of a document you are working on. At the bottom is a horizontal scroll line. This can be used to scroll the text in the window to the left or right.

Below the bottom margin of the window are the command lines. These show the basic commands for Word. Below the two command lines is a brief description of the highlighted option or instructions on how to proceed. At the current position the system indicates you can edit your document or press ESC to bring you to the Command Menu. Below the command lines the page number, a question mark, the name of the program, and the name of the current document are listed. The page number remains 1 until you have the system repaginate your document. If you use a mouse, the question mark is a quick way to get help from the system. To use this feature, move your cursor over the question mark and click the left mouse button. If you aren't using a mouse, the question mark doesn't appear. In this case you can get help by pressing ALT-H. At the bottom right side of the screen is the name of your current document.

It is assumed that you already know what the cursor does: it marks the position where your editing will appear. Thus, if you wanted to add text, you would move your cursor to the point where you wanted to make a change and perform your editing procedure. Since you will often be typing original text, it is easy to think of the cursor as the white block with a black diamond inside. The diamond is actually an end-of-text marker. It appears as a black diamond against a white block only when the cursor and the end block are located at the same position. This is the case when you are typing new text. At other times the end-of-text marker is a white diamond.

The cursor is a white block the size of an uppercase letter. When it is located over text or a symbol, the text shows up as black against the white of the cursor. As you type, the cursor moves to the right, pushing the text to its right across the line and down the page.

It is easy to get confused and think that the end-of-text diamond is the spot where your editing will begin; however, you should be careful to look for the solid block (with or without reversed text) to locate the cursor. Further, during much of your editing, the cursor may be extended to cover a block of text, ranging anywhere from a single character to the entire document. Anything that you do to the highlighted area affects the entire contents of the highlighted area.

If you use a mouse, you have another on-screen symbol to contend with: the mouse pointer. It is relatively easy to assume that edits will be made from the position of the pointer. This is only so if you point to the area where you want to make a change and click the left mouse button, which moves the cursor to the pointer position.

For the purposes of the current example, you want the screen to show many formatting marks. Such marks as tabs and paragraph end marks (paragraph symbols) help to illustrate what goes on as you type and edit. To set up this option from the keyboard, press ESC to bring the cursor to the command line. Next, select the Options field by pressing O or pressing TAB to highlight the word Options.

If you use a mouse, you can also move the mouse pointer to Options and click the left mouse button (although it may be easier to press ESC and then O). The bottom of the screen should look like this:

```
OPTIONS visible: None Partial Complete  printer display:(Yes)No  menu:(Yes)No
   default tab width: 0.5"   measure:(In)Cm P10 P12 Pt        mute: Yes(No)
Select option
Page 1   {·}                        ?              Microsoft Word: DOC1.DOC
```

Use the cursor or the mouse or press P to select Partial in the Options Visible field. Next, press RETURN or move the mouse pointer to Options and click the left button to accept the change and return to your editing screen.

To illustrate the three different marks (cursor, end-of-text diamond, mouse pointer), press RETURN several times. Position the mouse pointer somewhere in the middle of the screen. Press UP ARROW to move the cursor to the top of the page. Your screen should look like Figure 3-1.

```
COMMAND: Alpha Copy Delete Format Gallery Help Insert Jump Library
         Options Print Quit Replace Search Transfer Undo Window
Edit document or press Esc to use menu
```

Figure 3-1.   The screen with cursor, end-of-text diamond, mouse pointer, and codes displayed

ENTERING THE SAMPLE DOCUMENT

Now you are ready to type your document. Note that while you type, the system wraps words automatically from one line to the next within a paragraph. If a word is too long to fit onto a line, it wraps down onto the next line. In other words, when typing the sample shown here, you need to press RETURN only where indicated.

```
RETURN
March 3, 1986RETURN
Mr. Lester HicksRETURN
Kumquat Motor CompanyRETURN
Compton, CARETURN
RETURN
Dear Mr. Hicks:RETURN
RETURN
TABI must confess that when we received your offer to sell us the new Kumquat motor
car for our vehicle fleet, we were quite surprised. The idea of a new two-door car for
under $3,000 sounded almost too good to pass up.RETURN
RETURN
```

In this example, RETURN and TAB indicate returns and a single tab. For the rest of the text in this book, you should be able to tell where returns and tabs are required, unless otherwise instructed. The keys themselves will no longer be provided in the text.

In the next paragraph you enter, type the word *complete* in bold characters. To do this, hold down ALT and press B to turn on the bolding function. When you have finished typing the bolded word, hold down ALT and press SPACE to return to the normal type style.

NOTE: Microsoft Word offers you a variety of methods for selecting the character style for text. You may make your selection by going into the Format Character menu (discussed later), or you may use ALT key combinations to apply the special features to the text you are about to type or to text you have highlighted. To cancel the format change for text you are about to type, use the ALT-SPACE combination. (The ALT key combination is probably the fastest means of turning on a particular character style and is discussed a bit later in this book.) ■

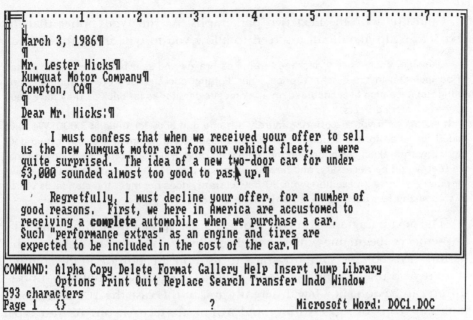

Figure 3-2.   The opening paragraphs of the sample document, DOC1.DOC

Now type the next lines, remembering to turn on and off the bolding of the word *complete.*

Regretfully, I must decline your offer, for a number of good reasons. First, we here in America are accustomed to receiving a **complete** automobile when we purchase a car. Such "performance extras" as an engine and tires are expected to be included in the cost of the car.

The text on your screen should look like that in Figure 3-2. Note that, depending upon whether you are in text or graphics mode and depending upon the color adapter and monitor you use, the word *complete* is displayed either in bold type or in color.

Continue with the next two paragraphs. As you type, notice that the text scrolls up about half a screen to allow you to type in more text.

Likewise, such "safety package" items as brakes and seat belts are also expected to be included in the purchase price. The "lighting package" features (headlights and taillights) have also been included on all domestic cars for as far back as they have been used on American cars.

It seems as if you are offering merely a frame and body for under $3,000. We have added the price for the "options" required to assemble a minimal, 4-cylinder, two-door model, with brakes, complete lighting, complete drive train, and other components that we feel would be necessary, and have determined that $17,000 is somewhat excessive for such a vehicle. In addition, your 30-day warranty does not meet the standards which this company has adopted for all of its fleet vehicles.

The next paragraph you type requires some special print functions. The last sentence, beginning with "should you wish," is bold. The ALT-B combination turns bold on, and ALT-SPACE turns it off. In addition to the bolding, you are also underlining the words *complete car.* As with bolding, underlining can be done in a few different ways. In this case the ALT-U key combination turns on underlining, and ALT-SPACE turns it off. As you type, bold, underlined text appears on the screen. When you turn off the special underline character, you are returning to normal text. To begin printing bold again, you must press the ALT-B combination.

Again, I am sorry that we must decline your offer at this time. **Should you wish to make a reasonable offer of a <u>complete car</u>, we would again be interested in considering your proposal.**

Very Truly Yours,

Your Name
Mgr., Fleet Operations

The last part of your document should look like Figure 3-3.

Before you make any changes to the document, you should save it. To do this,

Type: ESC T S RETURN

The method for saving and loading documents is discussed in detail in Chapter 4. What is important now is that you have already saved your original document; the document on the screen can be edited or even deleted.

```
   It seems as if you are offering merely a frame and body ¶
for under $3,000.  We have added the price for the "options"
required to assemble a minimal, 4-cylinder, two door model,
with brakes, comlete lighting, complete drive train, and
othe‖ components that we feel would be necessary, and have
determined that $17,000 is somewhat excessive for such a
vehicle.  In addition, your 30 day warranty does not meet
the standards which this company has adopted for all of its
fleet vehicles. ¶
¶
   Again, I am sorry that we must decline your offer at
this time.  Should you wish to make a reasonable offer of a
complete car, we would again be interested in considering
your proposal. ¶
¶
Very Truly Yours, ¶
¶
Your Name¶
Mgr. Fleet Operations¶
```

Figure 3-3.   The closing paragraphs of DOC1.DOC, showing underlined and bold text

Unless you give this edited document the same name as the original, your original will stay intact, uncompromised by any modifications that you may have made to what is present on your screen.

A number of things have happened since you first wrote the letter to Hicks. You have had a day to think about Mr. Hicks's original offer. Hicks has telephoned three times, trying to interest you in a special fleet price for the car. And he is beginning to be somewhat annoying. The revised letter you plan to send won't be quite as cordial as your original. To make the changes, you must use several editing features.

Overtype and Insert Modes

Two editing modes are available with Word: Overtype and Insert. The system is configured to begin in Insert mode. In Insert mode anything you type pushes whatever is to the right of it further to the right and down the page. To illustrate how this works, use the mouse (and the left button) or the cursor movement keys to move the cursor to the space before the word *sorry* in the last paragraph.

Type: **slightly**

before the word *sorry*. The text in the line moves over, the word *offer* drops onto the second line, and the rest of the paragraph is automatically adjusted.

In Overtype mode the text you type replaces the text it is typed over. Move the cursor on top of the *d* in *decline*. To activate the Overtype mode,

Type: F5

At the bottom of the screen, just before the word Microsoft, the indicator OT appears. This tells you that the Overtype mode is in effect. The lines at the bottom of the screen should look like this:

```
COMMAND: Alpha Copy Delete Format Gallery Help Insert Jump Library
         Options Print Quit Replace Search Transfer Undo Window
Edit document or press Esc to use menu
Page 1   {n}                        ?          OT Microsoft Word: DOC1.DOC
```

Return to the beginning of the document by pressing CTRL-PGUP.

It's been a day since you spoke to Hicks. Move the cursor so that it is located on the number 3 in the date. Type 4. The 4 replaces the 3.

NOTE: When you type numbers using Word, you should use the numbers on the top row of the keyboard. This is because the keypad is used for cursor movement functions and is also used to enter special characters into your document. Getting into the habit of using the top row for numeric entry avoids any confusion.

Because it causes original text to be deleted, few people prefer the Overtype mode. One advantage of the Overtype mode in Word is that the program highlights any text you attempt to overtype that precedes the spot where the cursor was located when you press the F5 key to activate this function. Thus the system warns you that you may be overtyping text that you don't want removed. So, to some degree, you are protected from delet-ing text you intended to keep. ■

Press F5 again, and OT is turned off. You are in Insert mode again.

You have found that the correct name of the Kumquat Motor Company is Kumquat Motor Car Company. Thus, you have to insert the word *Car* into the line containing the company's name. Move your cursor (using the cursor movement keys or the mouse and left button) right after the word *Motor* and insert a space.

Type: **Car**

The word *Car* is inserted in its proper space and the word *Company* is pushed over to the right. The rest of the text is unchanged.

NOTE: You can be somewhat creative in the way you type in your inser-tion. Whatever character your cursor is under when you begin typing remains on the page and is pushed to the right. In this example you could have placed your cursor under the *o* in *Company* and typed the following insertion: arSPACEC. The *C* in *Company* would have become the first letter in the word *Car*. The space and *C* at the end of your insertion would sepa-rate the two words and start the word *Company*. Any combination of key-strokes that accomplishes your desired goal is acceptable to Word. ■

Deleting Text

Deleting text using Word is somewhat different from deletion using some other word processors. The easiest way to delete small portions of text is by using BACKSPACE. When you BACKSPACE over text, it is removed from the screen and, in effect, gone forever.

However, the typical deletion gives you a second chance. When you make a deletion, the deleted text moves to an area of memory called the *scrap*. The contents of the scrap are listed at the bottom of your window, between the two curved brackets, {}. In effect, this is something like taking text out of your document and putting it into a temporary holding tray. The contents of the scrap remain until you delete other text (putting that text into the scrap), begin a new document, or turn off the system.

To make a deletion, highlight the area to be deleted and press DEL. The contents are moved to the scrap. To demonstrate this, move your cursor to the beginning of the first paragraph. To select the paragraph using the keyboard, press F10. To use the mouse, move the pointer into the left margin — the area of the selector bar. If you are in graphics mode, the arrow points to the top right. If you are in character mode, the pointer is slightly larger than lowercase letters. Click the RIGHT mouse button.

Once the paragraph is highlighted, press DEL. The contents of the paragraph disappear from the screen and are moved to the scrap. The bottom line, including the scrap, looks like this:

```
Page 1    {→I·must·con...pass·up.¶}   ?           SL·Microsoft·Word:·DOC1.DOC
```

You have decided not to delete this text, however. To restore the text from the scrap, press INS. The text is restored, and the scrap is again empty (or shows the contents of the previous scrap).

TIP: There may be times when you want to make an absolute deletion — that is, a deletion of text you know you'll never want again. This type of deletion can be made without disturbing the contents of the scrap. To perform this type of deletion,

Type: SHIFT-DEL

There may also be times when you want to replace existing text with text in the scrap. Rather than inserting text from the scrap and then deleting the text you don't want, highlight the text you want replaced by the scrap and

Type: SHIFT-INS ■

You should have learned enough by now to be able to make the revisions shown in Figure 3-4. Try to edit the letter so that it looks like the example in this figure.

Moving Text

Moving text follows the same procedure as deleting and restoring text. When you want to move text, first select it and then delete it. Next, move

March 4, 1986

Mr. Lester X. Hicks
Kumquat Motor Car Company
Compton, CA

Dear Mr. Hicks:

  I must confess that when we received your offer to sell
us the new Kumquat motor car for our vehicle fleet, we were
quite surprised. The idea of a new two-door car for under
$3,000 sounded almost too good to pass up. After looking at
your materials, it is obvious that your offer was too good
to be true and, in fact, smacked sufficiently of fraud.

  In America we are accustomed to receiving a **complete**
automobile when we purchase a car. Such "performance
extras" as an engine and tires are always included in the
cost of the car. Likewise, such "safety package" items as
brakes and seat belts are also expected to be included in
the purchase price. The "lighting package" features
(headlights and taillights) have also been included in all
domestic cars as far back as they have been used on American
cars. Being an American, you must be well aware of this.
To offer such an incomplete car, as you did in your letter
and phone calls, would appear to be either intent to defrad
this company, or incredible stupidity.

  You are offering merely a frame and body for under
$3,000. We have added the price for the "options" required
to assemble a minimal, 4-cylinder, two door model, with
brakes, complete lighting, complete drive train, and other
components that we feel would be necessary, and have
determined that $17,000 is obscenely excessive for such a
vehicle. What do you take us for?

  Your 30 day warranty does not meet the standards which
this company has adopted for all of its fleet vehicles. It
also begs the question--if Kumquat can't trust their cars to
last longer than 30 days, why should we? What do you know
that we don't?

  I am certain that you unserstand why we must decline
your offer at this time. **Should you wish to make a
reasonable offer of a <u>complete car</u>, we would again be
interested in considering your proposal.** However, you must
be aware that the obvious attmepts to misrepresent your
product would make us extremely wary of any future offers.

Very Truly Yours,

Your Name
Mgr. Fleet Operations

Figure 3-4. The revised DOC1.DOC

your cursor to the point where you want the text inserted and press INS. This then copies the text from the scrap into the new area and clears the scrap.

To move the third paragraph in DOC1.DOC so that it appears before the second paragraph, highlight the third paragraph (as described in the previous section and in Chapter 2). Press DEL to remove the paragraph to the scrap. Move the cursor before the beginning of the second paragraph and press INS to insert the text. Finally you will need to add a space to separate the two paragraphs.

NOTE: You should be careful not to make any other text deletions while the text that is to be moved is still in the scrap. If you do, the text you are moving is removed from memory. In some cases the UNDO command can be used to restore the deleted scrap, but the best prevention for this type of loss is avoidance of the loss in the first place. ■

Using the mouse, you can quickly move text — anything from a character to an entire document — without copying it into the scrap. The amount of text you select to move depends upon where you place the mouse pointer and which buttons you click. In addition, the same combination tells the system in which area to insert text. Table 3-1 lists the combinations and their effects.

Thus, to copy a sentence, position the pointer anywhere in the sentence to be copied and click both mouse buttons. The sentence is then highlighted. Next, position the mouse pointer at the point where you want to make your move, hold down CTRL, and click both mouse buttons. (Note that in order to complete a move, you must hold down CTRL and click both mouse buttons.)

Copying Text

Copying text is another function you may want to use regularly. The technique for this is similar to that for moving or deleting text. In this case, however, you highlight the text to be moved, select the COPY command, move your pointer to the place where you want to copy to, and press INS.

In the sample document, place the phrase "What do you take us for?" at the end of the third paragraph. To copy the phrase, move your cursor to its beginning. To select the sentence from the keyboard,

Pointer	*Button*	*Amount Highlighted*
In text	Left	Character
	Right	Word
	Both	Sentence
In scroll bar	Left	Line
	Right	Paragraph
	Both	Document

Table 3-1.   Moving or Copying Text Using the Mouse

Type: SHIFT-F8

Using the mouse, move the pointer under any letter in the sentence and click both mouse buttons simultaneously.

Next, select the **COPY** command (using the ESC-C key combination or the mouse). At the bottom of the screen the prompt "Copy to: {}" appears. Press RETURN to copy the text to the scrap. Next, move the cursor to the end of the next paragraph, type two spaces, and press INS. The text from the scrap is copied to the end of the third paragraph.

You can copy text by using a mouse in a manner similar to that used for moving text. The combinations of buttons and pointer position and their effects are listed in Table 3-1. However, instead of using the mouse buttons in combination with CTRL, you use them in combination with SHIFT. Thus, to copy a phrase like "What do you take us for?" you could highlight the phrase, move the cursor to the point where you wanted to copy it, hold down SHIFT, and click both mouse buttons.

TRANSFER FUNCTIONS

In the last chapter you performed some basic system start-up and editing tasks. You learned to delete, insert, move, and copy text. To a degree, these procedures are the basics needed for editing. But Microsoft Word has capabilities that go far beyond these basics. This chapter presents the extremely important file management procedures, including storing a document and creating edited copies.

THE TRANSFER MENU

Word's Transfer Menu, while foreign to virtually all other word processing programs, functions as the means for performing all your document handling functions. If you wanted to save a document, load a document, or do other things with a document, you would access these functions through this menu.

When you work on a document, a large chunk of the document is loaded into the system's memory. While you edit a document, changes are made to the contents of the system memory. For all intents and purposes, you can consider an entire document to be stored in RAM. Thus, if something were to happen to the computer while you were in an editing session, you would lose everything you did during that session. You should therefore regularly save your work on disk to avoid possible loss from system malfunction. It is recommended that, no matter what else you do, you should get into the habit of saving your work every fifteen minutes or so. Even though your computer may never lock up on you, it is still prudent to get into the habit of ensuring against the eventual catastrophe.

Saving a Document

Saving a document is a simple matter when you use Word. To save a document, you must first get into the Transfer Menu. You can do this in a number of ways. Using the keyboard,

Type: ESC T

This brings the cursor into the command line and selects the Transfer Menu. Using a mouse, you can move the pointer to TRANSFER and click the left mouse button. Be careful not to click the right mouse button, which automatically chooses the Load option. A screen with the Transfer Menu looks like this:

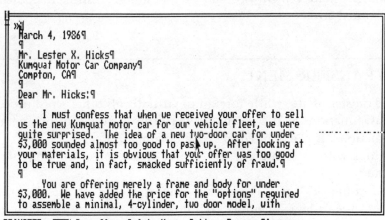

```
»
March 4, 1986¶
¶
Mr. Lester X. Hicks¶
Kumquat Motor Car Company¶
Compton, CA¶
¶
Dear Mr. Hicks:¶
¶
    I must confess that when we received your offer to sell
us the new Kumquat motor car for our vehicle fleet, we were
quite surprised.  The idea of a new two-door car for under
$3,000 sounded almost too good to pass up.  After looking at
your materials, it is obvious that your offer was too good
to be true and, in fact, smacked sufficiently of fraud.¶
¶
    You are offering merely a frame and body for under
$3,000.  We have added the price for the "options" required
to assemble a minimal, 4-cylinder, two door model, with
```

TRANSFER: ▆▆▆ Save Clear Delete Merge Options Rename Glossary

Select option or type command letter
Page 1   {}   ?   Microsoft Word: FIG35.DOC

To save the document while in this submenu, press S (for Save) or TAB to move into the Save field and press RETURN; using the mouse, point to Save and click the left button.

The system next prompts you for the name of the file. In most cases this will be the current name as it appears in the lower right corner of the screen. If you started the system without giving the document a name, you should give it a name now.

You may have revised DOC1.DOC as directed in Chapter 3. If you haven't turned off the system and you still have the revised DOC1.DOC on the screen, you should give this revised version a new name: DOC2.DOC. Simply type the new name over the old file name.

About Directories and Subdirectories Microsoft Word supports the use of subdirectories. When you work on documents, you can place them on any available disk drive or subdirectory. This concept may be unfamiliar to some users, especially those using Word on dual floppy disk systems.

As you work on your computer, you are using drives that have been given specific device numbers. For example, if you have a dual floppy system, your drives are probably labeled A and B. If you have a hard disk system, your two drives are probably labeled A and C, although you may have partitioned your hard disk to be categorized by the system as more than one drive, perhaps as C and D.

Since a hard disk is capable of storing a large number of files, trying to find any individual file on a single directory can be a very time-consuming and frustrating process. Microsoft, which developed the operating system that runs on your computer (if you are using MS-DOS 2.10 or PC-DOS 2.10 or later versions) allows for the provision of subdirectories. When you set up a subdirectory, you are creating a logical section for only a certain group of files.

When you set up Word, you probably created a subdirectory called Word (using the command **MKDIR WORD** or **MD WORD**), switched into that subdirectory (using the command **CHDIR \WORD** or **CD\WORD**), and copied your program files onto the subdirectory. When you load Word, you first change into the Word subdirectory (or use a batch file to do that for you) and enter your command to start Word. Your document files can similarly be stored in the Word subdirectory or other subdirectories.

For example, you may want to keep a separate document subdirectory for each major department. Thus, you may have a subdirectory called \acctg, a different one called \mktg, and a third called \engg (for accounting, marketing, and engineering). Using special subdirectories has a few advantages: it makes it easier to find any particular user's or department's files, it keeps the work for each department separate from the rest of the organization, and it makes file management easier.

The syntax for entering a name for the file that you want to save is as follows:

drive: *subdir* *subsubdir* *filename.ext*

where *drive:* is the drive number (usually A or C); *subdir* is the name of the first subdirectory (unless the file is stored on the same directory Word is loaded from); *subsubdir* is a subdirectory of the first subdirectory (this sounds more confusing than it actually is); and *filename.ext* is the name and file extension of the document you are saving.

Again, Word supports the use of subdirectories. Also, if you are saving the document to the directory Word uses to load the program, you don't need to type the name of the drive or subdirectory — your file is automatically saved there. Give this revised file the name DOC2.DOC. Press RETURN to accept the name and save the document.

Unformatted Files Before the document is saved, the word *formatted* appears to the right of the filename. Your response to this prompt indicates whether or not you want to save a formatted file. This is discussed in further detail in the section on file transfers.

This option allows you to do two different things. If you save the file as a formatted file, then when you print it or edit it, all the formatting (line spacing, character styles, and so on) remains with the document. This type of file is the most useful when using Microsoft Word, since it stores and reproduces the special attributes you give to the document.

If you choose to save an unformatted file, only the characters are saved; none of the information about line spacing, character styles, and so on is retained. This creates what is known as an ASCII (American Standard Code for Information Interchange) file. The ASCII code can be communicated between most computers and can be read by most word processing programs. Thus, if you were required to send a copy of the document to another computer and did not know the type of word processor used on the other computer, an ASCII file could be used.

Saving Versions of the Same Document Once you've saved DOC2.DOC, you may want to make some changes to the file that remains on your screen. After you've made your changes, the document is obviously different from the one you already saved. If you did not save this revised document before exiting Word, you would have no record of the edits when you next used the system. On the other hand, if you saved the revised document under the old filename (DOC2.DOC), you would replace the old document with the newly revised one and would have no record of what the "original" DOC2.DOC looked like. Thus, before you save an editing session, you must decide whether (1) you want to save your edited file separately from the earlier version, or (2) you want to save the file as a replacement of the earlier version.

In the first instance, in which you wanted to keep track of major revisions, you would select the TRANSFER SAVE commands and give the edited document a new name (for example, DOC3.DOC) before saving it. In the second case, you would accept the default and save the document to the old name (in this case DOC2.DOC). Microsoft Word makes it very easy to keep track of document revisions.

Microsoft Word allows you a variety of methods for saving a document. However, you may find that the quickest way is to use the keys: four keystrokes will save the current file to the current directory. If you aren't renaming the contents of the current editing session,

Type: ESC T S RETURN

to save your document.

If you want to change the name, you can do it almost as quickly.

Type: ESC T S

and then type the new document name (and directory, if appropriate) and press RETURN. Although the mouse is useful for many operations, the quick four-keystroke sequence is faster. Since you should be making regular saves, this quick key sequence could be less of a bother than using the mouse to get the same result.

Loading a File

When you started your current session of Word, you may have entered the system and loaded in a file. You will probably have few sessions where you only work on one document. Although you can load files by quitting and restarting Word, there is a better way.

From the Transfer Menu, you can instruct the system to load a document. From the keyboard,

Type: ESC T L

to get to the TRANSFER LOAD screen.

Using a mouse, you can get to this screen in two ways. The first way is to move the pointer to TRANSFER and click the left mouse button and then to move the pointer to LOAD and again click the left mouse button. The second way is to move the pointer to TRANSFER and click the right mouse button. For certain menus, the right button selects the item pointed at and another subordinate item. In this case the right button selects TRANSFER LOAD.

The TRANSFER LOAD menu looks like this:

```
TRANSFER LOAD filename: ▮                    read only: Yes(No)
Enter filename or select from list
```

You can type in the name (and drive and subdirectory information, if appropriate) for the file you want to load. However, you may not know the exact name of the file you want to load. In this case you can either press RIGHT ARROW on the keyboard or point to the name field and click the right mouse button to bring up the file directory of the subdirectory from which you loaded Word.

If you want a directory of the contents of a different drive or subdirectory, type the name of the drive and subdirectories, followed by *.* and then press RIGHT ARROW or click the right mouse button. Normally, Word gives you a list of files with the .DOC extension. A list of files appears on the screen. Once you find the name of the file you want to load, type in the exact name as listed on the screen and press RETURN or point to the desired file and click the right mouse button.

NOTE: You can load a file before you save the one you are currently working on. When you instruct the system to load, it prompts you to indicate whether you want to save the current document. Answering *y* saves the document using the name, drive, and directory it was last saved to. Answering *n* deletes the current document from system memory without saving it — in effect, loses it forever. If you press ESC, you are telling the system you don't want to load your document. You are then returned to your edited document. ■

Clearing a File

The TRANSFER CLEAR command is relatively straightforward. You would probably need this command if you were working on a document you decided you didn't want to save. For example, you might have written a letter you would not ever edit or record. Although you could highlight the whole document (by using SHIFT-F10 or by placing the pointer in the selection bar and clicking both mouse buttons) and then delete it, the entire document would be held in the scrap until it was replaced by other text. It would be preferable to clear the contents of a document completely.

In another case, you might have worked on several documents placed into more than one window. For example, you might have DOC1.DOC in one window, DOC2.DOC in a second, and DOC3.DOC in a third. You might decide that you no longer needed DOC1 or DOC2. After you saved DOC3.DOC, you still had three windows full of text. It would be convenient to clear all windows with a single command.

To do so, go to the TRANSFER CLEAR screen by using the keyboard or the mouse. The TRANSFER CLEAR menu line looks like this:

```
TRANSFER CLEAR: All Window

Select option or type command letter
Page 1   {}                        ?          Microsoft Word: SAMPLE2.DOC
```

Selecting to clear just a window clears the contents of the window you last worked in, leaving the other windows intact. Selecting to clear all removes the text from all the windows and brings up a single, empty window. By using the mouse or the keyboard, you may select either option. Again, it may be faster to use the keys rather than the mouse for entering this command.

Deleting a File

The TRANSFER DELETE command deletes documents from the disk. Be careful when you use this command: a deleted document can't be recovered.

This option can be useful if you've run out of space on your disk drive, or if you have finished working on a document you won't ever need again. Getting to this menu is simple. If you use the keyboard,

Type: ESC T D

If you use the mouse, point to TRANSFER, click the left mouse button, point to DELETE, and click the left mouse button.

The TRANSFER DELETE menu line looks like this:

```
TRANSFER DELETE filename: ▮

Enter filename or select from list
Page 1   {}                        ?              Microsoft Word:
```

You can type the name of the file you want to delete or do a directory search as already described. Once you've typed or selected the name of the file you want to delete, press RETURN and the system prompts you to confirm the deletion. If you use the mouse, point to the file and click the right mouse button to delete the file or point to the filename, click the left mouse button, and the system prompts you to confirm the deletion. Moving the pointer to TRANSFER DELETE and clicking the left button causes the file to be deleted. If you don't want to delete a file, press ESC to bring you back to the Command line.

Merging Files

The TRANSFER MERGE command is used to link two or more documents together. This is useful for a number of functions. If you prepared a proposal made up of many different parts, you might want to have the system automatically develop a table of contents and index for the entire document. Using TRANSFER MERGE, you could link the individual documents together in order and produce a correctly paginated, indexed document. In other cases you might simply want to print a document with correct, consecutive page numbers. Linking all the subdocuments together to form the whole would result in a single document with correct page numbering.

NOTE: TRANSFER MERGE should not be confused with PRINT MERGE, which is used for repetitive letters and other documents that combine data into a document. For example, if you wanted to print a set of letters, each individually addressed from the names in a mailing list, you would use PRINT MERGE, not TRANSFER MERGE. ■

Using TRANSFER MERGE is very simple. As with other Transfer Menu options, this command can be accessed using the keyboard or the mouse. The TRANSFER MERGE screen looks like this:

```
TRANSFER MERGE filename: ■

Enter filename or select from list
```

You can now enter the name of the next document — the one you want to attach to the existing document in the window. Press RETURN to complete the merge. (Although with the mouse you can complete the merge by pointing to TRANSFER MERGE and clicking a mouse button, it's quicker to press RETURN than to use the mouse.)

If you wish, you can load DOC1.DOC into the system and transfer merge DOC2.DOC. When you scroll through the document, you will see that DOC1.DOC is followed immediately by the text in DOC2.DOC. Again, TRANSFER MERGE is especially valuable when you need to "paste together" a document made of many smaller documents.

NOTE: You may initially be concerned that your system doesn't have sufficient memory to store a large document. This may be true. However, this isn't a problem for Microsoft Word, because it only stores a portion of a document at any one time. The rest of the document, no matter how large, is stored in a temporary file on the system's subdirectory. When the system repaginates, creates a table of contents or index, or otherwise moves through the large document, it is swapping text in and out of these temporary disk files. Thus, the concern about running out of memory by loading a large file is unfounded. A more valid concern, if your hard disk is almost full, is running out of space for the temporary files. ■

Changing Options

TRANSFER OPTIONS allows you to change your default document drive and directory. If, for example, you wanted to run Microsoft Word from the C: drive and \word subdirectory but to store the documents on the D: drive and \letters subdirectory, you would instruct the system to use that setting as the default for document storage and retrieval.

To get to this option, you can use the mouse or keyboard as already described. Type in the name of the drive and subdirectory you are storing your files to and accept this by moving the mouse to TRANSFER OPTIONS and clicking the left mouse button, or you can press RETURN. The system automatically stores and retrieves files from the new drive/sub-directory unless told to look elsewhere for the documents.

Renaming a File

Using TRANSFER RENAME is similar to saving a document under a new name; it tells the system to give the current document a new name. Note however, that it does *not* create a new document. For example, you may have a document that has gone through many revisions. Such a document might be named DOC2.DOC, revised from DOC1.DOC. If you have made your final revision and don't want to save DOC2.DOC, you can save the revision under a new name, DOCFINAL.DOC, perhaps.

Once you rename your revised document, the earlier one disappears from the directory. That is, if you loaded DOC2.DOC and revised it, and then renamed it DOCFINAL.DOC, the DOC2.DOC document would no longer exist. In principle, if you wanted to go back and see how DOC2.DOC looked before you changed it, you would be unable to do so, since only the modified document was saved. Be careful to use TRANSFER COPY when you want to save each version of a document. Use TRANSFER RENAME only when you don't want to save the earlier version.

If you mistakenly rename a document that you want to save, all is not lost. Your earlier document is saved, using the extension .BAK instead of .DOC, and should still be on your document disk. Thus, once you realize you have made this error, you can save your renamed document, and then load the original document, using the earlier name and the new extension (.BAK). If you accidentally renamed DOC2.DOC, you could retrieve it using TRANSFER LOAD and the name DOC2.BAK. Then, once your document was recovered, you could rename it DOC2.DOC.

Using the Glossary

The TRANSFER GLOSSARY commands include SAVE, MERGE, and CLEAR. A *glossary* is a special file that contains extended words or characters. (A glossary in Word is the same as "boilerplate" text—repeatedly used text stored in memory that can then be entered using a few keystrokes rather than many.) For example, if you planned to write many letters to the Kumquat Motor Car Company (as you did in DOC1.DOC and DOC2.DOC), you could load the phrase "Kumquat Motor Car Company" into a glossary, assign a simple key code, and have the system automatically insert the phrase for you.

To see how this works, load DOC2.DOC into your system (if it isn't already loaded). Now, using the mouse or the keyboard, highlight the phrase "Kumquat Motor Car Company." To do this using the keyboard, move your cursor to a spot in the line and press ALT-F9 to highlight the line. (You can also use ALT-F8 to highlight the sentence or use F6 plus the cursor movement keys to extend a highlight.) If you use the mouse, move the pointer to the line and click both mouse buttons. Next, select the COPY command from the command line. Do this either by pressing ESC C or by pointing to the word using the mouse and clicking the left button.

The system prompts, "COPY to: { }." This prompts you to determine what glossary listing you want to give to this text. (If you don't enter a name, the copy will be moved to the scrap. Once it is moved to the scrap, you can insert it into text by placing the cursor at the point where you want it inserted and pressing INS.) To give this phrase the glossary listing kmc,

Type: **kmc** RETURN

To check that the text has actually been moved to the glossary, position the cursor anywhere else on the page.

Type: **kmc**
      F3

When you type F3, the system looks in the active glossary to see if it can find a listing for kmc. When it finds the listing, Kumquat Motor Car Company, it replaces kmc with the longer listing. Glossaries can be very useful for repetitive text and boilerplate documents.

The TRANSFER GLOSSARY commands work in much the same way as the SAVE, MERGE, and CLEAR commands. In general, however, it is useful to develop a variety of glossaries if you often use different phrases for different departments. The use of glossaries can help streamline your editing in Microsoft Word.

RECOVERING FILES WHEN THE SYSTEM CRASHES

In spite of all the care you may take in regularly storing a document, something can still go wrong. The power may go out in your office. Your keyboard may lock up. For whatever reason, you may somehow exit Word without saving the file. All may not be lost. As already mentioned, your system stores parts of the document in temporary files. When you leave Word, these temporary documents are deleted from the system. However, if your exit from Word was unplanned, some of these temporary files might still remain stored on your Word disk.

To find these files from DOS, go to the directory from which Word was loaded.

Type: **DIR *.tmp** RETURN

The system may list some temporary files with strange numeric names. Of the greatest potential value are the date and time stamps attached to each document. From these, you may be able to tell approximately which files may have text you were working on before the system crashed.

To try to view these files, write down the complete name of the files and, still at DOS level,

Type: **Type** *filename***.tmp** RETURN

where *filename* is the name (or the numbers) of the temporary file you want to review. To stop the scrolling of the document, press CTRL-S. To restart the scrolling, press SPACE.

With luck, you may be able to load what remains of your original file, rename it, and Transfer Merge the temporary files that contain your text. You will probably have to delete many of the codes that came before and after the text, but at least a portion of the text can be recovered using this method. It's certainly far from elegant, but if you're lucky, it will work.

FORMATTING

In the previous chapters you learned how to set up and begin using Word, how to save and load your files, and how to set up a file for telecommunication or unformatted printing. This chapter shows how to make a number of important enhancements that take advantage of your printer's special capabilities and make your documents look much more professional than those produced by most other word processors. In addition, some of the many advanced features built into Microsoft Word are introduced in this chapter. Microsoft Word offers you a broad range of ways to print your text: depending upon your printer's capabilities, you can choose from eight different ways to print your letters and from many different ways to set up the overall look of your finished page.

CHARACTER FORMATTING

Word allows you to print characters in many different ways: bold, italic, super- and subscript, all uppercase, all lowercase, and so on. It allows you to mix different type styles in the same document, so that, for example, you can print a heading in a larger type size than main text. However, for the most part, these features are contingent on the capabilities of your printer. If you were using a daisy wheel or thimble printer, you would be able to change type styles (the system would stop the printer until you changed print elements) but could not print larger fonts or small caps. Using a dot matrix printer, you might not be able to have the system print larger characters or to get super- or subscripts to print.

The instructions in this chapter assume, for the most part, an ideal situation: that you use a printer that can handle all that Word can produce. If a feature doesn't work for you, it is probably be due to your printer's lack of ability to perform a certain function.

When to Change Character Formats

With so many different ways to print a character (not counting the different type styles your printer may support), it can be very tempting to try them all. Bolding, italics, single and double underlines, and so on all look great on paper. The other character types also make a definite statement when printed. However, you should exercise some degree of restraint when you use these features. Without a doubt, conservative use of such features as bolding and underlining can call attention to key points and make them stand out from the rest of the text. However, the use of too many special features detracts from the impact of each and results in a document that looks cluttered rather than clear.

Thus, you should use restraint when taking advantage of the many character-formatting capabilities. The examples in this chapter have somewhat overused the characters to show how to use the commands and how to format text, not to provide examples of particularly good page layout or practice.

Using and Selecting Character Formats

Formatting characters is basically very simple: highlight the text you want to change, go into the Format Menu, and assign attributes to your character. For this demonstration, call up the document called DOC2.DOC. Rename the document FORMCHAR.DOC. (To do this, go into the Transfer Menu and select the RENAME command.) This saves the original document and provides you with a copy of the document that you can alter without affecting the original.

Move your cursor to the line that reads "Kumquat Motor Car Company." Highlight the line by using the mouse or by pressing F9. You are going to print this line in bold print.

Get into the Format Menu by pressing ESC-F or by moving the mouse to the word Format on the menu lines, and clicking the right mouse button. (Note: The right button automatically made a double selection, selecting both Format and Character. You could have used the left button to select Format and then selected Character with the left button.) Your screen should look like Figure 5-1.

At the bottom of the screen is the Format Character Menu. This menu provides you with many of the options for printing text. To navigate through the options using the keyboard, press TAB to go forward or press SHIFT-TAB to move backward. As you come to each of the first seven options—Bold, Italic, Underline, Strikethrough, Uppercase, Small Caps, and Double Underline—you can respond by pressing Y for yes or N for no or by just tabbing through to leave a selection unchanged. Pressing the space bar will also move you through the selections within a field.

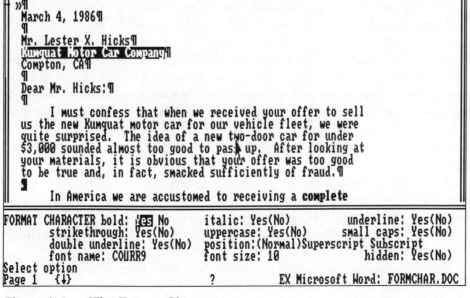

Figure 5-1.   The Format Character screen

While the first seven options are self-explanatory, others require clarification. The Position option allows you to select subscript, superscript, or normal type. This is useful for scientific formulas, such as the one for water (H_2O), or for mathematical expressions, such as 2^3.

To select from the remaining options, press SPACE or BACKSPACE to scroll from one to the next. The Font Name option allows you to choose which type style to use for the highlighted characters, depending on your printer's capabilities. To see which type styles are available on your printer (and, if you use a daisy wheel or other formed character printer, whether you have the appropriate print element), move your cursor to the Font Name field and press RIGHT ARROW. The screen display disappears and is replaced by a list of the fonts available for your printer. Depending upon the type of printer you use, the screen may show a list of type styles similar to that shown in Figure 5-2.

NOTE: Depending upon your computer system, you may be unable to get a listing of the font names on the screen. The selections, as listed in Figure 5-2, are somewhat indecipherable. In order to be able to determine what each name means, you may have to call Microsoft Product Support for a listing of what each font selection means. On most computers, however, you should be able to see which fonts are available. ■

To select a particular font, type its name, or press SPACE to move to the desired setting and then press TAB to move on to the next selection Font Size. Before moving on to Font Size, note that for your printer, you may have two options for the same font, one of which ends with a letter *D* (for example, Elite and EliteD). The font name ending with *D* indicates that the printer types each character twice, resulting in a darker, easier-to-read character.

Font size is a measure of the size of the letters you will print. The size of a character is measured in points; most standard text is 10 points. The higher the number of points, the larger the character will be. Thus, you may want to print a headline in 14, 16, or even 24 points, if your printer supports it, and print text in 10 or 12 points.

Another measurement often confused with print height (points) is print pitch. *Pitch* is the width of the character and is calculated by dividing the number 120 by the point measurement. Thus, if you were using a 12-point

```
COURR9 (modern a)              COURR10 (modern c)
GOTH6W (modern e)              GOTH9M (modern f)
GOTH9MR (modern g)             PC7 (modern h)
PCSS7 (modern i)               PCSS7R (modern j)
MX7 (modern k)                 MX9 (modern l)
MX9M (modern m)                MX9W (modern o)
MX10 (roman a)                 BKMAN9P (roman b)
BKMAN12P (roman e)             BKMAN18P (roman h)
BKMAN18T (roman i)             TAYL9 (roman j)
TAYL10 (roman l)               CASL10 (roman n)
SWIS10 (roman o)               SWIS12 (roman p)
SWIS14 (script a)              SWIS18B (script b)
SWIS18O (script c)             SWIS20D (script d)
BANK10 (script e)              PI10 (symbol a)




FORMAT CHARACTER bold:(Yes)No      italic: Yes(No)           underline: Yes(No)
         strikethrough: Yes(No)    uppercase: Yes(No)       small caps: Yes(No)
         double underline: Yes(No) position:(Normal)Superscript Subscript
         font name: COURR          font size: 10                hidden: Yes(No)
Enter font name or select from list
Page 1   {↓}                       ?             Microsoft Word: FORMCHAR.DOC
```

Figure 5-2.   A Font Selection list

pica font, your characters would be 10 pitch (120 divided by 12 equals 10) and you would then print 10 pica characters per inch. To further add to the confusion, a font's height and width are not the same: 72 points equal one inch in height, but a 72-point character would be 72/120 inch in width.

Other options are also available with some printers. Proportional spacing and microjustification are both related. A *proportional-spaced font* assigns more width to wide letters than it does to narrow letters — for example, the letter *w* is wider than the letter *i*. When printed, a proportionally spaced document looks better than one that isn't proportionally spaced. *Microjustification* adds spaces between words or characters (or both) to allow a line of text to end at the right margin. Where some printers perform normal justification by adding the same amount of space between each word (and can create some unsatisfactory printouts of short sentences), microjustification adjusts the space between words and between letters on a line. Both microjustification and proportional spacing are handled by Microsoft Word, and you shouldn't have to specify font size when using a proportional font.

The final option, Hidden, is somewhat beyond the scope of this current discussion. Basically, a *hidden character* instructs the system to do something; for example, it can be a code used to generate an automatic table of contents or an index. Your response to this prompt tells the system whether you want to see (and print) hidden characters. For now, leave the answer at No.

Once your selections are complete (in this case, you are bolding "Kumquat Motor Car Company"), press RETURN to accept the changes. Alternatively, you can make your selections by using the mouse and either clicking the right mouse button while pointing at your final selection or making your selection and pointing at FORMAT CHARACTER and clicking the left mouse button. Bold the highlighted line now. This line should be somewhat brighter than the rest of the characters on the screen.

You can also assign a variety of attributes to any highlighted text. For example, highlight the phrase "smacked sufficiently of fraud" at the end of the first paragraph. Next, bold and double underline the text. Next, highlight the word *accustomed* in the next line and set it in italics. Bold the word *complete* in the same line. Move back to the first paragraph and highlight the phrase "almost too good to pass up." Tell the system to set these characters in small caps. If you are in graphics mode, your screen should look like this:

```
[·········1·········2·········3·········4·········5·········]·········7····
»¶
March 4, 1986¶
¶
Mr. Lester X. Hicks¶
Kumquat Motor Car Company¶
Compton, CA¶
¶
Dear Mr. Hicks:▒
¶
    I must confess that when we received your offer to sell
us the new Kumquat motor car for our vehicle fleet, we were
quite surprised.  The idea of a new two-door car for under
$3,000 sounded ALMOST TOO GOOD TO PASS UP.  After looking at
your materials, it is obvious that your offer was too good
to be true and, in fact, smacked sufficiently of fraud.¶
¶
    In America we are accustomed to receiving a complete
automobile when we purchase a car.  Such "performance
extras" as an engine and tires are always included in the
```

Result	Key Command
Bold text	ALT-B
Underlined text	ALT-U
Italicized text	ALT-I
Strikethrough text	ALT-S
Double underline text	ALT-D
Type hidden text	ALT-E
Small caps	ALT-K
Superscript text	ALT-+ or ALT-=
Subscript text	ALT-− (ALT-minus)
Standard text	ALT-SPACE

Table 5-1.   Formatting Characters Using Key Commands

This method is fine for previously typed text. In fact, many operators may enter text without regard to font size, style, or format and then make the format changes as they revise the document. If you have many changes to make, however, the technique outlined here can quickly become cumbersome.

Using Key Commands to Format Characters   There's another, faster way to assign attributes to text (although you can't change fonts or character size or alter the hidden text prompt). To change the format for text, first highlight the text and then type the appropriate ALT key combinations to change the text. For example, you've already used the ALT-B key command for bolding. Character formatting commands and their results are listed in Table 5-1.

When you use style sheets (discussed in Chapter 8) you must hold down ALT and then press X before pressing the code for the character attributes (for example, ALT-X-B). Also, the character options are additive — that is, you can build up a number of special formats just by typing in the format instruction keys. For example, a bold, underlined, italicized, superscripted, small cap text string can be made by entering the commands for each option. There is no way to delete just one parameter from the list. To correct the list, you must start over by pressing ALT-SPACE and beginning again. Similarly, you must press ALT-SPACE to return to normal, non-formatted text whenever you use key commands to format characters.

The ALT key combination also allows you to set parameters for characters you are about to type. For example, if you wanted to type a paragraph of text in bold print, you would press ALT-B (or ALT-X-B). All subsequent characters would be bold until you press ALT-SPACE to reset the system to standard characters.

The ALT-E command tells the system that you want to type a hidden character. Depending upon how you set your system parameters, you may or may not be able to see the hidden text. In either case the hidden text is stored in the file, ready to be accessed whenever the appropriate function is selected. Word's ability to easily turn on and off print attributes makes it a powerful format-as-you-go text preparation system.

PARAGRAPH FORMATTING

Just as Microsoft Word allows you to modify the format of your characters, it also gives you a great deal of control over the look and layout of your paragraphs. Line spacing, margins, justification, indents, spacing between paragraphs, and many other features are available to you.

Hard and Soft Line Endings

Microsoft Word automatically wraps words that extend beyond the end of a line. You can type as much as you want without ever pressing RETURN. Pressing this key tells the system you have finished a paragraph. When you format a paragraph, the system automatically looks for the end of the paragraph, indicated by RETURN. Since you have configured your system to display some of the marks, you already have seen the paragraph symbol at the end of each paragraph.

At times you may want to keep a series of lines together and have the system treat all the lines as a single paragraph. For example, you might wish to move an address to the center of the page or possibly move it to the right side of the page for a special effect. If you were to define the address block as a single paragraph, you could issue a single command affecting the whole paragraph.

To end a line but not a paragraph requires a new command: the NEW LINE command. The NEW LINE command is a hard line ending. To make a new line,

Type: SHIFT-RETURN

An arrow indicates that you have entered the command and the cursor moves to the next line. When you format a paragraph made with such symbols, the entire paragraph is formatted.

To illustrate how this works, return to FORMCHAR.DOC. Move the cursor to the address line for Mr. Hicks and replace the paragraph marks (RETURNs) with NEW LINE commands. Highlight the paragraph. The paragraph should look like Figure 5-3.

Next, tell the system to center the paragraph.

Type: ALT-C

The centered paragraph looks like Figure 5-4. Next, move the paragraph so that it is flush right.

Type: ALT-R

```
Mr. Lester X. Hicks↓
Kumquat Motor Car Company↓
Compton, CA¶
```

Figure 5-3. Address lines modified with new line symbols

```
          Mr. Lester X. Hicks↓
       Kumquat Motor Car Company↓
            Compton, CA¶
```

Figure 5-4. A centered paragraph

The paragraph should now look like Figure 5-5. Note that the end of each line is flush with the right margin.

While you were manipulating the paragraph, you were also seeing how three of the four paragraph presentation options appear. The final option is to justify the paragraph. In *justified text*, lines of copy have aligned right and left margins. To see how justification works, highlight the first paragraph of the document. Next, enter the quick justification command, ALT-J. The paragraph should look like Figure 5-6. Except for the last line of the paragraph, the lines are aligned.

The UNDO Command   The UNDO command is useful in many different situations. It can return your system to the state it was in before you made a particular change. In the present example assume that you prefer an unjustified look for your paragraph. You can select the paragraph again and tell the system to left justify it or you can use the UNDO command.

To undo this justified paragraph using the mouse, point to the Undo prompt and press either mouse button. The paragraph then looks as it did before you justified it. If you want to see how it looked justified, repeat the

```
                        Mr. Lester X. Hicks↓
             Kumquat Motor Car Company↓
                        Compton, CA¶
```

Figure 5-5.   A flush right paragraph

```
      I must confess that when we received your offer to sell
us the new Kumquat motor car for our vehicle fleet, we were
quite surprised.  The idea of a new two-door car for  under
$3,000 sounded ALMOST TOO GOOD TO PASS UP.  After looking at
your materials, it is obvious that your offer was  too  good
to be true and, in fact, smacked sufficiently of fraud.¶
```

Figure 5-6.   A justified paragraph

procedure—undoing the UNDO. Thus, using this command you can toggle back and forth to compare text before and after a change. Using the keyboard,

Type: ESC-U

to issue the UNDO command. Again, it may be faster to use the key commands than it is to use the mouse for this particular command.

The UNDO command not only undoes commands related to format, but also deletes and "undeletes" text and works with many operations in Word. The system keeps your last editing step in memory (think of it as an UNDO box) and can move your new and old text into and out of that box. You should be careful, however, to use the UNDO command as soon as you realize you need to, because the next time you make any changes the new changes go into the undo box and your earlier modifications are gone forever (and can't be undone).

Hard and Optional Hyphens

When the system formats your paragraphs, it automatically wraps words that extend beyond the right margin of a line onto the next line. If you have a normally hyphenated word, the system may break the word into two words at the location of the hyphen. This is fine for certain words or phrases, where a split in the middle doesn't change the meaning or make the word read oddly, but for such things as item numbers or dates (such as 1-5-87), such a break would not be correct and could alter the meaning of the hyphenated material. Microsoft Word has provided a method for telling the system not to break a hyphenated string of characters.[7]

This method involves the use of what is referred to as a *hard hyphen*, a hyphen that always stays inside a particular string of characters and is never placed at the end of the line. Although this may result in making the previous line slightly shorter than it would be had the word been hyphenated, it is better than the alternative.

To enter a hard hyphen,

Type: CTRL-SHIFT-(CTRL-SHIFT-**hyphen**)

When you hold down CTRL and SHIFT and then press the hyphen key, a special hyphen is inserted into your text. This hyphen looks slightly different on screen than the other types of hyphens: it is wider and placed slightly lower on the line than the other hyphens.

NOTE: Microsoft Word provides for two other hyphens. The first is the hyphen you manually enter at the end of a line of text. The hyphen remains there only while it is needed. If you add words or change text and this changes the position of the hyphenated word on the line, the word will close up and the hyphen will disappear. Alternately, the hyphen can be put into text at the end of the line when you automatically check for hyphenation. Functionally, it is the same as the hyphen you manually put into your text.

The second type of hyphen is referred to as an *optional hyphen,* a hyphen that stays inside a word but doesn't print unless it is at the end of a line of text. Thus, you are, in effect, telling the system where to break a word in advance of knowing whether or not the word will need to be broken. It may be useful to enter optional hyphens in very large words or phrases to make it easier for the system to adjust the line widths of your document. To enter an optional hyphen, press CTRL - (CTRL-hyphen). Unless you have set up your system to show hidden characters, these optional hyphens remain hidden and won't print unless they are needed.

A problem sometimes occurs when you are typing a hard hyphen inside specially formatted text. Occasionally, the hard hyphen prints as normal text and causes the subsequent text also to be normally formatted (losing the special format that existed before the hard hyphen). The best way around this is to ignore the problem and then go back and highlight the text to which you want to assign the special character format. Next, assign the special format to the entire block of text; the hyphen then also carries the special format.

Line Spacing and Alignment

Getting into the Format Paragraph Menu is simple. Using the mouse, select Format and then select Paragraph. Using the keyboard, press ESC-F-P and the Format Paragraph Menu appears, as shown here.

```
FORMAT PARAGRAPH alignment: █Left█ Centered Right Justified
       left indent: 0"          first line: 0"        right indent: 0"
       line spacing: 1 li     space before: 0 li     space after: 0 li
       keep together: Yes(No)  keep follou: Yes(No)  side by side: Yes(No)
Select option                                        ▲
Page 1   {o}                        ?                Microsoft Word: FORMCHAR.DOC
```

You have already worked with the alignment options for paragraphs. These options can easily be selected using the ALT key combinations. You can also select alignment from within the Format Paragraph Menu by typing the first letter of your choice, by pointing to your preference and clicking the left mouse button, or by pressing SPACE to move the highlight to your choice of alignments.

The Left Indent and Right Indent fields are not exactly what you would expect. On most word processing systems, these indents would correlate closely with left and right margins. However, your page margins are set in the Format Division Margins Menu—the system already knows your margins. Thus, if you already had a 1-inch margin and wanted to start printing a paragraph 2 inches in from the left side of the paper, you would instruct the system to give you a 1-inch indent (1-inch indent plus 1-inch margin equals 2 inches). Remember that the left indent is relative to the preset margin and not to the edge of the paper.

The right margin is approximately the same as the left margin in terms of what a different setting will accomplish. If you were to set a right indent of 1 inch and already had a 1-inch right margin, your print would end 2 inches in from the right margin. Combining the left and right margins allows you to produce a narrower column that is easily recognizable and stands out from the rest of your text.

The First Line option provides you with flexibility in setting up your paragraph. As with left and right indents, it can be a positive or negative number. By varying the values, you can produce some interesting results. This option tells the system where to print the first line of text. Thus, if you wanted to indent the first line of a paragraph while printing the rest of the paragraph flush with the margin, you could set the first line indent at .5 inch. (Of course, you could always press TAB to accomplish this. However, you might want to change the first line indent in an entire document. By highlighting the entire document and then assigning the first line indent, you could change every paragraph in the document with a single command.)

This feature also lets you do what is known as an outdent. The *outdent* is a paragraph in which the first line starts at the left margin (or to the left of the rest of the paragraph), and the rest of the lines starts further from the margin. Thus, setting a left indent of .5 inch and a first line indent of −.5 inch would result in a paragraph in which the first line begins at the left margin, and the subsequent lines begin .5 inch from the left margin. The first line indent is measured relative to the position of the left indent—it is added to the position of the left indent. Thus, if you had a 2-inch indent and a −.5-inch outdent (or first line), the first line would begin printing 1.5 inches from the left margin.

The outdent is useful for calling attention to special paragraphs. There's another, probably more valuable, use for this capability: preparing tabular materials. In tabular or outline listings, an indent is used for each level of heading. The supporting text in a heading follows the indent for the subhead for the particular category. For example:

g. The Paragraph Mark—carrying paragraph and formats over.

In this example the first character g was indented (so .5 inch had to be added to the left indent figure to make the tab appear at the right position). The setting was for a 1-inch indent (the second and subsequent lines were to print 1 inch from the margin). The first line was set for −1 inch, which brought the cursor back to the left margin and allowed the tab to place the g at the right position. If a tab were not used before the g, a first line setting of −.5 inch would have accomplished the desired goal.

Obviously, making a new setting for each level of indentation is inconvenient. Microsoft Word provides you with the ability to copy formatting from one section to another. It also allows you to build and apply style sheets, which carry the formatting information for particular purposes—in this case for each level of an outline. These features are discussed Chapter 8.

To select the indents, you can point at the parameter you want to change, click the mouse button and type in the new number, or you can press TAB to move into the area you want to change.

NOTE: You can make these measurements in inches, centimeters, 10- or 12-pitch characters, or points. For now, it is probably easiest to work with the most familiar units of measurement. However, if you were to make your entries using points, you would be able to prepare a more accurate, more precise looking document, since you can break this measurement into 72 discrete divisions. You can change your unit of measure by using the Options Menu. You can also make your entries in different units by specifying the unit after the number. Thus, if you entered 72 pt, you would still have a 1 inch indent. The system would automatically convert the setting to your selected unit of measurement. ■

The next field, Line Spacing, allows you to tell the system how much space you want between lines of the paragraph: single spacing, double spacing, or some other type of spacing. For most standard documents, single, 1½, or double spacing is the response to this prompt. But if you were using a larger font, you would want to have more space between the lines for which those fonts are used. Microsoft Word defines one line as 12 points ($\frac{1}{6}$ inch). You can tell the system how much space you want between lines by typing in the number of lines (at $\frac{1}{6}$ inch per line) you desire. You can also type in decimal fractions of lines.

There are other ways to tell the system how much space you want between lines. You can type in a vertical measure in terms of inches (by typing in. or "), centimeters (by typing cm.), or points (by typing pt.). The unit of measurement must follow the number you select (that is, 1" or .4 cm.).

The system can also automatically adjust the space in the paragraph. Instead of typing in a number to indicate the amount of space you desire, type auto. The system then automatically adjusts the space based on the size of the largest character in each line. Thus, if you used a larger font, the system would automatically put more space between the lines containing large font text. When you returned to a small font, the space between the lines with the small font would automatically be decreased.

The Space Before and Space After prompts require you to supply the space to insert between paragraphs. Some Word users never put space between paragraphs while they do keyboard entry. Instead, they set the space before or after a paragraph using these parameters, and the system automatically separates the paragraphs. The measurements can be entered using lines, inches, centimeters, or points. There is no automatic setting for these parameters. If you use the Space Before parameter, the system will insert a space before the next paragraph. However, if the next paragraph begins a new page, that paragraph will begin at the top of the page and not be dropped down a line. Being able to do this automatically provides a more professional-looking document, saves paper, and saves the time it would otherwise take to make this adjustment.

The Space After parameter automatically inserts space following each paragraph. The Space Before and Space After parameters are additive. If you set one line before, and one line after, you would end up with two lines between each paragraph. Further, the Space After parameter always inserts a space, even when the next paragraph would otherwise begin at the top of a page. Since space between paragraphs is handled by the Space Before parameter, there is little reason to use the Space After setting.

The Keep Together prompt allows you to determine how to treat a paragraph that ends a page. If the paragraph is too long to fit at the end of a page, telling the system yes at this prompt makes the system move the entire paragraph to the top of the following page. This setting probably should not be applied to an entire document. If it were, your document would end up with many pages of different lengths. This option most appropriately fits tables, paragraphs, columns, or lists that shouldn't be broken up. (Remember that you can use the NEW LINE command to end a line but not to begin a new paragraph—this type of paragraph should most often be kept together.)

The Keep Follow option is useful when you want two paragraphs to be closely associated. For example, you may be preparing instructions or a section of a legal brief that requires a steady flow of thought. Separating the two closely related paragraphs may make it difficult to maintain the flow of thought between the two. In this case the system can be instructed to determine when the second paragraph should be printed onto the following page. However, instead of starting the next page with a new paragraph, it prints the last two lines of the first paragraph at the top of the next page.

If you were to set this option and apply it to an entire document, the pages of the document might be somewhat varied in length, since you would be forcing page breaks at specific locations. However, each page would then begin with the last two lines of the preceding page, which could make it easier to reassemble a document (since all pages would be logically joined to the ones following them). Automatically numbering pages is another excellent way to keep pages in order. The main use for the Keep Follow option is to retain a logical connection between paragraphs you don't want printed on two separate pages.

The final option on this menu, Side by Side, relates to multi-column pages. Using this option, you can produce side-by-side columns of text. This option and its use are discussed in Chapter 10.

Once you have indicated all your selections, press RETURN to accept the changes. Using a mouse, you could have moved your pointer to the words FORMAT PARAGRAPH at the top left corner of the menu and clicked either mouse button. You also could have moved it anywhere within the menu and used the right mouse button to apply your changes and get back into the document.

If you decided not to make any changes in the Format Paragraph or Format Character Menu, pressing ESC would bring you back into your document without any modifications being saved.

Using Key Commands to Format Paragraphs   There are also quick ways to change the look of your paragraphs from the keyboard. These are listed in Table 5-2.

It should be noted that these key combinations only work when no style sheet is attached. If you were using a style sheet, you would have to type ALT-X before entering the desired code (for example, ALT-X-C).

Some of the terms in Table 5-2 may require explanation. "Widen hanging indent" sets up the outdent. In the earlier example in which an outline was prepared, using this key combination would keep the first line of text

Result	*Key Command*
Centered text	ALT-C
Indent first line 1/2 inch	ALT-F
Justified text	ALT-J
Left-aligned text	ALT-L
Reduce left indent 1/2 inch	ALT-M
Widen left indent 1/2 inch	ALT-N
Open paragraph spacing (1 line before paragraph)	ALT-O
Standard paragraph spacing	ALT-P
Right-aligned paragraph	ALT-R
Widen hanging indent 1/2 inch plus tab	ALT-T
Double space lines	ALT-2

Table 5-2.   Formatting Paragraphs Using Key Commands

at the margin, and push all remaining lines to the right in one-half inch increments. Using this command twice would properly position the top line and place the body of the text at the correct spot.

The ALT-N command pushes the entire paragraph one-half inch to the right. As with the ALT-T command, its effect can be cumulative, resulting in indents of a multiple of one-half inch. In addition, it can be combined with other paragraph formatting commands. The ALT-O combination inserts one line before each paragraph.

The effect of each command is additive: you can get a double-spaced, justified paragraph with a two-inch indent and one-half inch hanging indent by pressing the appropriate combination of keys. If you make a mistake entering the formatting codes, you must return to your standard paragraph setting by pressing ALT-P and reentering your paragraph parameters.

Using the Mouse to Change Indents   Although you can change indents by entering numbers at the appropriate prompts while in the Format Paragraph screen, you can also make indent changes using the mouse. To do this, you must first get into the Format Paragraph Menu by using the mouse or the keyboard. (It's quicker using the keyboard — type ESC-F-P.) Three symbols should appear on the ruler at the top of the screen: a left bracket ([), a right bracket (]), and a first line indent symbol (|). The left and right brackets represent the left and right indents. Unless your first line and left indents are at different points, you won't see the first line indent marker.

To change the indents, move the mouse pointer to the tab symbol you want to move, hold down the right mouse button, move the symbol to the position where you want your new indent, and then release the mouse button. To demonstrate this, move the left indent to the 1-inch mark. You should see the first line symbol still at the left margin, and the left indent at the 1-inch position. The Left Indent field at the bottom of the screen shows a left indent of 1″. The First Line field shows a −1″ indent (meaning that it is still at the left margin). Again, the first line position is relative to the left indent, not the left margin. Your screen should look like Figure 5-7.

The mouse can, of course, be used to change any of the three settings. If you wanted to move the left indent and the first line setting so that they were at the same position, you would have to move each mark individually. (Note that although you can use the mouse to quickly set right and left

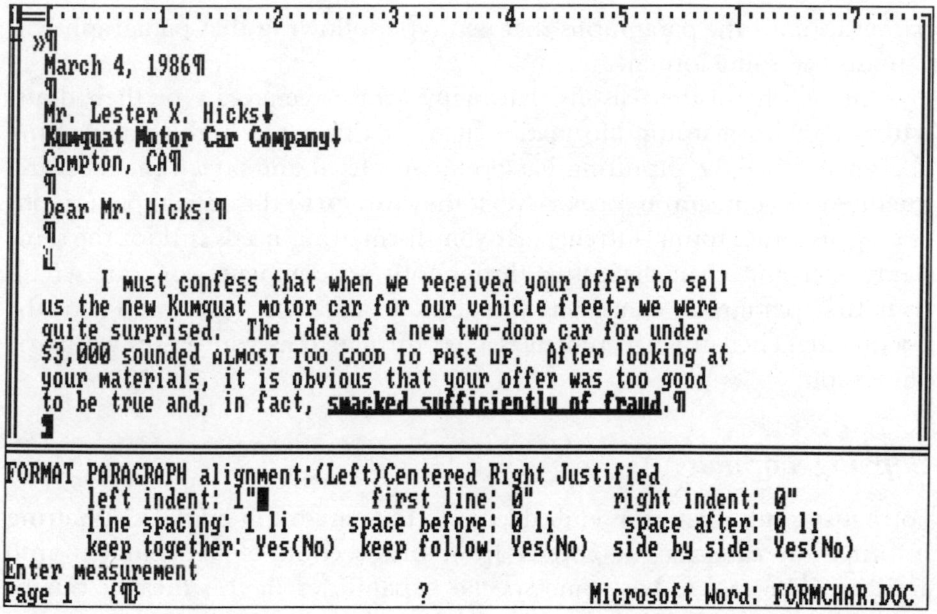

```
▐═[···········1·········2·········3·········4·········5·········]·········7···]▌
 »¶
  March 4, 1986¶
  ¶
  Mr. Lester X. Hicks↓
  Kumquat Motor Car Company↓
  Compton, CA¶
  ¶
  Dear Mr. Hicks:¶
  ¶
  ▒
      I must confess that when we received your offer to sell
  us the new Kumquat motor car for our vehicle fleet, we were
  quite surprised.  The idea of a new two-door car for under
  $3,000 sounded ALMOST TOO GOOD TO PASS UP.  After looking at
  your materials, it is obvious that your offer was too good
  to be true and, in fact, smacked sufficiently of fraud.¶
  ▊
```
```
FORMAT PARAGRAPH alignment:(Left)Centered Right Justified
     left indent: 1"▮          first line: 0"       right indent: 0"
     line spacing: 1 li      space before: 0 li      space after: 0 li
     keep together: Yes(No)   keep follow: Yes(No)   side by side: Yes(No)
Enter measurement
Page 1   {¶D}                         ?            Microsoft Word: FORMCHAR.DOC
```

Figure 5-7.   The Format Paragraph screen for a paragraph with an indent first line

indents and first line indents, if you are using indents that are in ½-inch increments, it may still be faster to use ALT key combination.)

Using the Paragraph Mark
In Formatting

The paragraph mark has a special meaning to Microsoft Word. With most other word processing systems, RETURN merely tells the system that you have completed a paragraph. With Microsoft Word, the paragraph mark tells the system much more. In addition to signaling the end of a paragraph, the mark also contains complete formatting information for the paragraph that precedes it. For this reason, if you make a change to one paragraph, all the paragraphs that you type following that paragraph will contain the same format.

This is one of the reasons that many Word operators type their drafts without any formatting information attached. They can highlight an entire document once the inputting has been completed and attach the most frequently used paragraph format. Next, they can go to the special paragraphs and apply other formats to them. If your formatting needs call for the same paragraph and character setup throughout a document, you can set up your first paragraph exactly as you want it and then type the rest of the document. The entire document is then formatted as you set up your first paragraph.

Copying Formats

Formatting information is embedded into the paragraph marks. Formatting information can also be copied from one section of a document into another. The mouse has some special capabilities in this area. It can be used to copy paragraph or character formatting.

To copy character formatting using the mouse, highlight the text (word, sentence, character, and so on) you want to reformat. Move the cursor to the character whose format you want to copy. Hold down ALT and click the left mouse button to copy the format.

Assume that you want to copy the bold and double underline of the last line of the first paragraph in FORMCHAR.DOC to the word *must* at the beginning of the paragraph. Using your mouse, highlight the word *must*. Next, move your pointer to any character in the phrase "smacked sufficiently of fraud." Hold down ALT and click the left mouse button. The word *must* is now bold with a double underline. To undo that format, point to another word in the document with the format you desire. Then hold down ALT key as you click the left mouse button to copy that character format.

Copying paragraph formats is also simple. To do this, highlight the paragraph you want to reformat. Next, move the mouse pointer to the selection bar (near the left margin) to the left of the paragraph whose format you want to copy. While holding down ALT, click the right mouse button.

Using the Keyboard to Copy Formats   The keyboard has a limited capability for copying formatting. In order to copy a format using the keyboard, you must first get into the Format Character or Format Paragraph Menu and make the changes in a block of text. Next, move the cursor to the text you want to copy the format to and press F4 to copy the last function performed.

Since your last action may have been to change a character's format, pressing F4 copies the changes to whatever area you highlighted. This works until you edit some text or make other changes within the system. For this method of format copying to work, you must do it immediately after your first format change is made. Otherwise, you may perform some other function and copy that operation into the new area. Applying style sheets or using the mouse is a better alternative than using the F4 key.

TAB FORMATTING

Microsoft Word normally sets up tab stops every .5 inch. In most cases this may be adequate for your needs. However, Word provides you with other options. To see these, get into the Format Tabs screen. To do this using the keyboard,

Type: ESC-F-T

Using the mouse, select Format by clicking the left button and select Tabs, again by clicking the left button. "SET CLEAR RESET-ALL" then appears on the screen.

Format Tabs Clear is used to clear individual tabs. When you use this option, you must indicate which tab(s) you want cleared. The system then clears the tab(s). Format Tabs Reset-All clears out all the tab settings on the line. You receive no confirmation for each tab setting.

Format Tabs Set is used to set up the tabs for your document or for a highlighted area. There are four types of tabs. The first type is the *left-aligned tab*. When you tab to a left-aligned tab and begin typing, your text moves to the right of the tab. This tab is normally used when typing text. A *center-aligned tab* is used for column headings and other types of headings. Any text typed at a center-aligned tab is centered around the position of this tab.

A *right-aligned tab* is approximately the opposite of a left-aligned tab. Any text typed at a right-aligned tab is pushed to the left of the tab. The effect of this type of tab is the same as if you were typing a right-aligned paragraph. This is useful when you want to emphasize key sections by putting section headings at the right margin instead of the left margin.

The right-aligned tab is also useful when you prepare tables (such as tables of contents), in which you use whole numbers, not decimals. You can type the numbers at a right-aligned tab, and all the numbers line up. For example, if you needed to use the numbers 5, 18, and 124, you would align the 5, 8, and 4 by using a right-aligned tab. The fourth type of tab, a *decimal tab*, is used to build numbers around a decimal point. In effect, you are aligning the decimal points.

When you set tabs from the keyboard, the first field is the position of the tab. You can type in the number for the position or use LEFT ARROW and RIGHT ARROW to move the tab to the desired location. As you do this, you see the highlight on the ruler moving and the numbers in the position line changing to reflect the ruler position. Once you have placed the tab where you want it, press TAB to get you to the next field, Alignment. This tells the system which type of tab you want. Type the first letter for the tab type or press SPACE to make your selection (or tab to the next field to leave the tab unchanged).

The *leader character* is the character printed between the point where you press TAB and the point where the tab (or first text around the tab) appears. In most cases this should be left blank. However, if you were building a table of contents, you might prefer to have dots connecting the section title with the page number. By selecting a leader character, you could use the desired symbol to connect the text with the tab. This is an easy way to get a professional-looking document. You can select the appropriate leader character by pressing SPACE or typing the desired leader character.

Once you are satisfied with your tab setting, press INS to set the tab in the document. If the ruler already has tabs set, you can quickly move from tab to tab by pressing UP ARROW and DOWN ARROW. To delete a tab setting, move to the tab you want to remove and press DEL.

Tabs can also be set using the mouse. First, select the type of tab you want to use, if it isn't already set. (For example, if you want a centered tab, you must select this attribute.) To do this, point at the attribute desired and click the left mouse button. Next, point to the position on the ruler where you want your tab to be located and click the left mouse button. To delete a tab, point to the tab you want to remove and click both mouse buttons. Once your tabs have been set, you may get back into your document by pressing RETURN or by pointing to the words FORMAT TABS SET and clicking the left mouse button.

PAGE/DIVISION FORMATTING

A page and a division are roughly the same thing in Microsoft Word. The Format Division Menu allows you to apply a format to either a page or a division. Before you print your document, you can have the system automatically break it down into pages. There may be times when you want to end a page before the system would automatically do so. For example, this may occur in a document made up of many sections. It is desirable to start each section on a new page. A division may also be useful if you want to change the look on a form or other nonstandard document.

You can place a forced page break symbol at the end of a section of a document to signal the end of a division. To do this,

Type: CTRL-RETURN

The system then adds a page break line. This appears as a solid line but is treated by the system as a single character. It is very simple to delete.

Get into the Format Division Menu. The first of three options is Margins. When you select this option, the Format Division Margins Menu appears at the bottom of the screen, as shown here.

```
═[·······1·······2·······3·······4·······5·······]·······7···
»¶
March 4, 1986¶
¶
Mr. Lester X. Hicks↓
Kumquat Motor Car Company↓
Compton, CA¶
¶
Dear Mr. Hicks:¶
¶
¶
       I must confess that when we received your offer to sell
us the new Kumquat motor car for our vehicle fleet, we were
quite surprised.  The idea of a new two-door car for under
$3,000 sounded ALMOST TOO GOOD TO PASS UP.  After looking at
your materials, it is obvious that your offer was too good
to be true and, in fact, smacked sufficiently of fraud.¶
¶
       In America we are accustomed to receiving a complete

FORMAT DIVISION MARGINS top: 1"    bottom: 1"      left: 1.25"  right: 1.25"
                page length: 11"    width: 8.5"     gutter margin: 0"
                running-head position from top: 0.5"   from bottom: 0.5"
Enter measurement
Page 1   {¶        }            ?            Microsoft Word: FORMCHAR.DOC
```

This menu is used to specify the type of paper you are using and the margins you desire. You will recall that the margins are absolute—you can't print outside of them—and indents are in addition to the margins you have already set. The basic default format for Word is to use standard letter-sized paper, as can be seen in the second line of the menu (8.5-by-11-inch paper). For legal-sized paper, the page length should be changed to 14 inches.

The margin settings are relatively straightforward. The left and right margins are set to provide 6 inches of text, evenly centered on the page. There may be times when you have to get text to fit into a certain page size. For example, you might have a letter that must take up only one sheet of paper. With the standard margins, the page might run a bit too long. One relatively easy way to adjust the length would be to widen your text area slightly (by decreasing the size of your margins). You could also creatively modify margins to lengthen a short document. The ultimate goal, of course, is to produce a document that fits into a desired space, yet doesn't look odd. (Note that another way to modify the size of a document is to change the printer pitch or alter the space between lines or paragraphs. Microsoft Word provides you with a wide range of tools for making minor changes to a document to make it fit into a desired amount of space.)

The gutter margin is used to allow extra space for binding your document. For example, you might be preparing a report to be staple bound. The edge of the paper closest to the binding requires an extra half-inch. By setting a gutter margin, you would allow extra space for this so that no text would be obscured when the document was bound. The gutter margin gives precedence to your page margins. That is, if you were using a one-half inch gutter, your margins would stay the same, but your text would be decreased by the one-half inch used by the gutter.

The gutter alternates from odd to even pages, so that if you were printing the pages back to back, the gutters would be correctly placed for binding. If you were not printing pages back to back, but printing only on the front of each sheet, you would not be able to use the gutter margin option to create a gutter. Instead, you would increase your left margin to accommodate the extra space required for binding.

Running-head position applies to headers or footers. This tells the system how far from the top or bottom of the page to begin printing your header or footer. Headers and footers (referred to in Microsoft Word documentation as *running heads*) represent text printed at the top or bottom of each page. Setting up headers and footers is discussed in Chapter 12.

As with the other Word screens, changes can be entered using the keyboard (pressing TAB and number keys) or the mouse. The margins can be applied to an entire document or to any number of divisions. Again, a division is defined as a page or as a group of text that ends with a required page break. Microsoft Word can determine which context you are applying your settings to.

Formatting Page Numbers

Another option on the Format Division Menu provides for the automatic numbering of pages as they are printed. When you get to the Format Division Page Numbers Menu, you have the option of specifying page numbering, the placement of page numbers relative to the top and left margins, and the way you want the numbers to appear.

The options for locating the page numbers are fairly clear. The Numbering prompt relates to how pages should be numbered with reference to other divisions. Continuous numbering carries over the page numbers from the previous division. For example, if the last division ended on page 10, the new division will begin on page 11.

The Start option is used to tell the system to begin numbering with the number that you assign in response to the At prompt. Thus, you may begin each division at page 1, if you wish. Or, if your new division is the beginning of a new chapter, you can begin printing at the correct number of the next page. Finally, you have a choice of numbering methods. Normally, the default (1) would be used to give you arabic numbers. However, you may choose to use uppercase or lowercase roman numerals (for example, for the preface to a book) or letters. Word supports any of the desired options.

Microsoft Word provides you with a wide range of methods for modifying and improving the presentation of text. Most of these methods can be accessed using the keyboard or the mouse, and menus won't often need to be accessed. Most of the Format Menu commands have been covered by this chapter. Additional options are covered in the appropriate sections of this book.

ADVANCED TEXT PREPARATION AND PRINTING

So far you've gone through many of the most important steps in preparing a professional-looking document. However, extra steps can be taken to improve your documents even more: searching for and replacing text or characters, spelling checking, repagination, and hyphenation.

SEARCH AND REPLACE

The Search function and the Replace function are different functions built around approximately the same constraints. In some ways the Replace function goes one step beyond the Search function: it not only finds a character string, but also finds it and replaces it with another string (or blank spaces, if you choose).

To use either command, you must specify the exact string to look for. If, for example, you asked the system to search for a single letter, it would find all occurrences of that letter. If you wanted to search for a single word, such as *the*, the system would find all occurrences of the word *the*, and it would also find the same key combination in many other words — mo*the*r, fa*the*r, *the*ory, and so on. In order to select a specific word, you must include the spaces before and after that word. Thus, to search for the word *the*, type SPACEtheSPACE. Unlike some other word processors, Word can also be told to search for the specific word. It is still a good practice to include the spaces before and after the word.

In addition to searching for text or numbers, you can search for other types of characters or for less specifically identified text. Using the question mark (?), you can tell the system to accept any character in that space. For example, when you tell the system to find the word, *ch?p,* it may search for *chip, chap, chop,* or any other word arranged as listed. If you were to tell the system to search for the string ???, the system would find all three-letter words.

To search for other types of characters, you must enter the carat (^), which is located on the 6 key on most keyboards, followed by a letter. Table 6-1 lists these characters and what they search for.

You can now try a Search. Load FORMCHAR.DOC back into the system and rename the file STEIGER. You have found out that Mr. Hicks is using a pseudonym: his name isn't really Hicks; it is Steiger. Further, his first name isn't Lester—it is Luther. And Kumquat Motor Car Company has adopted a new, more appropriate name, Lemon Motor Car Company.

Characters	*Search For*
^w	White space. Searches for any number and combination of spaces, tab characters, nonbreaking spaces, new line characters, paragraph marks, division marks, and manually inserted page break characters. The ^w character cannot be used in the "with text" command field (in the Replace Menu).
^s	Nonbreaking space
^t	Tab character
^p	Paragraph mark
^n	New line character
^-	Optional hyphen
^d	Division mark or page break character

Table 6-1. Special Search Characters

First, you want to change Lester to Luther. With the cursor located at the beginning of the document, select the Search function. Using the keyboard,

Type: ESC-S

Using the mouse, point to the word Search and click the left mouse button. The Search Menu looks like this:

```
SEARCH text: █
        direction: Up(Down) case: Yes(No) whole word: Yes(No)
Enter text
Page 1   {}                        ?              Microsoft Word: STEIGER.DOC
```

Type the text you want to search for, *Lester.* (Remember that it is preferable to type SPACELesterSPACE.) Next, press TAB to move to the direction prompt. This tells the system whether you want to search from the beginning to the end of the document (a Down Search), or from the end to the beginning (an Up Search). Since the cursor is at the beginning of the document, you must specify a Down Search. Since that is the normal Search default, press TAB to move to the next field.

For the next field, Case, you must specify whether you want to find an exact case match. For example, if you answered yes, the system would stop at all occurrences of the name *Lester,* but wouldn't stop at *lester.* If you answered no, the system would stop at all occurrences of the word, regardless of which letters were capitalized. Although you shouldn't have any occurrences of the name in a lowercase form, you would like to check for every appearance of the word. Leave the no response—this tells the system you don't want a case-significant Search.

The next field, Whole Word, allows you to specify whether you want to find the string only as a separate word or find each occurrence, whether inside a word or as a separate word. In the example previously given, using the word *the,* a whole word search would only find the word *the* and wouldn't find other words (such as o*the*r and whe*the*r). In most cases the answer to this prompt is yes. Tell the system yes now.

Once the Search parameters are set, you can begin a Search. Press RETURN if using your keyboard, or point to the word SEARCH and click the left mouse button (or make your selections with the mouse and click the right button when you've made your last change). The system begins its search and finds the first occurrence of the word. Change *Lester* to *Luther.*

NOTE: In this example, since you are replacing three letters in the middle of the name, you could have searched for the string *est* and changed it to *uth*. However, it is usually best to search for and replace the whole word, particularly when a string like *est* can be found in other words. ■

Now, check for any other occurrences of the word *Luther*. Using a mouse, point to the word SEARCH and click the right mouse button to begin the search immediately. Using the keyboard,

Type: ESC-S

to return to the Search Menu and

Type: RETURN

to begin the search. The system prompts, "Search text not found," indicating that it has searched the document and is unable to find another occurrence of this string.

Return to the beginning of the document (press CTRL-PGUP or use the mouse). You now want to replace every occurrence of *Hicks* with *Steiger*. In this case you want to use the Replace function. Select this function using the keyboard or mouse. The text you last searched for or replaced should still be in the Replace Text field. When you begin to type new text, the old text disappears from the screen.

Type: **Hicks**

Move to the next field (press TAB or use the mouse and click the left button). In the With Text field, type in the replacement for the searched text. In this case

Type: **Steiger**

Note that you can't replace text with blank space using the ^W command. You can delete text by leaving this field blank. If you want to do more than delete text (that is, add blank space where text used to be), you can do this in two steps: replace the text with some otherwise unused string, such as SPACEfSPACE, and then search for that string and type in the desired number of spaces.

NOTE: You can use nonbreaking spaces to enter blanks to replace text. A *nonbreaking space* is a special type of space, usually used between words in a special phrase to prevent the system from making a line break in a word with such a character. For example, if you used the phrase "vis-a-vis" in a document and did not want the phrase printed on two lines, you would use the nonbreaking space. To enter a nonbreaking space in normal text, press CTRL-SPACE. ■

Move on to the next field, Confirm, which is used to indicate whether you want to confirm a replacement before it is made. Telling the system no means that the system goes through the entire document (from the position of the cursor to the end of the document) and makes the change indicated each time it finds the searched-for text. Answering yes tells the system to prompt you before replacing text. Answer yes to this prompt.

The Case field is much the same as it is in Search mode. In this case not only will the system look for a case-exact match, but it will also make a case-specific replacement. That is, if you answer yes, telling the system to replace *Hicks* with *steiger* (no caps), it will type *steiger* every time it finds *Hicks,* but not when it finds *hicks* or any other capitalization variation. If you answer no to the prompt, the system will search for each occurrence of the string and replace it, matching the case of the original. Thus, it will replace *Hicks* with *Steiger,* and *hicks* with *steiger.*

The last field, Whole Word, is the same as it is in Search mode. Set your configurations to those illustrated here:

```
REPLACE text: Hicks█                    uith text: Steiger
        confirm:(Yes)No  case: Yes(No) uhole uord:(Yes)No
Enter text
```

Finally, tell the system to begin the process by using the mouse or by pressing RETURN. The system finds the first occurrence of the word *Hicks* and issues the following prompt at the lower left corner of the screen:

"Enter Y to replace, N to ignore, or press Esc to cancel."

Type: Y (or click the left mouse button for yes)

and the system makes the replacement.

The system continues to scan the entire document for all occurrences of the target text. It stops at the salutation and again prompts for replacement. Again, tell the system to replace the text. When the system can find no more words for replacement, it tells you how many replacements have been made. At the bottom left side of your screen, the system indicates "2 replacements made".

Finally, do a global replacement of *Kumquat* with *Lemon*. To do a global replacement, answer no in the Confirm field. The system replaces the word *and* the character format. Thus, the boldfaced *Kumquat* in the address line is now a boldfaced *Lemon*.

HYPHENATION

Before you print your document, it is a good practice to run a spelling and hyphenation check on the document. There are some good reasons for this. Word doesn't automatically hyphenate words as you type them. Word's automatic word wrap moves long words onto the next line if they won't fit on the previous line. When a long word pushes the line past the end-of-line position, the entire word ends up on the next line, leaving a somewhat shortened first line. But if you can hyphenate the long word, the beginning can go on the previous line and make it look less short. Besides improving the look of a paragraph (by making lines more uniform in length), this may also save a few lines in total document length.

Microsoft Word has the capability to search through the words in your document and hyphenate those words that can be split at the end of a line. While still in STEIGER.DOC, go to the Library Menu. The Library Menu looks like this:

```
LIBRARY: Autosort Hyphenate Index Number Run Spell Table
Select option or type command letter                    ▲
```

Now select the Hyphenate option.

The Hyphenate Menu presents you with two choices. First, you must decide if you want to confirm its hyphenation decision. If you answer *n*, the system will automatically hyphenate all the text for which it determines hyphens to be necessary. If you answer *y*, it will highlight each affected word and the suggested hyphen location.

Second, you must decide if you want to hyphenate words that begin with capital letters. In many cases these are proper names and shouldn't be hyphenated. If you choose to hyphenate capitalized words, you should also have the system confirm hyphenations to avoid hyphenating words that should be left intact. The hyphens the system inserts are soft hyphens. If you make changes in your document that move the hyphenated word to a different position on this or the next line, the hyphens will disappear from the word and your word will print normally.

As it is currently set up, the STEIGER.DOC won't present any hyphenation choices. However, by changing the line width, you can get the system to demonstrate this capability. Move the cursor to the first paragraph of text.

Type: ALT-N

to indent the paragraph one-half inch. Next, tell the system to hyphenate and to confirm hyphenation. Begin the process (by pressing RETURN or by using the mouse button), and the system scans the document. The system highlights the letter that follows the position in which the hyphen is to be placed. In this case the second *f* in *offer* is hyphenated. At the bottom of the screen, the system prompts you to confirm whether you want the hyphen. If you choose not to hyphenate the word at all, type N. You can also move the hyphen to a different part of the word by pressing LEFT ARROW or RIGHT ARROW. (The mouse won't work here.) Confirm the selection of hyphenation location. The system then highlights the second *f* in *sufficiently*. Again confirm the hyphenation decision.

Your hyphenated paragraph should look like the paragraph in Figure 6-1. If the paragraph looks different (it may have the hyphenated words in the middle of the line, with a hyphen inside the word), you should change one of your display options. To do this, select the Options Menu and answer yes to the printer display prompt. This displays the margins as the printer will print them. You don't want the paragraph indented, so

Type: ALT-M

to return the paragraph to its original margins.

SPELLING CHECKING

Before you print a document, you should, in most cases, perform a spelling check on it. Perhaps the term *spelling check* is somewhat unfortunate. This procedure does more than check for spelling errors: it looks for a more common form of error, the typing error, and it also checks for unfamiliar words. No matter how well you spell, the spelling checking procedure is

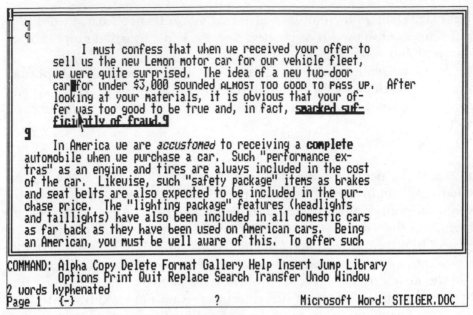

Figure 6-1.   A hyphenated paragraph

very valuable, since it can be used to check for typing errors. Many writers routinely check the spelling in everything they write to make sure that the typing is accurate.

In addition to basic spelling checking, you can add new words to the system dictionary, to a special dictionary for the document, or to a user dictionary. With luck, your document, STEIGER.DOC, has no spelling errors. However, it undoubtedly has words (proper names, city name) that the system doesn't recognize.

The spelling checking utility is accessed through the Library Menu. First, select Library, using the keyboard or mouse. Next, select Spell, again using the keyboard or mouse. The system prompts, "saving work file." Next, the Spell Menu screen appears with a variety of options. These options are Dictionary, Help, Options, Proof, and Quit. You can select any of the options by typing the first letter of the option, by using the mouse, or by pressing TAB or SPACE to move to the option. To check the spelling in your document, select Proof.

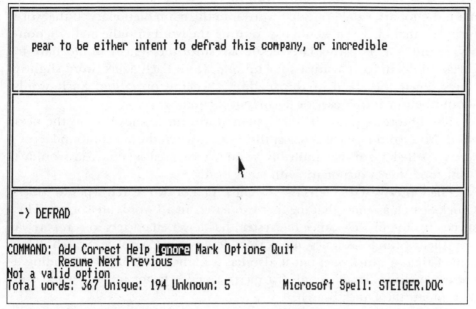

pear to be either intent to defrad this company, or incredible

-) DEFRAD

COMMAND: Add Correct Help Ignore Mark Options Quit
        Resume Next Previous
Not a valid option
Total words: 367 Unique: 194 Unknown: 5   Microsoft Spell: STEIGER.DOC

Figure 6-2.   A screen showing a sentence containing misspelled words and command lines for the Proof option

The system then checks all the words in the document against the system's master dictionary and a user dictionary. How many words were found, how many unique words were found, and how many words couldn't be found in the system's dictionary are indicated at the bottom of the screen. The suspect word is shown in the lower of the three partitions, and the word is shown in the sentence where it occurs. In this case the word *defraud* was incorrectly typed as *defrad*. Figure 6-2 illustrates the appearance of the screen.

You have several options here. If the word had been spelled correctly and it was one you would use in other documents, you could choose to add it to your dictionary. To add the word, you would select the Add option. The system would prompt you to specify which dictionary you want the word added to.

If you selected the user dictionary, the word would become a part of your special dictionary, with your own required terminology. Selecting the main dictionary would put that word into the main dictionary. If the word were one that only you would use, putting the word into the main dictionary would not be particularly desirable, since the system would have to check all documents against your unique word. Each added word slightly slows down the speed of the spelling checking operation. Such words should be put into a user or document dictionary.

The Ignore option tells the system you want to move on to the next word. You would probably select this option when the system found a correctly spelled word that probably wouldn't be used again. You wouldn't want to clutter a dictionary with such words.

The Options screen tells the system which of two search types to use. A Quick Search assumes that the first two letters in all words are correct. This speeds up the process, since the system has fewer characters to compare. A Complete Search assumes no correct letters. A Complete Search takes longer than a quick one, but it also has a higher probability of finding a correct spelling for the word. If time is a major factor in your work, you may prefer the Quick Search.

Help and Quit are obvious in their function. The Correct option takes you into another menu. You are asked by the system to enter a correct spelling. At this point, for small errors, it may be best to make the minor corrections your document may need. If you want to use the system to look through its dictionary to find the correct spelling of the word, press RIGHT ARROW, or point to the word *correct* and press the right mouse button.

This *should* bring up one or more words that closely match the misspelled word. The words found by the system appear in the middle window, as shown in Figure 6-3. If one of the words is correct, move the cursor to that word. You can accept the correct spelling of the word by pressing RETURN. If the incorrectly spelled word was capitalized, answering yes to the Adjust Case prompt will substitute the correctly spelled word with the same case.

As you go through your document, you can either have the system search for similarly spelled words or type in the corrected spellings yourself. For misspelled small words, it may be faster to type in the correct spellings. If the word is new to the system, or if your "misspelled" word is actually two correctly spelled words with no space between them, the system will prompt you to confirm that your correction is correct and that you want to save the corrected word. You will probably answer no to this query most of the time.

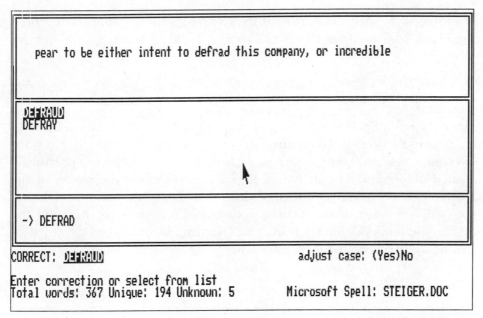

pear to be either intent to defrad this company, or incredible

DEFRAUD
DEFRAY

-> DEFRAD

CORRECT: DEFRAUD   adjust case: (Yes)No

Enter correction or select from list
Total words: 367 Unique: 194 Unknown: 5   Microsoft Spell: STEIGER.DOC

Figure 6-3.   A window showing dictionary selections that closely match the
misspelled word

You may prefer to mark a word and look it up later. When you mark a word, a symbol you select in the Spell Menu is placed in front of a suspect word. When you return to the edit screen, you can search for the mark and then check (or correct) the word. This option is good for technical, foreign, or other words that you want to check but can't check immediately.

To select the mark character, you must be in the Spell Menu. When you select Options, you can then choose which type of mark you want to use. In addition, you can speed the system somewhat by telling it to ignore all capital letters. But in most cases you will want to check words spelled with all capital letters in addition to those with either all lowercase or upper- and lowercase letters. The Next and Previous selections in the Proof Menu let you move back to words previously checked or ahead to words you want to check.

When you have completed correcting your document, you have the option of losing the changes, going back to the Proof Menu and checking your corrections again, or processing your document. Processing replaces the incorrectly spelled words with the correct spellings. To quit the spelling check at either level (Spell or Proof), type Q or select Quit with your mouse.

Dictionary Selection

From the main Spell Menu, you can select a dictionary to use in addition to the system dictionary. To do this, select the Dictionary option. If you want to create a new dictionary, type a name here. If you want to use a previously created dictionary, type its name. If you need to know the names of the available dictionaries, press RIGHT ARROW or the right mouse button, and you will see a list of the dictionaries available. Typing the name of the desired dictionary or highlighting and selecting the dictionary tells the system to use that selected dictionary when it proofs your document.

PRINTING

By now you should have a perfectly spelled, well-proportioned document, ready for printing. Printing is a virtually painless operation for most word processing operators. Before printing, you should repaginate your document, setting up page breaks where they make sense. You should also set up the printer.

The first step, for this one time only, is to set up your printer. From the Printer Menu, select Options. The Print Options Menu looks like this:

```
PRINT OPTIONS printer: RADIX
              draft: Yes(No)     queued:(Yes)No       copies: 1
              range:(All)Selection Pages      page numbers:
              feed: Manual Continuous(Bin1)Bin2 Bin3 Mixed
              widow/orphan control:(Yes)No          setup: LPT1:
Enter printer name or select from list
Page 1   {¶}                          ?          Microsoft Word: STEIGER.DOC
```

Respond to the first option by typing the name of your printer or by pressing RIGHT ARROW (or the right mouse button) to see the list of printers on files on your disk. The printer disk that came with your system has drivers for most printers.

Once the printer is selected (by typing the name, tabbing to the next field, or selecting with the mouse), you must tell the system whether you want to print in a draft or letter quality mode. This option applies most closely to dot matrix (but not laser) printers. Draft mode prints each character once. Letter quality mode prints each character twice. Obviously, a draft print takes about half as long as a letter quality print — the tradeoff is that the image is lighter and often much more difficult to read.

A *queued print file* is one put into a line (or queue) waiting for printout. When you queue a file to the printer, you can do your editing while the document is printing. However, you can't edit a document you are printing, and system response is slowed somewhat (since the system is handling the word processing program and the print function alternately).

The Copies field is used to determine how many copies of your document to print. The Range field is similarly straightforward. It is used to determine how much of a document you want to print. The default setting, All, instructs the system to print the entire document from beginning to end. Selection instructs the system to print text you have highlighted. Finally, Pages instructs the system to print selected pages. You may make more than one page selection at the Page Numbers field. For example, you could make the following selection: 3-6, 27, 45-999. As a rule, if you want to print to the end of a document, you can instruct the system to print to page 999 (or 99 for a shorter document), and the printer will stop after the last page.

The feed prompt is used to indicate whether you are using a sheet feeder or not, whether you are using manual or continuous feed paper, and how sheet feeder bins are used. These are also straightforward. The Mixed Bin option assumes that your first page is loaded from Bin1, and subsequent pages from Bin2.

The Widow/Orphan Control prompt relates to treatment of a paragraph that ends a page. If that paragraph can't be printed without leaving a single line at the end of one page (widow) or a single line at the beginning of the next (orphan), answering yes to this prompt forces the system to break the page so that at least two lines of each paragraph print at the end or beginning of a page.

Finally, you must tell the system where to address the print output. In most cases you will probably use a printer with a parallel interface; also this printer will normally be connected to the port called LPT1. However, you may also use more than one printer — perhaps one printer for fast, medium quality drafts and a second (or third) printer for better quality print. In this case you may have your draft printer connected to LPT1 and your high quality printer connected to LPT2 or LPT3, or COM1 or COM2.

You may also have a printer with a serial interface. If so, you must tell Word which communication port you are using. Microsoft Word then sends the printer output to the selected communications port.

NOTE: Using a serial communications port requires slightly more setup than does setup for a printer port. Such items as data transfer speed, parity, and stop bits all have to be set to match the printer to the system. The printer setup manual supplied with Word provides the most current information on how to do this. ■

Once you set your printer options, they remain with the document until you reset them. In addition, when you start a new document, all information remains the same, with the exception of the information about how much to print — the default for each document is to print the entire document. If you haven't done so yet, make the required settings now.

Pagination

What you have developed until now has been a one-page document. If you were to begin a document and type thousands of words, the system would still indicate that you are only on page 1 (as shown at the bottom left corner of your screen). The process of pagination, as performed by Word, involves calculating the length of each line, adding these lengths, and making the breaks between pages.

Pagination can be done in two ways: attended and unattended. Unattended pagination tells the system to repaginate the document automatically, without stopping. Whether you get widows and orphans in your final printout depends upon your setting for that parameter in the Print Options Menu.

To employ unattended pagination, answer the prompt "Confirm Page Breaks?" with an *n*. This method is faster than attended pagination. If you choose to confirm page breaks, the system will stop at the position on each page where it suggests that the page be ended. You can press UP ARROW to move the page break higher up on the page. You may be able to move the end down a limited number of lines by pressing DOWN ARROW. The system won't let you end a page below the end of a sheet of paper or where it will encroach on a footer.

If you have previously repaginated, or have entered required page breaks, the system will ask you to confirm the page break. The system indicates that the current page has a page break symbol but is not long enough for a regular break. In other words, if you confirm the page break at this prompt, the page will be shorter than the others.

Once you respond to the prompt by answering *y* or *n* and pressing RETURN or by selecting with the mouse button, the system then goes to the beginning of the document and begins the repagination process. Once you've repaginated, the system provides you with page numbers for all the paginated text. The number appears at the bottom of the page. In addition, an arrow appears at the left margin to indicate the end of each page.

NOTE: Before you repaginated, or while you were editing your document, you may have inserted required page breaks. These breaks are easily deleted, should you change your mind about the positioning of the breaks. During pagination these breaks are respected and a page (regardless of length) is broken before these marks. ■

Note that as you add new text, the page numbers won't increase. In order to get a correct number of pages, you must again repaginate. Also, if you insert or remove text from a previously paginated document, the numbers won't change (and you must repaginate in order to get correctly spaced, numbered pages).

NOTE: There are alternatives to automatic pagination. If you were working on a document set up for automatic indexing or automatic table of contents preparation, the system would paginate while it worked on developing the index or table of contents. However, it is still preferable to go through a normal repagination before you create an index or a table of contents. ■

Types of Printing

You should now be back at the main Printer Menu. This menu presents you with a variety of options. Two of the first three, Printer and File, tell Word where you want the selected page(s) to print. Once you have repaginated, you can choose to print your document to the printer or to a file. If you choose to print to the printer, the file will begin printing.

Printing to a file transfers the document, with all format codes intact, into a document file on your hard or floppy disk. When you select Print File, you are prompted for the name you want to give this file. (The effect of this procedure is essentially the same as that of an unformatted Transfer

Save.) This file name can include an extension, if you prefer. You should be careful not to give it a name that is already in use, since this records the file over the previously named file. In the event that you do give the file a name already in use, the system prompts to check that you really want to record over the file.

A file prepared this way is stripped of special formatting features. Such a file can be printed on any printer from DOS level, using the PRINT *filename.ext* command. The file can also be telecommunicated.

Print Direct puts the printer into a typewriter mode so that everything you type is echoed onto the printer. This mode is useful for filling in forms. You can't see the text on your screen, and the text is not printed until you press RETURN. Thus, to some extent, even as a forms completion tool, it is of marginal value because you are required to estimate how many spaces you must indent from the margin to complete any items not at the left margin. To return to the main command line from Print Direct, press ESC.

Print Glossary prints the contents of your current glossary. The glossary is discussed in Chapter 8. Print Merge sets up the system to print documents with merged text and data. This capability and the options involved are discussed in Chapter 9.

Queued Printing

A print queue is, literally, a lineup of print jobs. If you chose queued printing in the Print Options Menu, you instructed the system to place the document in a line (or queue) of documents to be printed. The Print Queue Menu gives you control over the documents in the queue with four options: Continue, Pause, Restart, and Stop.

The Stop option stops printing of all documents in the queue. The Continue, Pause, and Restart options work hand in hand. If you wanted to go into direct printing or to print a document immediately (without placing it in the queue), you would want to select Pause. If the printer was paused in the middle of a page, you would probably have difficulty lining the paper up in exactly the same position it was in before you paused the printer. If, on the other hand, you paused the printer to make a phone call, pressing Continue would tell the printer to continue printing from the point where it paused. The Restart option tells the system to print the document from the beginning (or from the first page selected in the Print Options Menu). Again, this is useful if you stopped printing mid-page and removed the paper.

WINDOWS

Microsoft Word differs from most other word processing programs in many ways, including the terms it uses for common word processing functions and the mouse interface. Yet another key difference, its windowing capability, may be one of the most striking.

Using windows, you can have up to eight different documents active on your screen at any one time. You can expand or contract your windows to suit your current needs: you can look at many parts of the same lengthy document; review earlier versions of a document you are editing; refer back to earlier correspondence; and copy text from one window into another. Thus, although you often can do quite well without windows, the added power that windows provide can be valuable.

The mouse is probably most useful when working with windows. For many of Word's functions, it may be faster and easier to use the keyboard than it is to use the mouse. Not so with windows. Using a mouse, you can open and close windows with ease: you can highlight areas to be moved and copied and easily change the size of windows. In short, use of the mouse greatly eases the operation of windows.

TYPES OF WINDOWS

There are basically two types of windows, vertical and horizontal. To show how the two windows look, load in your document, STEIGER.DOC. The first window you will work with is a vertical window.

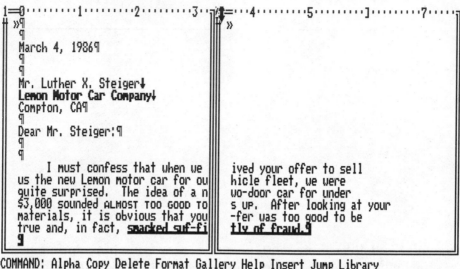

Figure 7-1. Vertically split windows

If you are using a mouse, move your cursor so that it points to the ruler on the screen. Your pointer changes from an arrow into a box (or from a small blinking box into a taller box, if you are in character mode). Move the pointer so that it is at the 3.5-inch mark. If you don't currently have a ruler, go into the Window Options Menu and tell the system to show a ruler. When you've positioned your mouse pointer, click the left mouse button to split the screen into two windows. The screen looks like the one in Figure 7-1.

If you are using a keyboard, you can also make the split. To get to the Window Menu, press ESC-W. The system gives you four choices: Split, Close, Move, Options. To create a window, you must tell the system to split the screen into a window.

Type: S

A new screen appears. You must now specify the type of split you want: vertical, horizontal, or footnote. In this example you want a vertical split.

Type: V

The next menu (which is basically the same as the one for a horizontal split) is shown here.

```
WINDOW SPLIT VERTICAL at column: ▓   clear new window: Yes(No)

Enter number
Page 1   {¶}                         ?              Microsoft Word: STEIGER.DOC
```

You must now determine where to make the split. Type 35 (for column number 35). The Clear New Window prompt allows you to split a window within your existing document or to create a new, clear window. In this case, to remain consistent with the example using the mouse, you would not want to clear the new window. Once you have indicated where you want the vertical split and told the system that you don't want to clear a new window, press RETURN to tell the system to execute the command. Your screen should look like the one in Figure 7-1. Your cursor is in Window 2. There are a few ways to tell which window the cursor is in. First, you may be able to see your cursor. Second, the window number at the upper left corner of the window is reversed in the active window (that is, black number on a white background rather than white number on a black background).

You are still editing the same document. To demonstrate this, type a few spaces. The first line in both windows moves. Although you are in the same document, you don't have to have the same portion of the document visible in both windows. To demonstrate this,

Type: CTRL-PGDN

The beginning of the document is in Window 1, while the end of the document appears in Window 2. The vertical window doesn't provide you with a view of the full width of the document.

Using the keyboard, you can scroll the document across the screen in two ways. You can use the cursor movement keys to pull in the text beyond the outer edges of the window. For example, if you moved your cursor into the beginning of a paragraph and held down the right arrow key, the text would scroll from right to left until you reached the end of the line, at which time the screen would jump back to the beginning of the first line. You can also press SCROLL LOCK to scroll across the screen, using the cursor movement keys to move the text. In this mode the screen scrolls in a manner that closely resembles what would happen if you cut out a cardboard window and slid it over a page of text.

Using the mouse, scrolling is even simpler. To make the text scroll from top to bottom, place the pointer on the scroll bar at the left side of the window you want to scroll. Clicking the left mouse button moves your text up, while clicking the right mouse button moves it down. To scroll left to right, use the bottom scroll bar to determine the amount you wish to scroll. Again, the left button moves your text to the left, and the right button moves it to the right. The distance of the pointer from the top of the page (for up-down scrolling), or from the far left corner of the window (for left-right scrolling), dictates how much of the screen you want to scroll.

Again, if you want to scroll to a particular portion of a document, moving to the approximate position on the scroll line and pressing both mouse buttons will quickly move you through a document. For example, to move to the middle of your document, you would point at the middle of the scroll bar and click both buttons simultaneously. The system would then bring you to the middle of your document.

Moving from one window to another using the mouse is also simple: just place the mouse pointer anywhere within the window you want to go to and click the left mouse button. Using the keyboard, you can press F1 to move to the next window. SHIFT-F1 moves you back one window. If, as in this case, you are in your last window, pressing F1 will bring you back to Window 1.

Closing a Window

Using the keyboard or mouse, it's easy to close a window. With the mouse, however, it is also easy to close the wrong window. To close a vertical window, move the pointer to the bar at the right side of the window you want to close. The pointer changes its shape. Click both mouse buttons and the window closes. You may run into problems when you point to the left of the window you want closed rather than the right. Try closing the second window now, if you are using a mouse. You again have a single window, with the entire document in it.

To demonstrate where you might run into difficulty, again open a window at column 35. This time, point to the column and click the right mouse button. When you open a window this way, you start out a new, clear window. Note that the bottom of the screen shows no document name attached to this window.

Now close Window 1. Point at the bar at the right corner of the window (or to the left of the scroll bar of Window 2). If you are in graphics mode, you will see that the shape of the pointer changes from a double arrow to a box when you pass through the two scroll bars. This doesn't happen if you are in character mode. Next, hold down both mouse buttons. Window 1 is cleared, leaving you with an empty screen.

If you have made any changes to the contents of Window 1, the system will prompt you to indicate whether you want to save or lose your edits or to cancel the window-clearing operation. Thus, Microsoft Word gives you a fail-safe method to prevent you from deleting text inadvertently. If you are in a hurry or are overconfident, however, you can easily lose your edits. Once a window has been deleted, the contents can't be recovered.

Using your keyboard, you must first get into your Window menu and select the Close option. Next, you have to tell the system which window you want to close. If you are trying to close a window that contains a document you edited, the system will prompt you to save or clear all changes. This won't always work in a window with an unnamed document.

Horizontal Windows

The horizontal window may be of more value than the vertical window for most Word users. This is because you can see the entire width of a line (unless line length exceeds the normal seven inches or so that the screen can display). To open or create a horizontal window by using the mouse, move the pointer into the bar on the right side of your window. Point to the position where you want to make your split and click the left mouse button. If you wanted to create a clear window, you would click the right mouse button.

Using the keyboard, you should proceed in much the same way as with a vertical window. In this case split the window at row 14. Using the mouse, make the split at the approximate middle of the screen (using the left mouse button). The screen should look like Figure 7-2. Pressing F1

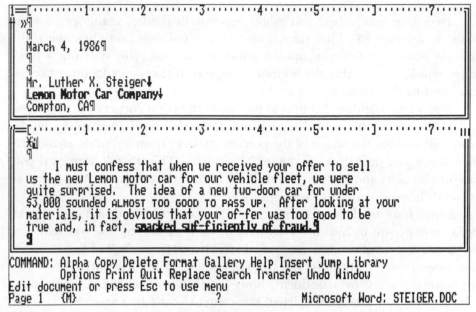

Figure 7-2. Horizontally split windows

moves you from one window to the next (or back to 1). Scrolling is also performed in the same way as in vertical windows.

To close a horizontal window using the mouse, point to the right side of the window to be closed and click both mouse buttons. Again, if the contents of the window you are closing have not been saved, the system will ask if you want to save them.

WINDOW OPTIONS

Before you begin manipulating text in your windows, you should become familiar with the window options available. Using these options, you can get more information about each window and easily tell them apart. To get to the Window Options Menu,

Type: ESC W O

Using the mouse, select Window in your command line and then select

Options; in both steps be sure to use the left mouse button. The Window Options Menu looks like this:

```
WINDOW OPTIONS window number: 2█  outline: Yes(No) show hidden text:(Yes)No
                background color: 0   style bar: Yes(No)         ruler:(Yes)No
Enter number
Page 1  (M)                      ?              Microsoft Word: STEIGER.DOC
```

The first selection from this menu tells the system which window you would like to change. The Outline prompt has to do with the outlining function, to be discussed in Chapter 11. In general, this option is really quite practical. When you select to show your outline, you can have the general outline of a document in one window and the working document in another.

The Show Hidden Text prompt relates to text and commands normally not printed. For example, if you wanted to have the system automatically prepare an index or table of contents, you would embed hidden commands preceding the item to be indexed. Just before printing, and after pagination, you would have the system search for all hidden index marks, and an index or table of contents would be automatically generated. If you plan to automatically generate indexes or tables of contents, you should probably leave this option on. Just before repagination this option can be turned off.

The Background Color option is of much importance when you use multiple windows. If you use many windows or have many generations of the same document, it may be confusing if all the windows look alike. For many similar documents, there may, in fact, be large sections of identical text. In this case, if you have a monitor and graphics card that supports it, you can apply a different color to the background in each window.

For example, your current document, STEIGER.DOC, is adapted from FORMCHAR.DOC, which was taken from DOC2.DOC, which grew out of DOC1.DOC. You may have all four documents on the screen at once, so you can switch from one window to the other and see how your document changed. To avoid confusion, you may leave STEIGER.DOC as white text against a black background; FORMCHAR.DOC as white text against a red background; DOC2.DOC as white text against a green background; and DOC1.DOC as white text against a yellow background.

To see which color backgrounds your computer/monitor/graphics card is capable of, move into the Background Color field and press RIGHT

ARROW or the right mouse button. The screen clears and the system displays the available colors. In most cases you must be in the character mode to make use of the background color feature, although this feature may be supported in the graphics mode if you have an extended graphics monitor and adapter.

In addition, some monochrome graphics cards may be able to produce a background pattern (instead of a color), which may be valuable in differentiating one window from another. Using a colored background may also be easier on the eyes than the stark white against black to which Microsoft Word normally defaults. It may be worthwhile to try various background colors to see which looks best to you.

The Style Bar prompt relates to the use of style sheets. A *style sheet* is a record containing the formatting information for a particular type of paragraph or character. For example, you might create a style sheet for section headings—this sheet might automatically center and boldface all the text to which it is applied. When a window has a style bar attached, you can see the name of the style sheet used for each paragraph in your document. This moves the text slightly to the right on your page and creates a space in the left margin where your style sheets are attached. If you use style sheets, it may be valuable to have the style bar displayed.

Finally, the Ruler prompt is used to determine if you want the ruler displayed at the top of the screen. You have already turned this feature on and off. There is probably little reason not to use the ruler bar. It helps you instantly identify all the tabs, the type of tabs, the margins, and, perhaps most importantly, to determine where you are on a page when your text is more than eight inches wide. You should usually leave the ruler displayed at the top of the window. Once you have made your selections for window options, press RETURN to accept the changes and get back to your document or use the mouse to get back to editing.

Copying a Window

You have seen how you can look at two parts of the same document. This may be valuable when you need to confirm (or copy) passages from one part of the document to another. Although you could do this without windows—by copying text to be moved into the scrap, and then moving to the point where you want to move the text—this is somewhat difficult for a very long document.

For now, assume that STEIGER.DOC is thirty pages long. You want to copy the paragraph that begins "You are offering merely a frame and body for under $3000" to the end of the document, just before the final closing. If this was a thirty-page document, you'd have an awful lot of text to go through to get to the point of insertion. (Although pressing CTRL-PGDN would bring you to the end of the document, assume that instead you would have to move through the document, which would be the case if you wanted to copy something to or from the middle of the document.)

Create a horizontal window in the middle of STEIGER.DOC. Next, move the text in the window to the bottom of the document. (For a long document, you may want to point to the bottom of the scroll bar with the mouse, click both mouse buttons, and then work your way up to the point of insertion. From the keyboard, pressing CTRL-PGDN works nicely.)

Another way to get to a specific page (if you've already paginated your document) is to use the Jump function. Jump can be accessed using the mouse or the keyboard. When you call up the Jump command line, you get two options: Page and Footnote. Jump Page moves you to the page number you select. Jump Footnote moves you to the footnote number you select. Again, you can jump to a page in text if your text has already been paginated. This may be quicker than trying to find text with the mouse or DOWN ARROW.

Now that you've made your second horizontal window, make sure that the cursor is in this window. Next, move to the line just above "Very Truly Yours." Next, move into Window 1. (Using your mouse, simply point to the window and click the left button. Using the keyboard, press F1.)

Now move the cursor to the paragraph you want to copy and highlight the paragraph. (Using the mouse, point to the scroll bar to the left of the paragraph and click the right mouse button. Using the keyboard, move the cursor into the paragraph and press F10.)

Next, tell the system you want to copy the text. Using the keyboard, type ESC-C. Using the mouse, point to the word Copy in the command line and click the left mouse button. Press RETURN. (Note that if you typed anything at the "copy to where?" prompt, you would have created a glossary containing the entire paragraph. In this case just pressing RETURN copies the text into the scrap.)

Once the text is in the scrap, move back into Window 2. Your cursor should again be placed above the line, "Very Truly Yours." Press INS or point to the word Insert and select it with the left mouse button. The text is then placed in the chosen spot. To move, not copy, text, you would delete the text into the scrap and insert it at your target location.

Loading Another File

When you make changes in a document, you should give the document in the new window a different name. This way, you are automatically creating and updating a new file based on the earlier original. In this case the TRANSFER RENAME command is useful. To use this command, be sure that the cursor is in the window you want to rename and select this option. Once a file is renamed, it is treated as different from its original. Any changes to this version are not reflected in the earlier document.

When you want to copy from one document to another, you must put both documents into separate windows. Doing this is simple. First, you should create a clear window. Move your cursor into the clear window and transfer load the second document. The document is then placed into the previously clear window.

As already discussed, you can have up to eight windows, although this is impractical for most purposes. The only time when this may be of special value is when you are transferring or referring to blocks of information or numbers that don't have to use much window space. You can load up to eight different documents into windows, load different parts of the same document into windows, or create any combination of documents and clear windows, up to the maximum number of windows.

When you load data into a new window, more system memory is needed to keep track of the window contents. If you were loading many very large documents into the windows, you might run out of system memory.

The TRANSFER LOAD command is used to load documents into selected windows. If you try to load a document into a window that already has text, the system will prompt you to determine whether you want to save the current text in the window, to simply delete it and replace it with the selected file, or to abort from loading the file into that window. You should be careful when transferring files into a currently used window — once the text is deleted (if not saved first), it can't be retrieved.

Transfer Clear

The TRANSFER CLEAR command removes the contents of a single window or all windows at once. When you select the Transfer Clear function, you have two choices: Transfer Clear Window or Transfer Clear All. Transfer Clear Window deletes the contents of the currently active window. If you try to clear the window without saving your text, the system will prompt you to do so. Transfer Clear All tells the system you want to delete the contents of all the windows and, in effect, return to a single, empty window. If you select this option, the system will prompt you to consider saving all window documents that haven't yet been saved.

AUTOMATIC FORMATTING WITH STYLE SHEETS

One of Word's key strengths is its ability to apply formats to text automatically. In a typical letter, for example, you would probably use a variety of different text formats: the top indent might differ for a letterhead, for an address block, and for a salutation line. Your typed text would definitely be differently spaced and use different margins than the text above it. And your closing, salutation, signature line, title, and other comments might also be differently formatted.

If you prepared legal documents, these might require special formats for text, signature blocks, case numbers, and so on. Although you could adapt fairly rapidly to preparing a basic form for these documents using a standard word processor or typewriter, being able to type your text without complicated formats and then quickly attach the exact format required would speed up the preparation of your documents considerably.

Each format setup is referred to as a *style*. A style can have formatting information that applies to a character, paragraph, or division, or any combination of the three. Thus, you can create a style that centers text, bold prints it, has two-inch left and right margins, and is double spaced—and avoid having to go into the required menus or to type the necessary commands to set up these parameters. The styles you use can be saved in a *style sheet*. This sheet is a recorded document that contains the predefined styles supplied with the program. You may have a separate sheet with styles for each type of document, for each client, or for any special usage, or you may have a single style sheet with many (up to 103 user-definable) different styles.

ADVANTAGES

In addition to the speed of formatting achieved by using a style sheet, there are other benefits. First, you can redefine a style and change all areas of a document where the original style was used. For example, you may have a document using a standard paragraph style that features double-spaced text. All these paragraphs will have a style called SP attached to them. After printing out the document with double spacing, you may want to change *just those standard paragraphs* to single spacing. Although you can change the entire document to single spacing (by highlighting the document and going through the Format Paragraph Menu), this may be troublesome, since you only want to change the text paragraphs, not the entire document. To change only those paragraphs with the SP style, you can change the parameters for SP from double to single spacing. Once the change is saved, all such SP paragraphs change according to the new style.

The second advantage is consistency. A single set of styles and style sheets can be used for all your documents. Rather than try to set up duplicates of your formats, you can use predefined styles to format the text. In this way the format(s) for your documents remain consistent from document to document. On a larger scale a corporation or word processing department can develop standard formats for its communications. The word processor operators can then routinely apply the standard format to all documents. For complicated setups a standard, predeveloped format (or style) can save a lot of time that would otherwise be required for "reinventing the wheel."

A Potential Disadvantage

Although Word's style capabilities can greatly enhance the ease of document preparation, in addition to improving the appearance of your documents, a minor problem may arise due to use of style sheets. In order to take fullest advantage of the style sheets, you should type your document without extra spaces or built-in paragraph or division formatting. When you make changes to one area affected by a particular style, the text in that area reflects whatever style is applied to it. To some extent, the codes involved in getting Word to produce special characters or typefaces cannot be communicated. In order to transmit a file prepared by Word to another computer, database, or bulletin board, special formatting must be removed from the document, or a method described in Chapter 14 must be used to set your format into the document.

One way to remove formatting is to perform a Transfer Save and save the text without formatting. Microsoft Word then puts the document onto the disk as straight text characters. Even though your style sheets may specify double spacing and extra lines between paragraphs, when you do an unformatted save, only single lines separate paragraphs. In addition, a RETURN is placed at the end of each line. If you don't place an extra line between paragraphs, the unformatted document will also place only a single RETURN between paragraphs. In most cases a file saved this way looks a lot like one very long paragraph rather than a group of paragraphs.

Although you can get around this spacing problem by printing your document to a file, there may be times when you forget to do this. A problem you may encounter when you print a document to a file rather than to paper is that, depending upon the printer you use, you may also be printing to the file control codes for the printer. Thus, before you print to a file, you may also have to tell the system you are using a generic printer that doesn't require special formatting codes. Use of styles and style sheets can be of tremendous value to you, but you must remember that if you plan to produce a straight, unformatted file that can be communicated to other computers, you must print to a file rather than store the document as an unformatted document — and even this can be problematic.

USING STYLE SHEETS

Microsoft Word allows you to see the style applied to each paragraph in your document. This ability is addressed as a window option. To demonstrate this, again load the document called STEIGER.DOC. Take a close look at the left side of the screen.

Next, tell the system to display the style bar. To do this, get into the Window Options Menu. Select the Style Bar option, using the procedures for moving through menus that have already been discussed. Your screen should look like this:

```
WINDOW OPTIONS window number: 1    outline: Yes(No) show hidden text:(Yes)No
                 background color: 0  style bar: YES No              ruler:(Yes)No
Select option
```

Accept the option (yes), and you are returned to your document. You should notice that an area to the left side of the text has opened up and an asterisk appears at the beginning of each paragraph. Your screen should resemble Figure 8-1. You should note that the three address lines, which were ended by using the NEWLINE command rather than RETURNs, are treated as a single paragraph. You should also note that no asterisks appear to the left of the first paragraph.

The asterisk indicates that no formatting instructions were applied to the text. In the case of the first paragraph, a number of format changes were made: the top line was indented and a variety of type styles, in addi-

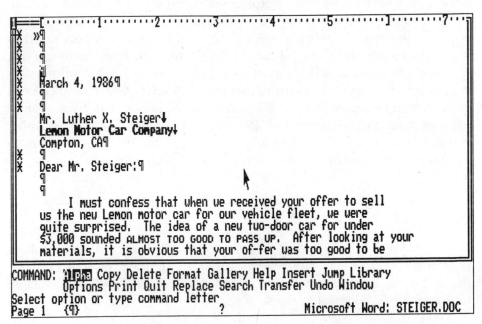

Figure 8-1.   The STEIGER.DOC with style bar and asterisks

tion to the double underlining, was used. When a paragraph differs from the standard block paragraph, no asterisk appears (since the paragraph *has* already been formatted) and no style designation is shown.

Attaching a Style Sheet

In order to use a style sheet in a document, it must first be attached. When you attach a style sheet, you tell the system that you will use the styles (formats) already recorded onto the sheet. To attach a style sheet, you must get to the Format Style Sheet Menu. Do this by using the mouse (Select Format, Style, and then Sheet) or the keyboard (press ESC-F-S-S). Since at this point you may not know which style sheets are available, you can have the system indicate which are already recorded into the system.

When you are in the Format Style Sheet Menu, the prompt should look like this:

```
FORMAT STYLE SHEET: C:\WORD\NORMAL.STY

Enter filename or select from list
Page 1   {¶}                        ?              Microsoft Word: STEIGER.DOC
```

To see what other style sheets are available, point to the selection area highlighted on the menu line and press the *right* mouse button or press RIGHT ARROW. If you are using a floppy disk system, these files will have to be loaded onto the floppy you use to load Word. The screen then lists the available style sheets. The screen should resemble Figure 8-2. Select the style sheet called FULL.STY.

After the selection is made, you are returned to the document. The document now looks different than it did when you created it. The system has attached the style SP (for standard paragraph) to the paragraphs in STEIGER.DOC. You should notice a line of space between each paragraph. This was inserted because the style SP is set up to place one space between paragraphs.

NOTE: You can set styles to do virtually everything that can be done from within the various format menus. In this case you've added a line between paragraphs. If you are like many writers, you automatically enter two RETURNs at the end of each paragraph. This would not be compatible

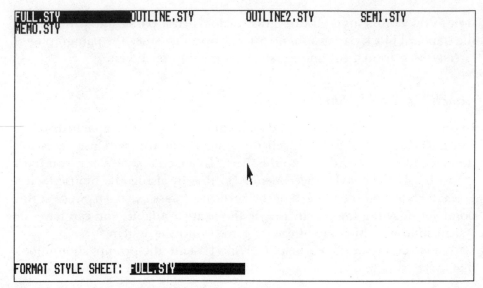

Figure 8-2. The list of available style sheets

with the style you created. You have two choices: to alter your method of writing by consciously remembering not to press RETURN twice or to change the style to fit your writing style. Remember that it is often easier to change the style to fit your needs than to try to modify your methods to suit the system. Microsoft Word is designed to provide you with much flexibility in preparing your documents, but the system is also flexible. It can (and should) be set to suit your style and needs, and not the reverse. ■

Reviewing Styles

So far, you've attached a style sheet called FULL.STY. At this point you don't know what styles have been recorded into the style sheet. Further, you only have a general idea what the style called SP does. You know that it is single spaced, inserts a line before each new paragraph, and is not right justified, but there are other parameters (such as type style) that you can't identify yet.

To view, edit, and modify style sheets, the Gallery Menu is used. Basically, the Gallery Menu is to style sheets what the standard menu is to text. Select the Gallery function. The screen of text has been replaced by a screen full of listings for the styles built into the currently active style sheet (FULL.STY). The first screen of styles looks like Figure 8-3. The two menu lines in the command area of the screen allow you to perform any desired modifications to the existing style sheet, in addition to giving you the ability to copy, delete, or combine style sheets.

Since your original goal was to find out how SP was set up, you can do this now. Press PGDN or use the mouse to move down one screen until SP appears. This should be style number 7 on your screen. SP is a typical listing. The first item is the number of the style in the style sheet directory. This particular style is given the number 7. The next item is the one- or two-key identifier (referred to in Microsoft documentation as the *key code*). This identifier is used to attach a style to a selected portion of text. To the right of the key identifier is the *usage block*. This tells you whether the style applies to a paragraph, character, or division. (This is set up when you define each style.) Following the usage information is a variant number.

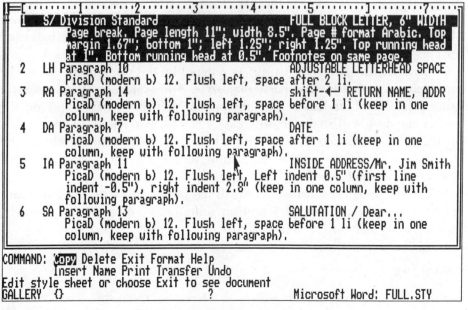

Figure 8-3. The style sheet displayed on the screen

The *variant* is a number assigned to a particular style identifying its application to a character, paragraph, or division. For example, you may have 20 different paragraph styles: styles for address blocks, signature blocks, indented paragraphs, and so on. The system allows you to give a variant number to each new style you use. Further, you can define one standard for paragraph, character, and division styles—these are automatically applied to your documents unless you apply other styles.

Since SP is the style for a standard paragraph, this format was applied to the text in STEIGER.DOC. Further, a standard character style and division style were also attached to your document. If you look at the first style on the sheet, you will see the style called S/ (for standard division—the slash (/) is also the division character). Although you don't see the code for this standard (or for the character standard) in the style bar, these styles apply to your document. Only paragraph formats appear in the style bar on your screen. If you make changes to your standard paragraph, such as indenting or changing the spacing, the style code will be removed from that paragraph.

The next item on the style line is a brief remark about the style. Normally, you would type this in as a reminder of what the style is for or how to use the particular style. In this example, the remark for SP style is "STANDARD PARAGRAPH." The next style, CL, carries the remark "COMPLMNTRY CLOSING/Sincerely," telling you what the style is used for and giving you an idea of how the paragraph is usually begun.

The final line(s) in the listing are entered by the system and reflect the formatting applied to that particular style. For example, SP uses a style generically called modern b; with the printer that this system is set for, the font name is also listed—in this case PicaD 12, a double density pica, printing at 10 characters per inch. (The 12 represents the height of the character, and 120 divided by the height reveals the pitch, or number of characters per inch.)

Next, the style is indicated as a flush left paragraph with one line space before each new paragraph. Scanning some of the other styles, you will quickly note many other types of format.

Changing Styles

Changing a style is very easy. There are a few ways to do this. First, you can select a style and type in the key code that causes a change. For example, if you want to change your standard paragraph spacing from a left alignment to justified, you can highlight the SP definition and

Type: ALT-J

Figure 8-4 shows the standard paragraph style before you change it to justified. Figure 8-5 shows the style description after you change the format to justified. Now that you've made the paragraph change, assume that you also want to remove the space before each paragraph and to change the type style.

To do this, the best thing is to go into separate format menus. Select the FORMAT command. The menu looks like this:

```
FORMAT: Character Paragraph Tabs

Select option or type command letter
GALLERY {}                              ?           Microsoft Word: FULL.STY
```

NOTE: The menu you get when you select Format from the Gallery Menu varies depending upon the style usage you want to modify. For example, if you wanted to change the format of a character style, you would immediately go to the Character Attributes Menu; if you wanted to change the format of a division style, you would be given the choice of setting margins, page numbers, or layout. ■

At this level you are able to change the format for characters, paragraphs, or tabs. Select Paragraph and change the line spacing to 2 and the

```
7    SP Paragraph Standard              STANDARD PARAGRAPH
     PicaD (modern b) 12. Flush left, space before 1 li.
```

Figure 8-4.   The style sheet listing for a standard paragraph, left aligned

```
7    SP Paragraph Standard              STANDARD PARAGRAPH
     PicaD (modern b) 12. Justified, space before 1 li.
```

Figure 8-5.   The style sheet listing for a standard paragraph, justified

```
7   SP Paragraph Standard                    STANDARD PARAGRAPH
       PicaD (modern b) 12/24. Justified.
```

Figure 8-6.   The style sheet listing for a standard paragraph, double spaced with no space before the paragraph

space before to 0. Once this is done, accept these changes. You are not returned to your document, but to the highlighted style listing for SP.

In addition, although the style listing doesn't indicate line spacing as such, the number representing the size of the character has changed. As shown in Figure 8-6, the type has changed from 12 to 12/24. The 12/24 indicates that the character is 12 points high and that 24 points are used between lines. Thus, although the system doesn't indicate double spacing, it applies two-line spacing to each line of text. To further illustrate, if you were to set line spacing to 1.5 lines, the type would be listed as 12/18 (12-point characters, with 18 points between lines). Word is essentially a typesetting program—it works with spaces rather than lines.

When you use other type sizes, you should be careful to check the spacing between lines. Since it is possible to print characters taller than 12 points, it is possible to print lines of text that overlap each other. For example, if you were to specify single spacing and a PicaD font 16 points high, you would get a text character larger in size than the space between

```
7   SP Paragraph Standard                    STANDARD PARAGRAPH
       PicaD (modern b) 16/12. Justified.
```

Figure 8-7.   The style sheet listing for a standard paragraph, showing 16-point type on 12-point line spacing

Figure 8-8.   Standard paragraph after changes

lines. In this case the system would not prompt you for a correction but would show a somewhat illogical character layout, such as that shown in Figure 8-7. Note that this would print lines with overlapping text.

When you use characters larger than the standard line height or much smaller than standard line height, you must set the style to accommodate for the new character height and to produce text that is neither too close together nor too far apart. Choosing the automatic option for line spacing (in the Format Paragraph Menu) tells the system to adjust the spacing automatically for you. Next, change the Space Before setting to 0 lines. Finally, return to the Gallery command line. The format line should look like Figure 8-8. To see what effect the standard paragraph change has on your document, exit from the Gallery Menu. Do this by highlighting the word Exit and pressing your right mouse button or by typing the letter *e* on your keyboard. The salutation line and first paragraph should look like Figure 8-9.

Whatever changes are made to a style apply to all areas that use that style. This is true in the case of line spacing, width, and margins. However, it is not always the case in a paragraph in which other character formats are used. In such paragraphs Word is not especially consistent. In some cases changing a font in the style area causes the character style to be changed in the paragraphs where the selected style is applied. In other cases, if you've entered such things as bolding, italics, underlining, or superscripts or subscripts, the system may assume that you still want the preset paragraph format—but won't apply the character format.

Thus, if you wanted to change the type style throughout a document, simply making the change in the style bar wouldn't always work—it might be necessary to highlight all the areas to be changed and make those changes using the FORMAT CHARACTER commands.

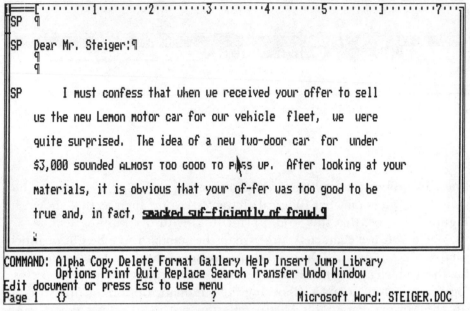

Figure 8-9. The first paragraph of STEIGER.DOC with a new SP applied

NOTE: When you use style sheets, if you want to apply new character formatting, Word will not replace specially formatted characters. In other words, even if you redefine the characters throughout a document, the special formats—bold, italic, underlined, and so on—take precedence over the changes that are to be made later. Thus, you will not lose special character formats even if you change style sheets or change the format for an entire document. ■

GALLERY COMMANDS

The Gallery option can be thought of as something like a different Edit mode. Instead of editing text documents, its only purpose is to edit and manage style sheets. Most commands and procedures used to edit text can be used from the Gallery Menu to modify style sheets. There are some functional differences between the Standard editing mode and the Gallery editing mode.

GALLERY COPY Command

Gallery Copy copies a highlighted style into the scrap. To demonstrate, return to the Gallery Menu and move the cursor to highlight SP, the standard paragraph style. Next, select the COPY command. The name of the usage and variant (in this case Paragraph Standard) is copied into the scrap. Next, move to the end of the style sheet and select Insert. The style is inserted into the next position and the number in the listing is increased by one. In the case of FULL.STY, the copy of SP is given the number 14.

Since you can't have two styles by the same name or key code, you should rename the style now. Select Name and the Name command line appears. This command line looks like this:

```
NAME key code: SP            variant: Standard
          remark: Standard Paragraph
Enter key code
```

The key code is the code used to attach this format to your text. It must be one or two letters or numbers, excluding the letter *x*, which is used to call on standard speed formatting commands (discussed in "Speed Formatting" in this chapter). The two-letter/number code should be unique — it can't be used elsewhere in the style sheet. Also, it should give a clue to the contents of the style listing — for example, *SP* means *standard paragraph.*

Assume for now that you want to change this format to a single-spaced paragraph. Call this paragraph P1 — a paragraph with 1 line spacing. Go to the next field, Variant. Do this by using the mouse or pressing TAB. A variant is, in effect, merely a number that you select from a catalog of available styles from the style sheet. The number has little or no meaning, but each style must be attached to its own variant.

To get a list of the available and used variants, press the *right* mouse button or press RIGHT ARROW. The screen should look like Figure 8-10. Some of the variant numbers are followed by key codes enclosed in parentheses. These correspond to styles already defined on the style sheet.

Tell the system to call this variant variant 1. The next field requiring response is Remark. This field allows you to give a brief description of what the style does or how it should be used. In this example use the remark "Stan. Par. 1 Space." Once the changes are completed and accepted, you are returned to the Gallery listing. The style sheet listing now looks like the illustration at the top of the next page.

```
     PicaD (modern b) 12.
i4  P1 Paragraph 1                              Stan. Par. 1 Space
     PicaD (modern b) 12/24. Justified.
 ‣
```

Up to this point, however, you haven't changed the spacing to single space. To do this, select Format. Next, tell the system that you want to format the paragraph. Finally, make the changes as you normally would in Edit mode (as already described). Once the change to single spacing has been made, your style listing changes to reflect a standard type size of 12, not 12/24 as it was for double-spaced type.

In many cases it may be simpler to copy and modify a predefined style than it is to create one completely from scratch. However, there may be times when you want to create a completely new style. In this case use the INSERT command. Defining a new style using Insert is basically the same as naming a style using the NAME command. The Gallery Insert command line looks like this:

```
Standard (SP)       Footnote        Heading level 1    Heading level 2
Heading level 3     Heading level 4 Heading level 5    Heading level 6
Heading level 7     Index level 1   Index level 2      Index level 3
Index level 4       Table level 1   Table level 2      Table level 3
Table level 4       1               2                  3
4                   5               6                  7   (DA)
8   (NA)            9   (TI)        10  (LH)           11  (IA)
12                  13  (SA)        14  (RA)           15
16                  17  (RI)        18                 19
20                  21  (CL)        22                 23
24                  25              26                 27
28                  29              30                 31
32                  33              34                 35
36                  37              38                 39
40                  41              42                 43
44                  45              46                 47
48                  49              50                 51
52                  53              54                 55
56

NAME key code: p1            variant: Standard
      remark: STANDARD PARAGRAPH
Enter variant or select from list
GALLERY  {Paragraph Standard }        ?          Microsoft Word: FULL.STY
```

Figure 8-10.   The list of paragraph variants

```
INSERT key code: [#]           usage:(Character)Paragraph Division
         variant: 2            remark:
Enter key code
```

However, you have one more menu item to answer, the Usage item. You have to tell the system whether the style applies to a character, paragraph, or division. Once this is done, future format changes will relate to this selected usage.

GALLERY PRINT Command

The GALLERY PRINT command prints the contents of the selected style sheet. To print the style sheet, merely make sure your printer is turned on (the system uses the current printer configuration) and select Print.

GALLERY TRANSFER Commands

The Gallery Transfer Menu acts in much the same way as the Transfer Menu functions in Edit mode. When you select Transfer, you see the following Transfer Menu:

```
TRANSFER: Load Save Clear Delete Merge Options Rename
```

TRANSFER LOAD is used to load a style sheet into the Gallery. The technique is basically identical to performing a Transfer Load for a document. You still have the capability of defining directories to search for a style document. All style sheets must use the extension .STY following the style name. When you load a file, it replaces the contents of your current gallery style sheet. If you have made changes to your current style sheet, you will be asked whether you want to save changes, to ignore changes, or to abort the new Transfer Load.

Similarly, TRANSFER SAVE is useful for saving style sheets you have created. In this chapter you've made a change to your Standard Paragraph, and you've created a new style, P1. Since it may be a good idea to retain the standard style sheet, FULL.STY, you should create a new style sheet with the changes you have made. Also, since you expect to do all your letter writing using the styles on the newly modified sheet, call this style sheet

LETTER. Select Transfer Save and give the new style sheet the name LETTER. The system saves the style sheet and automatically adds the extension .STY. The next time you want to write a letter, you can load and attach the LETTER.STY style sheet to your document. Many users find that using a predefined style sheet (one included with Microsoft Word) and modifying it to suit their needs is easier than creating a completely new style sheet.

TRANSFER CLEAR is used to clear the contents of the gallery window. You will be prompted by the system if you attempt to clear the styles without saving any changes.

TRANSFER DELETE deletes a style sheet from the system. Once the style sheet has been deleted, it is unrecoverable. You should be certain that you want the style sheet deleted. (Note that if you do mistakenly delete a style sheet, it is sometimes possible to recover a style sheet using a file recovery utility program. These utilities work best, however, if you immediately attempt recovery — any new file could destroy the directory information that could be used to find the "deleted" style sheet. You can also delete a style sheet at DOS level using the DOS DELETE (or DEL) command.)

The Gallery TRANSFER MERGE command allows you to append another style sheet to the one you are currently working with. For example, creating separate style sheets called LETTER and ENVELOP may work well when the two types of documents are prepared separately. However, you may need a style sheet combining both styles. To easily combine the two sheets, you can use the MERGE command.

Assuming that you already are using the LETTER.STY style sheet, select Transfer Merge. The system prompts you for the name of the merge file. Type ENVELOP RETURN. The system appends ENVELOP to LETTER. This merged file can then be saved under a new name. If your merged file has duplicate style names, the first occurrence of each code will be saved and all further same-name styles will be deleted. For example, you may have a different standard paragraph in each style sheet that you merge. The first standard paragraph is the one that remains with the new merged style sheet. Thus, before you save the merged style sheet, you should check for duplicate key codes and change the key code for any that you want to save.

The Gallery TRANSFER OPTIONS comand allows you to specify the drive and directory path your style sheets will be saved and loaded from.

This is a default setting — in actual use you may instruct the system to load a style sheet from any drive or directory.

The Gallery TRANSFER RENAME command is used when you load a style sheet you want to modify. Once the sheet is loaded, you should rename it. Later, when you want to save the style sheet, it's already renamed and you won't have to worry about changing the style sheet that you originally loaded to modify.

The GALLERY UNDO Command

Finally, the Gallery UNDO command is used to return a style to its condition before your last change. By toggling the Undo on and off, you can see the style before the change and after the change.

APPLYING A STYLE

Once a style sheet is attached to a document, you can apply styles to any portion of the document you desire. A number of styles are automatically applied to your document and are in effect until you change them. For example, you've seen and modified the standard paragraph. In addition, a standard division is applied to the document. It specifies line spacing, margins, and so on. The standard character is already built into your standard paragraph.

NOTE: If you don't attach a style sheet to your document, the styles recorded into NORMAL.STY will affect your document. If these standard settings aren't appropriate for the documents you are preparing, you can change these styles so that they conform with your needs. From then on, your documents will take on the standard appearance without the need to attach a style sheet to the document. This may result in some time savings to you. ■

When you finish typing a paragraph, the current format or style in effect is carried over to the following paragraph. Thus, if your first paragraph used a style called P1, all subsequent paragraphs would also be P1 until you applied a different style to them. To apply a style, hold down ALT and type the letters of the style name. Thus, to apply the style P1 to a paragraph, make sure the cursor is in the paragraph and

Type: ALT P1

To demonstrate, exit from the Gallery Menu and return to your document, STEIGER.DOC. Next, move the cursor into the first paragraph.

Type: ALT P1

(Note that you don't have to hold down ALT while entering the second part of your command. It may be simpler to hold down ALT while typing the first letter and then to type the second letter or number of the code than to hold down ALT while typing both letters.) Your first and second paragraphs now look like Figure 8-11. Notice that the style name is in the left margin and that the first paragraph is single spaced, while the second is double spaced—just as the two styles were set up to do.

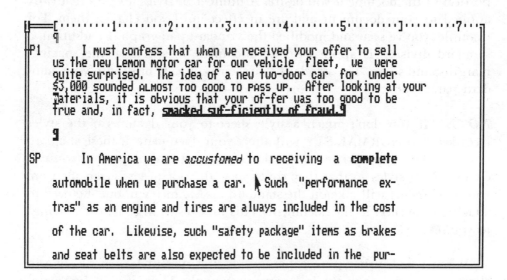

Figure 8-11. STEIGER.DOC with two different paragraph styles applied

When you apply a division style, the page is ended and a new page started. When a division style is applied, there is no indication of the style in the style bar at the left of the screen. The character styles can be applied either to highlighted text or to text you are about to input into the system. When you apply these styles, there is no indication in the style bar at the left margin.

Speed Formatting

Earlier in this book, you learned about using speed formatting keys. The ALT key combinations you learned were useful for changing character and paragraph formatting. When you have a style sheet attached, however, these keys don't work in exactly the same way. In order to use the speed formatting commands, you must insert an x into the formatting command.

For example, to bold an area of text, the standard command is ALT-B. When you have applied a style sheet, you must instead press ALT X B. If you set up a style whose code began with an x, you would not have access to the speed formatting commands.

TIP: If you were using the same type style throughout your document(s) and the only formatting changes were things such as bolding, underlining, and italics, you might be able to set these attributes up as separate styles. Thus, the style for a bold character could be set up on your style sheet as *b*, the style for an italic character could be named *i*. In other words, you could set up your character attribute styles to correspond to their normal speed formatting commands. Once this is done, you can just type the normal speed command and avoid having to type the x before the formatting key. This only works for character styles and applies only to a specific type style. It is roughly, but not completely, equivalent to the standard speed formatting commands. ■

Using styles can automate the formatting of your documents in addition to creating a standard appearance for all your documents. Once you've used style sheets and ventured to modify styles to suit your specific needs, you'll probably wonder how you ever word processed without them. In many ways using style sheets is an easy way to create documents that look typeset. Style sheets are especially useful in addressing laser printer output.

Unfortunately, the behavior of Word as regards style sheets is somewhat idiosyncratic. If you use styles for all the formatting in your document (character, paragraph, and division), your results should be consistent and predictable. However, once you have used speed formatting commands, character style may not automatically adjust back to a standard paragraph setting.

It is a good practice to develop a style for every aspect of your document's format—characters, paragraphs, and divisions—and to avoid speed formatting altogether. Thus, you should probably attempt to create a gallery that can handle all format changes in the documents you create. There is an added advantage to this. Since changes in your styles are reflected in the text they are attached to, you can quickly make major changes in your document by modifying the styles and avoid making laborious changes paragraph by paragraph.

BOILERPLATE AND MERGED DOCUMENTS

Microsoft Word provides you with tremendous abilities to format and edit any type of document. Many word processor operators frequently prepare what are commonly called "repetitive letters." These letters or documents are built around two basic components: a frame letter and a data document that inserts the appropriate data into the frame. For example, those letters that you probably get from Ed McMahon every few weeks are one of the ultimate examples of a repetitive letter—on a basic form your name (spelled more or less correctly) is inserted into the space for the "possible ten million dollar winner!"

Word provides you with the ability to create such merged documents. Another type of document, prepared using boilerplate text, has already been briefly discussed. This is done in a sort of "oriental restaurant" format: once you've recorded frequently used words, phrases, or passages, you can then put their abbreviations together to create a complete document.

USING THE GLOSSARY FOR BOILERPLATE DOCUMENTS

As you use Word, you may find that many words or phrases are used repeatedly in your word processing functions. For example, the year remains the same for 365 days, and months change only every 30 days or so. If you are doing a lot of letters, why type the name of the month each time you begin a letter? Wouldn't it be simpler to type *J* each time you wanted to type *January*? Using Microsoft Word, you can set the system to extend your abbreviations for you.

In the previous example, you could have all the months encoded into one- or two-letter abbreviations and always available for you. One possible abbreviation scheme would be as follows:

JA	January	F	February	MR	March	AP	April
MA	May	JN	June	JL	July	AU	August
SP	September	O	October	N	November	D	December

You may also plan ahead and enter the next four years:

7	1987	8	1988	9	1989	0	1990

To see how this works, begin a new document and name it LETTER1. While you are preparing the documents in this section, assume that you are preparing the letters for a company that does mail order sales. This company requires a few different types of letters: acknowledging receipt of an order; announcing shipment of an order; apologizing for an item being out of stock; and, perhaps, letters offering alternative items.

Now you can create a standard document and put your letter together using standard components. First, set up the dates so that they are easily accessible for whenever you need to insert them into your letters. To do this for January,

Type: **January**SPACE (be sure to put a space after January)

Next, tell the system you want to save the text into the glossary. (Glossary is the name of the file that holds the boilerplate text.) To do this, highlight the word and the space after it and select the **COPY** command. The screen should now look like Figure 9-1.

Next, type the glossary abbreviation listed previously.

Type: **JA**

NOTE: Microsoft Word's Glossary feature is not case specific—thus, you can type the desired abbreviation any of four ways—Ja, ja, jA, or JA—and still be able to use the Glossary function. In addition, regardless of the case

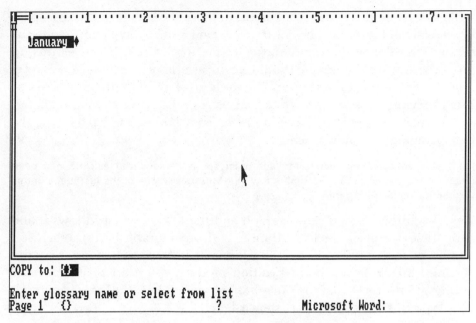

Figure 9-1.   Highlighted text to be saved to the glossary and the prompt
for a glossary listing at the bottom of the screen

you use to store or retrieve a glossary listing, the extended glossary setting
remains the same. Note also that Word has some automatic glossary entries
that work for you. If you wanted to enter the current date, you could do this
simply by typing Date and pressing F3 to print the date into your document. Similarly, you could have the system insert the time by typing Time
and pressing F3. ■

Now that you've stored January in glossary listing JA, it's time to show
how it works. Delete the word January from your screen. Now type JA (or
Ja, ja, or jA) and then

Type: F3

When using this feature, be careful to place the cursor in the first space beyond the abbreviation. If you try to extend your abbreviation while the cursor is inside the abbreviation, the feature won't work. If you set this up properly, the word January should again appear where the JA was previously. Enter the abbreviations for the rest of the months and years as listed previously.

To create some of the paragraphs for your boilerplate letters, type the first paragraph as shown here.

I am pleased to inform you that your order for a Personalized Necktie has been received. You are one of the fortunate few who will receive one of the last items in this very limited collector's series.

Next, highlight the entire paragraph and the RETURN that follows it and copy these into the glossary, calling it 1y (for paragraph 1, yes). When you do this, your screen should look like Figure 9-2. Now delete the paragraph.

Since this truly is a limited edition product, you must prepare a letter telling the customer that the order has arrived too late. Call this paragraph 1N. Type in the paragraph as shown here.

I am sorry to inform you that we have run out of Personalized Neckties. Response to our offer was much larger than we had prepared for. However, we would like to substitute a set of Personalized Dish Towels, an even better value, for the Personalized Neckties. If this is not acceptable, please return our shipment, which should arrive in the next few days.

Next, you have a *maybe* letter for your special customers, who may be able to get this necktie even though their order was late. Type the following paragraph, saving it and the next space beyond it as 1M.

Your order for our Personalized Necktie has been received. Unfortunately, all stocks of our first shipment have been sold. However, we expect a special, second shipment very soon and should be able to fill your order within the next two months. If you choose not to wait, we will be happy to refund your payment.

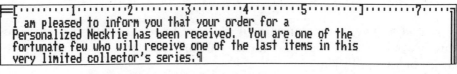

Figure 9-2.   The paragraph recorded into glossary as 1y

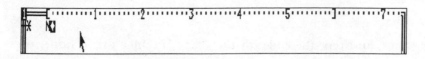

Figure 9-3.   The glossary listing for the date before F3 has been pressed

Next, prepare a standard closing paragraph, including two spaces after the paragraph to separate it from the closing and signature block. Call the paragraph shown here cl1.

We appreciate your business and thank you for your order with us. Your future trust and confidence are extremely important to us. We hope to serve you again very soon.

Finally, prepare and record the closing and signature block. Call this sig1. The signature block should be like this:

Sincerely,

Freddy Marcos
Sales Manager

FM/am

Be certain that all the text you have typed so far has been stored to the glossary and deleted from active memory.

Now you want to write a letter to a man named George Smith. Rename this document (using Transfer Rename) SMITH1. First, assume a date of November 28, 1987. At the top of the page, type N F3. The text line should look like Figure 9-3 before you press F3 and look like Figure 9-4 after you press F3.

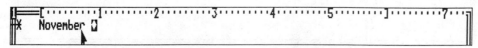

Figure 9-4.   The glossary listing for the date, extended after F3 has been pressed

Now,

Type: **28**,

press SPACE and type the code for the year (7). Once this is done, press F3 and the entire date appears.

NOTE: Depending on your needs, you may also want to prepare a second set of year numbers that would automatically insert the comma and space before the numbers (that is, after the month and date and before the year), and the RETURN and space between the year and the salutation. Although this could have been done when you set up your year defaults, it may be more meaningful to include a comma in a separate code to easily distinguish one type from another. In other words, the code "7" would be expanded to "1987", and the code "7," would be expanded to ", 1987 SPACE SPACE". ■

Now press RETURN twice to place a space between the date line and the beginning of the address block.

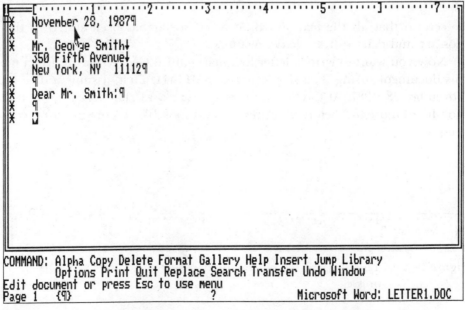

Figure 9-5. The beginning of the sample boilerplate letter

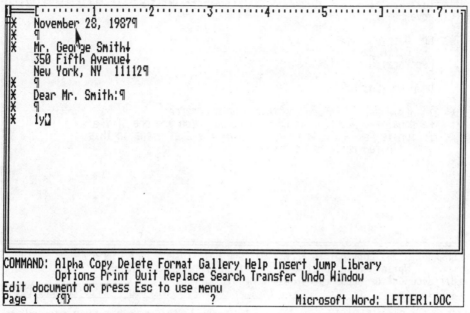

Figure 9-6.   The glossary listing 1y before F3 has been pressed

Type the following address, using the NEW LINE command rather than pressing RETURN, so that you can change the format of the entire address block later, if you desire.

Mr. George Smith
350 Fifth Avenue
New York, NY 11112

Note that the address is fictitious: the street address is the Empire State Building, the zip code is not correct, and it is assumed that no real George Smith actually works at that address. Add two RETURNs, a salutation line, and another space. Your screen should look like the one in Figure 9-5.

Mr. Smith was lucky enough to have his order arrive while you still had supplies of your product. Therefore, you want to send him a confirmation letter. To do this requires very few keystrokes. First, insert the "yes" paragraph, which you saved to the glossary and called 1y.

Type: 1y F3

Before you press F3, the screen looks like Figure 9-6; after you press F3 to expand the code, it looks like Figure 9-7. Next, using the techniques

```
═══[··········1··········2··········3··········4··········5··········]··········7···]
✗   November 28, 1987¶
✗   ¶
✗   Mr. George Smith↓
    350 Fifth Avenue↓
    New York, NY  11112¶
✗   ¶
✗   Dear Mr. Smith:¶
✗   ¶
✗   I am pleased to inform you that your order for a
    Personalized Necktie has been received.  You are one of the
    fortunate few who will receive one of the last items in this
    very limited collector's series.¶
✗   ▯




COMMAND: Alpha Copy Delete Format Gallery Help Insert Jump Library
         Options Print Quit Replace Search Transfer Undo Window
Edit document or press Esc to use menu
Page 1   {¶}                      ?              Microsoft Word: LETTER1.DOC
```

Figure 9-7.   The glossary listing 1y, extended after F3 has been pressed

already discussed, add the closing paragraph, cl1, and the closing and the signature line (sig1). The body of the letter should look like Figure 9-8. You can further practice this technique by assembling other versions of the letter using the "no" and "maybe" paragraphs.

The main goal when using boilerplate text is to reduce the amount of input required to produce a document. Thus, this technique works best for paragraphs and large strings of words. Word accepts glossary item names up to 31 characters long. The size of all entries is limited by system memory. Thus, if you have a fully loaded computer system, you should have few problems with running out of memory space. However, if you are using a small system (less than 640KB of memory), the system may reach its system limits quickly and may not be able to handle extensive glossaries.

When you set up your glossary items, you used the COPY command. This copied the extended version of your word into the glossary, assigned it an abbreviated name, and stored the word in the glossary. The word was left on the screen. If, however, you wanted to move the word into the glossary, yet not leave it on the screen (as you did when you prepared the items

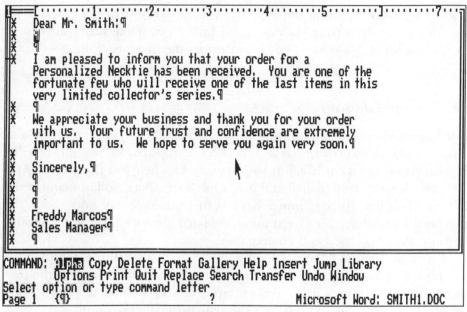

Figure 9-8. The body of SMITH1.DOC

for this file), you could have used the **DELETE** command instead of the **COPY** command. In other words, when you delete to a glossary, the effect on the screen is the same as if you had merely deleted text from the screen — except that in addition to going into scrap, your text is also stored in the glossary.

Viewing the Glossary Contents

In order to see the contents of the glossary, you can view the glossary or print out the contents. To view the glossary, select text (any text), and select the **COPY** command. This brings you to the menu shown at the bottom of Figure 9-1. When you get the "Copy to" prompt, press RIGHT ARROW or point and click the right mouse button. The screen then shows the abbreviations in the glossary. Of course, if you have more than a screen full of abbreviations stored in your glossary, you can scroll through to view the multiple screens of data. Once you've seen the directory and found the abbreviation for the listing you want to use, press ESC to return to where you were before scanning the glossary. You can also print the glossary. To do this, select Print from the command line. Next, make sure your printer is on and select Glossary. The system prints the glossary.

Editing the Glossary

Editing glossaries is somewhat different from other operations in Word. Unlike normal text editing and style sheet manipulation, not all the editing functions are completely at your command when you use your glossaries. You have already created and used glossary listings. So far, many of the listings you have programmed have been unused. Since you check the extended text before you give it an abbreviated glossary form, there should be no need to go back and change it.

If you do want to change a listing, however, this is simple. Simply type the replacement as you wish it to appear and record it to replace the previously saved glossary item. For example, if you wanted to record years with the comma and space before the year printed, you would

Type: ,SPACE1987SPACE RETURN RETURN

then use the **COPY** or **DELETE** command to get to the scrap/glossary option line. Next, you would tell the system you want to call this new string 7. The system would make the replacement for you.

NOTE: Be careful when replacing glossary items. The system does not prompt you for confirmation when you delete one glossary entry and replace it with another. ∎

The Transfer Menu provides options for dealing with glossaries. Select Transfer Glossary, and you are given three options: Merge, Save, and Clear. The **CLEAR** command removes from the system the settings made during your present editing session. This option can also be used to delete a glossary file from the system disk.

For example, if you had developed a glossary for your necktie promotion and no longer needed it, selecting Transfer Glossary Clear would present you with two choices. If you wanted to completely remove the current glossary, pressing RETURN would delete the entire contents of the glossary. To remove particular items, you would press RIGHT ARROW or the right mouse button to bring up a listing of the glossary abbreviations. You would highlight the item you wanted to delete and press RETURN or the right mouse button. Whether you wished to remove a single entry or an entire glossary, the system would prompt you to confirm your decision. This would be your last chance to change your mind. Telling the system yes would result in deletion of the directory or the entry.

Transfer Glossary Merge is used to bring up a glossary. When the system first starts, the default glossary, NORMAL.GLY, is loaded. In many cases this is the only glossary you will ever need. As you use it, it will grow to include your additional glossary listings.

However, there may be times when you want to create a special glossary. For example, if you were in a word processing department or company that did work for a variety of disciplines, it might be easier and faster to have a separate glossary for each discipline, such as a legal glossary and a medical glossary. However, you might also want to combine the basic listings in the NORMAL.GLY glossary. You can merge these listings using the Merge option. To do this, use the MERGE command (and the RIGHT ARROW or right mouse button) to call up the names of the glossary files in the system and add these listings to those you are already using.

You should be careful when merging an old glossary file with one that you created during a current or previous work session. The glossary entry that you load last takes precedence — it replaces any earlier listing with the same abbreviation.

TIP: If you want to use more than one glossary, you should load the least important glossary first. This way, if any abbreviations are duplicated, the most important abbreviations would take precedence. ■

Unlike other editing functions, the glossary does not employ a TRANSFER LOAD command. Your system always starts with NORMAL.GLY in place. To load a glossary, merge the desired glossary into your document.

The Transfer Glossary Save option allows you to save a revised glossary or to give a glossary a new name. When this option is selected, you can save the glossary to the current name by accepting that default, or you can type in a new name for the glossary. In most cases you will save it to the current glossary name. Remember that a glossary should be added to and updated to make your work easier. When you identify text you type often, put it into the glossary. Tailoring a glossary in this way can help enhance your productivity and the pleasure you get from word processing.

The Glossary function also offers predefined entries that stay with the system. The first two, date and time, automatically insert the date or time into your documents. The date is in the form that you would use for beginning a letter; time is also in a standard format. Page prints the page number for your desired pages at the time of printout. Footnote automatically inserts the character required for automatic footnote numbering.

Timeprint and dateprint automatically insert the time and date into your document at print time. Using this option, you can write a letter that may be used for many months; however, each time it is printed, the current date or time is printed. All of these options are discussed in more detail in Chapter 12.

For now, it is also useful to note that these predefined entries can be embedded into another glossary entry. For example, if you were to enter a letterhead or address line into a glossary, you could also include dateprint as part of the glossary entry and automatically tell the system to print the address and the date of printing. Creative use of the predefined entries can result in a great deal of flexibility.

CREATING MERGED DOCUMENTS

Probably the most frequent use of merged documents is the repetitive letter. This type of document is actually made up of two parts—a frame document and a data document. The *frame document* contains the body of the letter—everything that prints in all copies of the letter. It may, for example, contain a heading, date line, signature block, and, possibly, all the text. Microsoft documentation refers to the frame document as the main document, so the words *frame* and *main* are used interchangeably throughout this section.

The *data document* contains the information that changes from letter to letter. This information is typically identifying data: name, address, and perhaps some other special information. At print time the system combines both documents to produce a merged letter.

The first step you should take, whether you choose to prepare the data document or the frame document first, is to decide what data you need and how you plan to integrate it into your document. Alternatively, you may already have a large body of data previously created or converted from a database program. It is important to know how these data items (referred to as *fields*) are named. For example, your file may have a field called Address.

This could contain as little as the street number or as much as the street number, street name, city, state, and zip code. Knowing in advance how the data fields are (or will be) set up enables you to prepare a merged document correctly.

For the example in this chapter, you are preparing a letter selling a necktie embroidered with the symbol of the customer's political party. The data you want to record are built around the following fields: Title, Name, Street, City, State, Zip, Salutation, Party.

The Data Document

Your data document is made up of two parts, a header paragraph and the data. The header paragraph tells the system the name of the data fields. Each field can be separated from the next by pressing TAB or entering a comma. However, you should be careful, once you've defined a *field separator,* to consistently use that separator when you create a data document.

Start a new document, called MFILE1. Next, create the header paragraph. Type the paragraph exactly as it appears here:

```
[·········1·········2·········3·········4·········5·········]·········7···]
X   Title,Name,Street,City,State,Zip,Salutation,Party¶
X   ◘
```

When entering the field names, be careful not to put spaces between the delimiters (commas or tabs) and the field. If you included a space, you would also have to include a space in the frame document to call up the field.

Once the header paragraph is completed, you can begin typing the data. Note that the system places your data into appropriate fields based on a count of delimiters. Thus, if you were preparing a data record that didn't need a particular field, you would still have to enter something into the field. In this example, whatever you put into the second field, Name, would be treated by the system as name data. To make a blank field, type the delimiter. In this example, if you wanted to leave the Title field empty, you would type a comma.

Since the system uses the comma as a delimiter that separates the fields, you must enter fields containing a comma somewhat differently. For example, if you wanted to write to Rodney Cooper, Jr., the system would normally look at the name Rodney Cooper as one field, and the Jr. as the entry for the Street field. Obviously, this wouldn't do. In order to tell the system to ignore the punctuation inside a field, you must enclose the data in quotation marks (" "). Thus, Mr. Cooper's name should be entered as

"Rodney Cooper, Jr.",

Using the quotation marks creates another possible problem. What do you do with text that prints with the quotation marks? For example, what if Rodney Cooper's nickname was "Hot Rod"? Merely enclosing the nickname in quotation marks would confuse the system. Using a single quotation mark around the quote would tell the system you are entering a few fields and leaving out delimiters. The system would see "Rodney Cooper" as the first field, enclosed in quotation marks; Hot Rod as the second field; and "Cooper, Jr.", as the third field, again enclosed by quotation marks. Clearly, single quotation marks would not work.

For this reason, you must put double quotation marks before and after any quoted data. Thus, the correct way to enter the name in the field is this:

"Rodney ""Hot Rod"" Cooper, Jr.",

When you finish entering each data file (the record for each person, company, and so on), end the list by pressing RETURN. This distinguishes one record from another.

Type in the following records as they appear here:

Mr.,"Rodney""Hot Rod""Cooper, Jr.",2312 Oakfoot Lane,Hasbrouck Heights,NJ, 07604,Mr.Cooper,Democrat

Mr.,Hobart Norris,1724 Kitchener Way,Seattle,WA,98022,Mr. Norris,Republican

Mr.,Harry Appell,28891 Washington Lane,Portland,OR,97219,Mr. Appell,Technocrat

Your screen should now look like Figure 9-9. (If you have changed your system's normal gallery, the spacing for the lines (or between the lines) may be different.)

The Frame (Main) Document

Now that you've created the data, it's time to create the main document. Take advantage of Word's windowing abilities. Since you must match up the field names in the data file with the field names in the main document, it is extremely valuable to have the header paragraph visible on the screen while you create the main document.

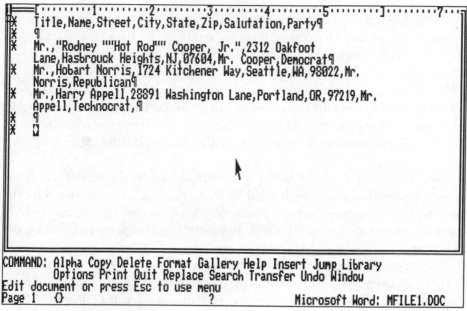

Figure 9-9.   The data document for MFILE1

Create a new window for the main document, splitting the window just below the header paragraph. To do this using your mouse, move the pointer to the line on the right of the screen and point just below the header paragraph. Press the right mouse button to create a new window. Using the keyboard, type ESC-W-S-H-3, and tab to respond *Y* to the "clear new window" prompt, and then press RETURN.

Name this new document (the main document) MLETR1. Now tell the system where to find the data file. To do this, you must type the word *DATA* (all uppercase), followed by the name of the data file. This must also be enclosed by brackets. To enter the left bracket, type CTRL-[. For the right bracket, type CTRL-].

The data statement at the beginning of the document should look like this:

<<DATA mfile1.doc>>

Of course, this line does not print — it merely tells the system where to find the file with the data to be merged. If your data document is in a different drive or directory, provide that information to the system also.

Next, prepare the letter. For each field, you must indicate where the merge is to appear. To do this, type the name of the data field enclosed in the same type of brackets you used at the beginning of the letter.

TIP: If you write many letters with the same field names, you can save time by storing the names, including their brackets, inside a glossary. In addition, you may be able to store fields with different character attributes under different glossary headings (as is illustrated shortly). ■

Merely typing the name of the field surrounded by the brackets tells the system more than just which field to take the data from; it also tells the system about character format. Microsoft Word applies the same character format to the contents of the field as you did to the first character of the field name.

For example, assume you are working with the first data file and want to type "Rodney "Hot Rod" Cooper." If you entered the command to insert the name like this, <<Name>>, the system would print "Rodney "Hot Rod" Cooper." On the other hand, if you entered the command with the first character in Name italicized, the entry would print *"Rodney "Hot Rod" Cooper."* Similarly, underlines, boldface, changed font size or style, or otherwise differently formatted treatment of the first letter in the field would be applied to the entire field.

Now type the letter exactly as it appears in Figure 9-10. Be careful to insert the spaces after the merge instructions. You should be aware that the system inserts the exact contents of each merge field—all punctuation in the setup document must work around the merged field.

Merge Printing

Once the frame (main) document is completed and you are certain that the fields in the main document match those called out in the data document (again, checking the header paragraph can ensure a perfect match), you are ready to print your document. To do this, be sure that the cursor is in the main document window. Word looks in the active window to find the name of the data document before performing a merge printing task. Next, go to the Print Menu. Set your printer options, if necessary, and then select merge print. If all is in order, the system will indicate that it is merging text and will soon begin printing. To cancel printing, press ESC, just as you would with regular printing.

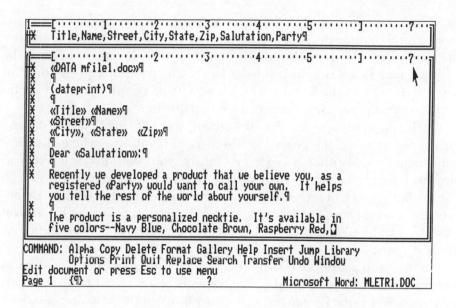

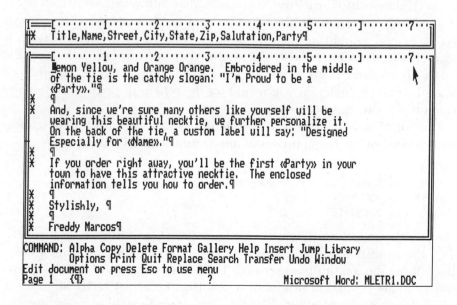

Figure 9-10.   Two screens showing the merge document, MLETR1

Conditionals

For simple repetitive letters, the preceding instructions may be adequate. However, the real world isn't always that simple. What if you had another data field called Company Name? If you set up your document to print the company name each time it printed a letter, what would happen when an empty field was reached? That is, what about the people on the list who don't have company names attached to their listing?

When you made up your data document, you left this field blank. In a normal merge print, the system would insert a blank line where the company name would otherwise go. Obviously, you wouldn't want this to happen. Instead, the empty field should be skipped during printing.

Or what if you had a special product you only wanted to offer to Democrats and you didn't want to create a special letter specifically for Democrats? Or maybe you wanted to print a special paragraph for each major political party.

The way you accomplish these tricks is by using *conditionals* — logical statements that can be applied to the contents of a selected field. The primary statement is the IF statement. In general, when the situation described by the IF statement is true, the instruction that follows the IF statement is executed (or printed); when the situation is false, the instruction is ignored. ENDIF is used to indicate that the situation affected by the IF condition is ended. If the situation is false, the system then continues just beyond the ENDIF. For example, in a case in which the company name might not always be part of the letter, you would set the system to print the company name only if one has been entered.

The form and syntax for a new address block containing the conditional statement for the company name would look like this:

```
<<Name>>
<<IF companyname>> <<companyname
ENDIF>> <<STREET>>
<<CITY>> <<STATE>> <<ZIP>>
```

Note that the condition (IF companyname) is enclosed in its own brackets. When the condition is met (there is an entry in the Companyname field), what follows the condition is executed. That is, the contents of the Companyname field are printed, followed by a new line. Finally, ENDIF signals the end of the conditional effect. If the Companyname field were empty, the system would skip to the text immediately beyond the ENDIF indicator and print the contents of the Street field.

You can also match for text or numbers. For example, you may have a special print run on ties with the name Smith already embroidered onto them. In this case you may want to build a special paragraph into your letter offering these special ties to all addressees named Smith.

The syntax for entering the command to compare text fields is this:

<<IF *field name*="text to match">>*text to print* <<ENDIF>>

For example, the instruction and special paragraph for all Smiths should look like this:

<<IF Name="Smith">>We are also pleased to announce that a very limited edition of our popular MY NAME'S SMITH ties is now available. They are available in Navy Blue only and cost only $29.95. Use order number SM-88.
<<ENDIF>>

The instruction specifies that only letters addressed to people named Smith include this paragraph. (Technically, this wouldn't work, since the command searches for the word Smith. To make this work, you would have to set up your files to include a Lastname and a Firstname field.)

You can also check for numeric matches. For example, if you had a special product for California, you might want to include a paragraph only in letters to the Californians on your list. Since California is the only state with zip codes starting with the number 9, you can have the system select all the zip codes greater than 89999.

Before you see how this is done, it is important to introduce another command, ELSE. ELSE is in some ways a corollary to the IF command. ELSE takes effect when IF is false. The syntax for an IF-ELSE statement is like this:

<<IF *condition*>>*text if true*<<ELSE>>*text if false*<<ENDIF>>

In this example, you have two different sets of ties: one for California and one for the rest of America. A sample paragraph, including the conditionals, might look like this:

<<IF Zip>89999>>We have recently received a shipment of ties that say I'm Proud to be a Californian. These are a true bargain at $19.95. Use order number CA-22.<<ELSE>>We have recently received a shipment of ties that say I'm Proud to be an American. These are a true bargain at $19.95. Use order number US-22.<<ENDIF>>

In addition to matching for numbers greater than one you specify (using >, the greater than symbol), you can match for equal numbers (using =, the equal sign) or for numbers less than that desired (using <).

You can also *nest* conditionals. This means that you can apply a condition to a condition. For example, you could select for all Californians named Smith. This nested condition would look something like this:

<<IF Zip>89999>><<IF Name=Smith>>*desired text*<<ENDIF>><<ENDIF>>

The desired text is the special text applied to those letters where the condition is satisfied. You must have a symmetrical amount of IF and ENDIF statements.

You can also view the contents of each data listing before it is printed by using the NEXT conditional. In this case you are telling the system to show you the contents of each data file that matches your parameter. For example, if you wanted to see each record for California before it printed, you would place the following command right below the DATA command that started the page.

<<IF Zip>89999>><<NEXT>><<ENDIF>

Note that you didn't close the expression with the bracket. If you had done so and also pressed RETURN, the effect would have been to print a blank line and feed the next sheet of paper. In this case, the RETURN at the end of the line is sufficient for ending the conditional statement.

Still other commands can be used in preparing form letters. One such command, SET, can be used to substitute a string of text for the contents of a field. For example, you might want to change the salutation from the formal one you are currently using to "Dear Friend." To do this, at the second line (or third line, if you use the NEXT command) of the document, you can employ the following syntax:

<<SET Salutation=Friend>>

There are two other uses for the SET command, both of which are closely related. The first use is to prompt you to type in the value for a variable. For example, you can employ the following syntax:

<<SET Salutation=?>>

The system prompts you to type a new salutation for each new record. The system does this by flashing the "Value" prompt in the command lines. You must then enter a response (in this case, a salutation).

The other use for SET is very similar. In this case you specify how you want the system to prompt you. For the current example, the following line should work well.

`<<SET Salutation=?Type a Salutation>>`

NOTE: The SET command requests a response from you *only the first time the merge print is run*. The answer you give to the prompts that SET provides are used for all the documents. Thus, if you changed the salutation to Sir, all letters would be printed with that response, whether addressed to men, women, or children. This conditional is more appropriate for data that does not vary from letter to letter than for item-by-item modifications. ∎

The ASK command is used to prompt the operator to type in the data for a field. For example, you might want to print a series of merged letters to people whose addresses are taken from a mailing list. You might already have the rest of the letter ready to run with its current settings. In this case the ASK command would prompt for information for each record.

For example, you may want the system to ask for the name of the addressee. The syntax for this is as follows:

`<<ASK name=?>>`

As each document is prepared to print, the system prompts you with a "Value" prompt and the message "Enter Text" in the command line. As with the SET command, you can also include a prompt after the question mark. Unlike SET, however, ASK prompts for an answer as it gets to each new record.

Form Letters Prepared Without Data Files Using SET and ASK, you can prepare form letters without referring to a data document. In this case, when you activate Print Merge, the system asks for typed entries to the prompted fields. Once all the prompts have been responded to, the system prints the document, complete with merged data.

Merging Documents You may prefer to print a number of short documents as if they are all one long document. For example, if you were writing a book, you might want to keep each chapter separate from the others on your disks but to print the entire book as one document. To do this, you could use the INCLUDE command. The syntax for the INCLUDE command is simple: INCLUDE *docname*. Docname is the name and extension of the file to be printed after the INCLUDE command, including path information, if the new text is on a different drive or directory.

For example, to print three chapters together as a single document, you would (1) place at the end of Chapter 1 the command, <<INCLUDE CHAPTER2.DOC>>; (2) place at the end of Chapter Two the command, <<INCLUDE CHAPTER3.DOC>>; (3) merge print the three documents. The system would automatically print the files, linking them as indicated by the INCLUDE command.

You can use this command to link other documents to the end of a document or to link them at any point inside a document. In addition, you can create a document that prints linked files. In the preceding example, you would not have had to go into any of the three chapters to make them print as a single document. Instead, you could have created a document that accomplished the same thing. This document would look like this:

```
<<INCLUDE CHAPTER1.DOC>>
<<INCLUDE CHAPTER2.DOC>>
<<INCLUDE CHAPTER3.DOC>>
```

Mailing Labels and Envelopes

Mailing labels and envelopes are easy to produce using Word's merge printing capability. You simply develop a frame document that contains the formats for the items to be printed. As a rule, continuous labels are seven lines long. Thus, you must write your master label document to print a total of seven lines per file. Also, you should be certain to change the DATA command at the top of the page to reflect the name of the current data file you are printing.

Preparing envelopes is similar. Most envelopes are about 28 lines long. With some printers, you may be able to scroll the first envelope so that the place for the first line of the address is right under the platen. If you set up 28-line page lengths, you may be able to feed the next envelope into the feed area at the back of the printer. As one envelope prints, it rolls the next envelope into the printer. When it ejects the printed envelope, it scrolls the next one to the right place under the platen, ready for printing. With a little practice and fine tuning, envelope printing can become almost automatic.

Organizing Data Files

In many cases you may have a large data file containing much more information than you may need for any single letter. For example, the sample file you created in this chapter contained a political party affiliation field. There may be few occasions when you need to use the information in the field. However, there is no harm done (other than increased storage requirements) by preparing a data file containing more information than you need. When you merge print, the main document only retrieves the data from the fields specified in that document. The system ignores fields it doesn't need.

Thus, it is probably prudent to create one large list with all the information you need, instead of creating many small lists with subsets of the data. (Again, large databases increase storage requirements, and may also slow down data retrieval; however, having a large master list saves a lot of file swapping and sorting.) Word also allows you to sort text based on a number of parameters. This is discussed in Chapter 14.

COLUMNS AND MATH

One of the most serious limitations of many early word processing programs was their inadequate procedures for creating columns. Although most programs could use fairly rigid formats for numeric columns, text columns and columnar math were difficult, if not impossible, to produce. Microsoft Word has very powerful column and mathematical capabilities. You can produce columns that look like newspaper columns, or you can produce side-by-side columns of related text (the type usually used for catalog listings). For mathematical material, column totals can be automatically computed and recorded in the appropriate places.

In this chapter you create simple tables and columns and progress to complicated multicolumn text formats. The once intimidating columnar tasks that were difficult (but possible) using a typewriter, and impossible using many word processing programs, become well within your understanding and reach.

BASIC TABLES AND COLUMNS

Much of what you will be doing will probably be tables of numbers. Typically, a table includes a heading for each column and aligned columns of numbers. These tables are usually set up with a tab stop for each column. With Microsoft Word you have the ability to specify which type of tab you want to use for your table. When you type whole numbers, you use a right-aligned tab, which makes all the numbers flush right. For decimal figures, a decimal tab aligns all the numbers in the column over a preset decimal point.

In most cases you probably want to use a different tab setting for column headings. For these headings you must apply a different format. If you have a standard layout for your tables, you should record the settings into a style sheet so that they can be called up and applied to the areas whose format you want to change.

You can now create a simple table. This table is included as part of your letter to Steiger, who wanted to sell you a fleet of Lemon cars. In this first setup, you use the standard left or right tabs. Begin a new document called TABLE1. Next, set up your tab stops. You must first get to the Format Tabs Menu. Using your keyboard,

Type: ESC F T

Using your mouse, select Format and then select Tabs. The Format Tabs Menu is shown in Figure 10-1.

A ruler should appear at the top of your screen. You want to start with a clear ruler — that is, you don't want any tab settings from previous formats to influence your current setup. Thus, select the Reset-all option to remove all tab settings and bring you back into the Main Menu. Now that the tabs are cleared, you want to enter your new tab settings. Again, return to the Format Tabs Menu and select Set. The screen looks like Figure 10-2.

The table you want to produce looks like this:

Item	*List Price*	*Fleet Price*
Tires	$700	$698
Brakes	$250	$195
Windshield	$600	$597
Lighting Package	$4500	$3750
Wheels	$350	$350

```
FORMAT TABS: Set Clear Reset-all

Select option or type command letter
Page 1   {¶}                          ?        Microsoft Word: TABLE1.DOC
```

Figure 10-1.   The Format Tabs Menu

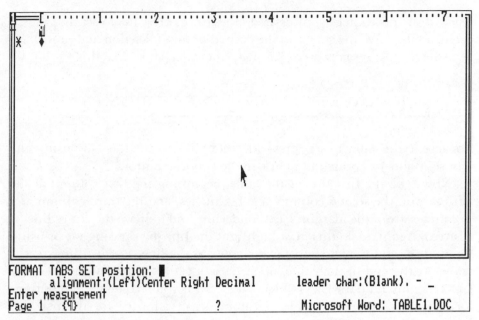

Figure 10-2.   The Format Tabs Set Menu

First, you must set tabs for the column headings. In this case you could have gone with the system's preset tabs at 0.5 inch increments. You can reset those now.

To do this using a mouse, point to the position on the ruler that corresponds to every 0.5 inch. Next, click the left mouse button to leave the left tab symbol. When you place a tab symbol on the ruler, you see the position displayed on the command line.

If you place a tab where you don't want it, there are two things you can do: you can delete the tab mark using the mouse, simply by pointing at the tab you want to delete and pressing both mouse buttons; or you can move the tab mark. To move the tab mark, point at it, press and hold down the left mouse button, and move the pointer to the position where you want the tab moved. The column position can be seen in the Format Tabs Set Menu area. When you release the mouse button, the tab is at the new position.

Using the keyboard only is also relatively easy. Use RIGHT ARROW to move the cursor to the desired tab stop. The cursor moves on the ruler and the tab set position in the command line changes. When the cursor has reached the position of your desired tab setting, press INS to set the tab. To delete a tab, move the cursor to the desired point of deletion and press DEL.

After you've set tabs every 0.5 inch, the ruler looks like this:

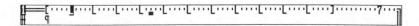

To accept the tabs as set, press RETURN. To accept the tabs using the mouse, point to Format and click the left mouse button.

Now type the first line of the table, beginning the first column at the left margin, the second column at 2 1/2 inches, and the third column at 4 1/2 inches from the margin. Next, underline and italicize the entire line (if desired). Again, to do this, first highlight the line (by pressing F10 or using the mouse) and then assign the attributes to the line. Begin filling in the table. At the end of each line, don't press RETURN—instead, use a NEW LINE command (SHIFT-RETURN). This way, if you change the tab settings for the table, the entire table is automatically adjusted for the new tab settings.

As you fill in the table, you will see that everything is lining up properly, until you get to the line for the lighting package. If you entered the line using the current tab settings, the table as you've typed it so far would look like this:

```
[············1·········2·········3·········4·········5·········]·········7···
q
Item→→    →    →    →   List·Price→    →   Fleet·Price¶
q
Tires→    →    →    →   $→   700→ →    →   $→   698↓
Brakes→   →    →    →   $→   250→ →    →   $→   195↓
Windshield→    →    →   $→   600→ →    →   $→   597↓
Lighting·Package→ →    →   $→  4500→→    →   $→  3750↵
```

(Note that in this illustration OPTIONS visible Complete was selected so that the new line character and tabs could be seen.) Notice that in the List Price column, the number 4500 is not aligned with those above it. A simple way to correct this is to delete the tab before the 4500 and insert spaces between the number and the dollar sign until the column looks right. With most other word processing programs, this is a good fix.

However, with Microsoft Word you can make a much more elegant repair by using the right-aligned tab. When you tell the system to use this

```
[····L····L····L····L····L····L····L····L····L····L····L····]·······7···]
¶
Item→→      →    →    →     List·Price→    →      Fleet·Price¶
¶
Tires→      →    →    →     $→    700→ →   →      $→    698↓
Brakes→     →    →    →     $→    250→ →   →      $→    195↓
Windshield→ →    →    →     $→    600→ →   →      $→    597↓
Lighting·Package→ →  →      $→    4500→ →  →      $→    3750¶
```

Figure 10-3.   A table created using right-aligned tabs

type of tab, all characters scroll to the left of the tab. First, highlight the paragraph. Next, return to the Format Tab Set command line. Delete the left-aligned tab at 3.0 inches, and set a right-aligned tab at 3.3 inches. You have already seen how to enter and delete tabs using the keyboard and mouse. To change from a left-aligned tab to a different style, use the mouse to point to the alignment box or press TAB. Select the right-aligned tab. Next, delete the left-aligned tab at 5 inches and place a right-aligned tab at 5.3 inches. Once these changes are made, accept the new tabs.

Your table should now look like Figure 10-3. To show that the format carries through to the rest of your table, enter the last line of the table. As you type the numbers, the column fills from the right, pushing each number to the left as a new number is added.

For this or any other table, you must set your tab settings to allow enough space for the largest entry in each column. If, for example, you had only allowed for three digits to be placed into the price column, Word would have had a problem accepting the fourth number and instead would have typed beyond the tab mark. To show this, continue typing numbers in any of the numeric columns. Once you have seen how this works, restore the numbers to their correct condition. Any changes you make to the tab settings in the ruler for your table affect the appearance of all the text in the table.

Assume you have now received a more accurate price list for the preceding table. This list includes prices to the penny. So you must now replace the previous figures with decimal numbers. In actual practice you would probably just make modifications to the existing table. However, in this case make a copy of the table, and make changes to the copy. To do this, highlight the entire screen. (Press SHIFT-F10 or, using the mouse, point to the scroll bar and press both mouse buttons.) Next, select the COPY command and copy the table into the scrap. Finally, move a few lines down on the page and press INS to place the table on the screen.

You can see that it makes sense simply to replace a right-aligned tab with a decimal tab. To do this, again go to the Format Tabs Set Menu and make your changes. When you scroll to the right-aligned tab and change the alignment to decimal, the right-aligned tab is automatically changed — you don't have to delete the right-aligned tab and record a decimal tab over it.

Although it appears to make sense to replace the right-aligned tab with the decimal tab, this really doesn't work properly. The number after the decimal point encroaches onto the position of the tab (at the 3.5-inch mark). Thus, you should go back and delete the right-aligned tab at the 3.3 inch and 5.3 inch marks, and insert a decimal tab at the 3.1 inch and 5.1 inch marks. Setting up the tabs so that you get exactly what you want sometimes takes some time and experimentation. If you prepare your tables with the complete coding visible on the screen, it is easy to tell exactly what's going on (why your format works or doesn't work).

Finish typing the table, correcting it to show the decimal values as illustrated below.

```
[····L····L····L····L····L····3D···L····L····L····5D···L····]·········7··
¶
Item→→    →    →    →    List·Price→    →    Fleet·Price¶
¶
Tires→    →    →    →    $→ 699.99→→    →    $→ 698.99↓
Brakes→    →    →    →    $→ 249.99→→    →    $→ 195↓
Windshield→    →    →    $→ 599.99→→    →    $→ 597.45↓
Lighting·Package→    →    $→4500.00→→    →    $→3749.99↓
Wheels→    →    →    →    $→ 349.99→→    →    $→ 349.98▮
```

You can see that by changing the tab styles and settings, you have altered the look of the table. By altering the position of the tabs, you can widen or narrow a table of numbers.

NOTE: The system normally starts with tabs located every half inch. This approximate setting was used when the table was developed. Notice, however, that the tabs at .5, 1, 1.5, and 2 inches were unnecessary — the first required tab was at 2.5 inches. If you removed the first four tabs from the format line, you would end up with a useless table, because the system would not automatically delete the tabs from the text you typed. If you remove tabs from the ruler, you must also remove the corresponding tabs from the text affected by your changes. ■

Column Editing

As already discussed, any changes made to the ruler for a column affect all the contents of the column, as long as the column is prepared as a single paragraph — that is, by pressing SHIFT-RETURN to enter a new line character rather than by pressing RETURN to end each line. Microsoft Word allows you to move, edit, copy, or delete text columns of any size. First, you must select the column you want to edit. Move the cursor to any corner of your desired column. Press SHIFT-F6, telling the system you are selecting a column. Next, move the cursor to the opposite end of the column you want to select.

To see how this works, switch the position of two columns, so that the Fleet Price column is to the left of the List Price column. There are two ways you can make the switch. The first, and probably most obvious, is to move the List Price column to the right of the Fleet Price column. When you do this, however, the extra tab following the List Price column turns the Fleet Price column into a jumble of text. After you make this move, you must make adjustments to the tab spacing between columns and the new first column.

The other way to make this change is to insert the Fleet Price column before the List Price column. Again, you must make adjustments to the tab spacing between columns, but these can be accomplished in a somewhat simpler manner by copying the tabs that previously separated the two columns and inserting them between the two columns.

In either case you must be careful not to move the new line symbol, or the copy won't work correctly. Looking at the table, you can see that if you were to try to copy the column and its heading, you would be including the new line symbols. Therefore, it is best to copy the numerical columns first and then move the column heads. This is also a good practice, since it is less likely to confuse the system with two different column formats. (Remember, the columns employ decimal tabs, while the column heads all employ left-aligned tabs.)

Whenever you copy a column, you should also be aware of whatever changes might be required to fit the new spacing — that is, if you move a wide column into the space previously occupied by a narrow column, you will have to change the format to accommodate the change in column widths.

Highlight the dollar sign ($) in the number 698.99.

Type: SHIFT-F6

Now point to the 8 in the number 349.98. Using the mouse or cursor movement keys, you can build a column of almost any size. You should also notice that in the bottom line of your screen, the indicator CS appears, signifying that you are currently in Column Select mode.

The highlighted column is shown in Figure 10-4. Now, since you want to move the entire column, you must place it into the scrap. Select the Delete function to move the column into the scrap. Move the cursor so that it is on the first dollar sign in the List Price column.

Type: INS

The Fleet Price column is now inserted before the List Price column. The table should look like Figure 10-5.

Next, readjust the spacing between the columns. The easy way to do this is to copy the two columns of tabs that were (and still are) placed after the numbers in the List Price column. The highlighted tab columns are shown in Figure 10-6. Insert the column immediately before the dollar sign in what were the List Price column figures. A column of tabs still follows the numbers in this column. Further, the column is not aligned around the decimal point, because you haven't copied the tab that would otherwise have followed this column of numbers.

To fix this, it may be easiest to insert again another copy of the two columns of tabs before the dollar sign and delete one column of tabs. Alternatively, you can reset the tabs for this second column so that the

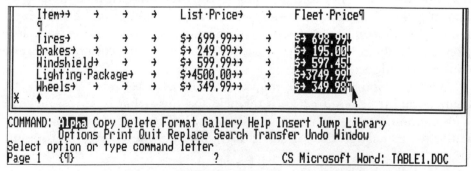

Figure 10-4.   The highlighted Fleet Price column in Column Select (CS) mode

```
┌─────────────────────────────────────────────────────────────┐
│  Item→→    →     →     →    List·Price→   →    Fleet·Price¶   │
│¶                                                             │
│  Tires→    →     →     →    $→ 698.99$→  699.99→   →   →   ↓  │
│  Brakes→   →     →     →    $→ 195.00$→  249.99→   →   →   ↓  │
│  Windshield→     →     →    $→ 597.45$→  599.99→   →   →   ↓  │
│  Lighting·Package→     →    $→3749.99$→  4500.00→  →   →   ↓  │
│  Wheels→   →     →     →    $→ 349.98$→  349.99→   →   ↖   ¶  │
│✕  ♦                                                          │
└─────────────────────────────────────────────────────────────┘
COMMAND: Alpha Copy Delete Format Gallery Help Insert Jump Library
         Options Print Quit Replace Search Transfer Undo Window
Edit document or press Esc to use menu
Page 1   {$→698.99ı$...$→349.98ı}    ?         Microsoft Word: TABLE1.DOC
```

Figure 10-5.   The Fleet Price column switched with the List Price column before the headings have been switched

```
┌─────────────────────────────────────────────────────────────┐
│  Item→→    →     →     →    List·Price→   →    Fleet·Price¶   │
│¶                                                             │
│  Tires→    →     →     →    $→ 698.99$→  699.99→  ██ →   ↓    │
│  Brakes→   →     →     →    $→ 195.00$→  249.99→  ██ →   ↓    │
│  Windshield→     →     →    $→ 597.45$→  599.99→  ██ →   ↓    │
│  Lighting·Package→     →    $→3749.99$→  4500.00→ ██ →   ↓    │
│  Wheels→   →     →     →    $→ 349.98$→  349.99→  ██ ↖   ¶    │
│✕  ♦                                                          │
└─────────────────────────────────────────────────────────────┘
COMMAND: Alpha Copy Delete Format Gallery Help Insert Jump Library
         Options Print Quit Replace Search Transfer Undo Window
Edit document or press Esc to use menu
Page 1   {$→698.99ı$...$→349.98ı}    ?     CS Microsoft Word: TABLE1.DOC
```

Figure 10-6.   The highlighted tab columns in Column Select mode

column is right-aligned—this should align the tab symbols and make it easy to copy and move them. (In this case it won't work, since the column is wider than the space between tabs.) The best way to handle this spacing problem right now is to use the first method: insert the double tab column from the scrap, delete one of the columns, and then delete the tabs after the last column of numbers. You may also have noticed a block shape between the tab symbols in the scrap. These symbols represent the end of a row, and they also help remind you that your scrap contains columnar data.

Finally, switch the two column headings. This can be done with the normal editing methods. It may be easiest just to switch the words *List* and *Fleet,* since *Price* is common to both labels. The new table should look like

Figure 10-7. (Note that Microsoft documentation advises that when you move a column, you should move the heading first. There is little real advantage to this, so you can do whatever seems right for you. The key is to keep track of which numbers go with which column heading.)

When you copy columns, it is best to copy the column with its trailing tab headings — this way, you have a better likelihood of producing properly spaced columns. However, even with its advanced column manipulation, Word may still require some degree of trial and error and tab reformatting to make column manipulation produce a table that is correct in appearance. Do not use a proportional font to print tables. Word allows a variable amount of space for each character, so even a perfectly aligned table may not print correctly with proportional spacing. Also, if you plan to add a new column at the right side of an existing table, you should insert a tab character following the current right-most column. This way, the system provides space between the old right column and the new right column.

Column Insertion

Inserting a new column is also simplified using Word's Column Select mode (activated using the SHIFT-F6 key combination). When you want to create a new column, move your cursor into the column to the right of

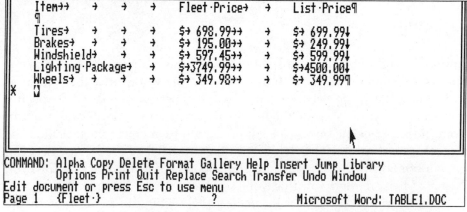

Figure 10-7.   The table with the Fleet Price and List Price columns and headings switched

where you want to insert your new column. Activate the Column Select mode and highlight the column to the right of where you want to insert a new column. Next, press TAB to insert a new tab character in the column to the right of the one you selected. The number of rows that columns are inserted into equals the number of rows in the column that you highlighted.

Once this new column is defined by the tab character, you can highlight the new tab and begin filling in your column. Again, remember that if you add a tab to your table, you must also make a change in the ruler to accommodate the extra column.

COLUMNAR MATH

Microsoft Word's number calculation capabilities can be used to calculate numbers inside of text or numbers in columnar form. This capability provides more power than most other word processing programs that only work on numbers in columns or don't do calculations at all. You will most frequently want to calculate numbers in tables rather than inside text. Other word processors may handle addition and subtraction, but few handle multiplication, division, or percentages as Word does.

Operators

Operators specify which mathematical function you want to perform. If you highlight a column of numbers, Word initially assumes that the numbers are to be added. If you want to subtract a number, you can specify this in two ways: by placing a hyphen, or a minus sign if your numeric pad has one, in front of the number (so the system adds a negative number), or by enclosing the number in parentheses to indicate it is a negative number.

To multiply a number, place an asterisk (SHIFT-8) in front of the number to be multiplied. This symbol (*) is a universal computer symbol representing the multiplication operator. The accepted symbol for division is the slash (/). Placing this symbol in front of the number that is to be the divisor tells the system that you want division.

The percent sign is also used, but only makes sense for multiplication or division. This symbol must be placed after the number of the percent you are specifying. An operator (either * or /) should appear before the number of the percent you are specifying. In many ways the percent sign is extraneous: to specify a number like 25%, it may be easier to substitute its decimal equivalent, 0.25. For anyone with a mathematical background, using decimal equivalents is clearer and less ambiguous.

Unlike most programs, Word calculates from top to bottom or left to right. Consider the simple equation, $1+2*3$. Depending on the order of calculations, you can get two different answers. Most computers do the multiplication first, then perform addition. If this were the case with Word, the answer to this equation would be 7 ($2*3=6$, $6+1=7$). Word, however, solves the equation in what is probably a more logical order and arrives at 9 as the answer ($1+2=3$, $3*3=9$). There may be few occasions where you need to mix calculations; however, it's important to know the order in which Microsoft Word calculates numbers.

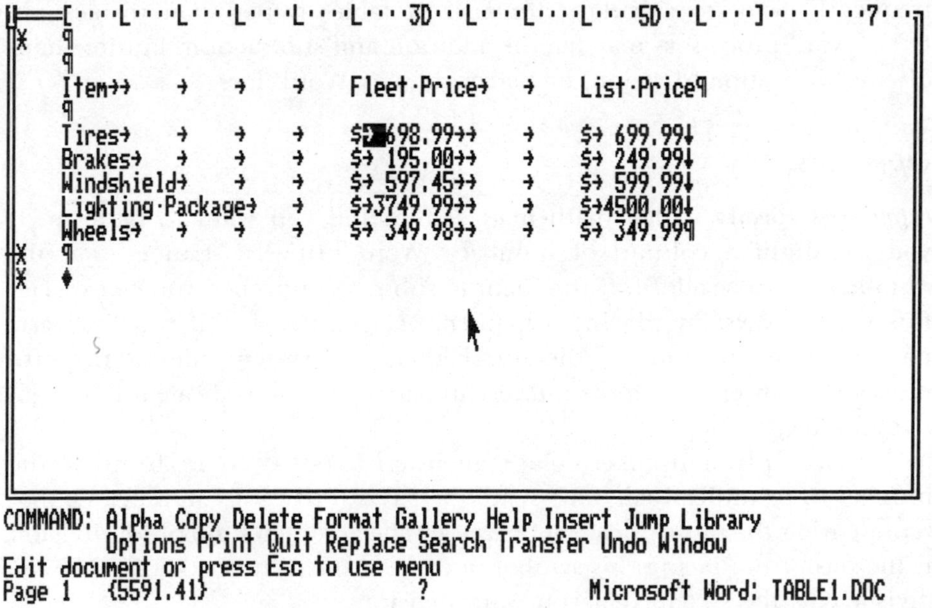

```
[····L···L···L···L···L···3D··L···L···L···5D··L···]·········7···
 ¶
 ¶
Item→→    →    →    →   Fleet·Price→    →   List·Price¶
 ¶
Tires→    →    →    →   $→ 698.99→→   →   $→ 699.99↓
Brakes→   →    →    →   $→ 195.00→→   →   $→ 249.99↓
Windshield→    →    →   $→ 597.45→→   →   $→ 599.99↓
Lighting·Package→   →   $→3749.99→→   →   $→4500.00↓
Wheels→   →    →    →   $→ 349.98→→   →   $→ 349.99¶
 ¶
 ◆
```

```
COMMAND: Alpha Copy Delete Format Gallery Help Insert Jump Library
         Options Print Quit Replace Search Transfer Undo Window
Edit document or press Esc to use menu
Page 1   {5591.41}              ?              Microsoft Word: TABLE1.DOC
```

Figure 10-8.   The total for the figures in the Fleet Price column, displayed in the scrap

Figure 10-9.   The table with the totals for each column separated by an
underline

Calculating numbers is really very simple. Use the Column Select mode
(SHIFT-F6) to highlight the numbers you want to operate on. Next, press F2
to tell the system to calculate the numbers. The total appears in the scrap at
the bottom of your screen. For now, assume that you want a total cost for
the Lemon car options. Select the Fleet Price figures, using the Column
Select mode. Next, press F2. The selected column is no longer highlighted,
and the total appears in the scrap, as shown in Figure 10-8.

Now that you have the total in the scrap, it should be placed at the
bottom of the column. This isn't as easy as just typing the word *Total* and
entering four tabs. In order for the number to appear correctly, you must be
sure that the tabs you are using are carried over into this new Total line.
Before you begin the new line, return to the end of the table and insert a
NEW LINE command in front of the paragraph symbol (which indicated
the end of the table and also contained the format for the entire paragraph).
Be careful not to delete the paragraph mark, since this will remove the tabs
and leave you with a table that looks disorganized.

Once you've added a new line symbol, you can type the word *Total* and
tab to the point where you want to add the dollar sign. Add one more tab
and press INS to place the total in its correct position. Run a total for the
List Price column and place it at the bottom of that column, again remembering to push the paragraph symbol to the right rather than delete it.

The final touch is to put an underline between the last listing in the
column and the total. Do this by selecting the listings and using the ALT-U
command. The table should now look like Figure 10-9. Finally, remove the
formatting marks (using the Options Display None option). The finished
table looks like Figure 10-10.

```
Item                    Fleet Price        List Price
Tires                   $  698.99          $  699.99
Brakes                  $  195.00          $  249.99
Windshield              $  597.45          $  599.99
Lighting Package        $ 3749.99          $ 4500.00
Wheels                  $  349.98          $  349.99
Total                   $ 5591.41          $ 6399.96
```

Figure 10-10. The table with the formatting marks removed

Subtotals and Multicolumn Totals

It seems almost axiomatic that if you work with one numerical table, you will probably work with many. This is probably because there's a tendency to take a set of figures and work with them — add varying rates of interest, make deductions for depreciation, and so on. In many cases, you may have two related tables, one placed above the other, and want to run a total for both. Using Word's mathematical capabilities, it's no problem to run a total of either table. However, if you want to calculate a total of two different tables, you have to be careful.

In your document, TABLE1.DOC, you should have two tables: a beautifully formatted table with decimal figures and a so-so looking table using whole numbers. Assume for now that the two tables had different components — that the top table listed items like radio, heater, spark plugs, engine, and hood. You want to calculate a subtotal for both classes of items — those in the upper table and those in the lower table — and finally to generate a total of all items. Ignore the fact that you've switched the Fleet Price and List Price columns and that the item headings are the same. What you want to do is demonstrate how a total is obtained.

The first rule when doing math on more than one table is to compute the grand total first. The reason for this should be relatively obvious: since Word calculates all the numbers in a column and doesn't distinguish between subtotals and item entries, it adds any subtotals to the other entries in the column, which can result in a total twice the size of the correct amount (or produce other weird numbers if the two columns are of different signs).

Return to the top of the first table. The screen should look something like Figure 10-11. Highlight the first column and carry the highlight (using Column Select mode) through to the last line of the first column in the second table. (Do not include the Total line — remember, you don't want to add the total into this calculation.) Also, don't be concerned about enclosing the dollar sign or the heading of the second table in the highlighted column — Word ignores anything but numbers and mathematical operators.

Type: F2

Your total for the first column in the two tables shows up in the scrap. Push the paragraph down, using the NEW LINE command and pressing TAB, enter a Grand Total line, and insert the one-column total. Do the same for the second column, again inserting that column's total. The second table should look like Figure 10-12.

Finally, go back to the first table and calculate column totals. Create a Subtotal line and place the totals in their correct position. The screen

```
⌶━━[····L····L····L····L····L····L····L····L····L····L····L····]·········7···⌝

   Item                    List Price          Fleet Price

   Tires                $     700          $     698
   Brakes               $     250          $     195
   Windshield           $     600          $     597
   Lighting Package     $    4500          $    3750
   Wheels               $     350          $     350
 ⌇
 *
 *
 *
 *
 *
   Item                    Fleet Price         List Price

   Tires                $   698.99         $   699.99
   Brakes               $   195.00         $   249.99
   Windshield           $   597.45         $   599.99
   Lighting Package     $  3749.99         $  4500.00

COMMAND: Alpha Copy Delete Format Gallery Help Insert Jump Library
         Options Print Quit Replace Search Transfer Undo Window
Edit document or press Esc to use menu
Page 1   {6399.96}               ?            Microsoft Word: TABLE1.DOC
```

Figure 10-11.   The two tables for which a grand total is to be calculated

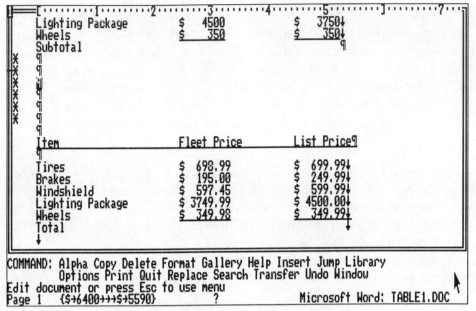

Figure 10-12.   The grand totals for the fleet and list prices for the two tables, displayed in the scrap

should look like Figure 10-13. Again, remember that you should add the grand total first and then calculate subtotals. When drawing totals, then, work from the bottom up. You can now save the document containing these tables.

TIP: You can run continuous subtotals without worrying about adding them into the total if you create a calculation window at the bottom of the screen. This way, when you have arrived at a total for each column, you can not only place it at the bottom of the column, but you can also place it into your other window and use Microsoft Word's math capabilities to add the collected subtotals. If you are working with many subtotals or sets of lengthy columns, this may be less of an interruption of the work flow. This is yet another example of how an extra window can make your work somewhat easier. ∎

It can be a tremendous time saver if you develop a style sheet for each basic type of table you prepare. By applying the predeveloped style to a table, you can avoid much of the trial and error involved in setting up each

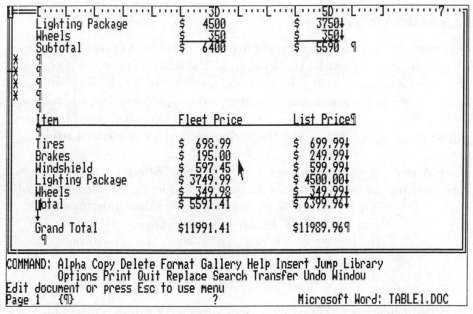

```
Lighting Package           $    4500        $   3750↓
Wheels                     $    350         $    350↓
Subtotal                   $    6400        $   5590  ¶
                    ¶
***                 ¶
***                 ¶
***                 ¶
                    ¶

Item                   Fleet Price       List Price¶
                    ¶
Tires                      $  698.99       $  699.99↓
Brakes                     $  195.00       $  249.99↓
Windshield                 $  597.45       $  599.99↓
Lighting Package           $ 3749.99       $ 4500.00↓
Wheels                     $  349.98       $  349.99↓
Total                      $ 5591.41       $ 6399.96↓

Grand Total                $11991.41       $11989.96¶
                    ¶
```

```
COMMAND: Alpha Copy Delete Format Gallery Help Insert Jump Library
         Options Print Quit Replace Search Transfer Undo Window
Edit document or press Esc to use menu
Page 1    {¶}                        ?        Microsoft Word: TABLE1.DOC
```

Figure 10-13.   The subtotals for the first table, entered after the grand totals
                   have been calculated

table. In addition, it is a good idea to use as few tabs as possible when
setting up a ruler. This makes it easier to see which tab is influencing
which column of text or numbers and also leaves you latitude in adding
new tabs when you add more columns. (Note that in some instances you
may want to place text or numbers in an exact position. Using Word's
alignment options, you can position columns just about anywhere you
want them. In the first table you could have used spaces instead of a tab to
properly align the larger number.)

When you use spaces within a column, it is a good idea to use hard
spaces. A hard space tells the system that, no matter what, you want those
spaces in your text or column. It also tells the system to keep any text
affected by the column from being split onto two lines. In most cases the
system ends each line on a standard space. If you use hard spaces, you can
keep your figures together. On some word processors you must use hard
spaces in numeric columns to assure that the numbers in the column align
properly. For any numerical columns that aren't automatically set using
decimal or right-aligned tabs, you should use hard spaces before numbers.

COLUMNAR TEXT

One of many important features of Word is its ability to prepare columnar text. This feature provides you with great flexibility in formatting your text and has capabilities still missing from some other word processing programs. One application that is a tremendous problem for virtually any other word processor on the market is the multicolumn setup. The following example is similar to one the author created for a medical book.

Drug Name	*Suggested Dosage*	*Side Effects*
Amoxicillin	50 mg. four times daily. Therapeutic course should run for 10 days. Prophylactic dosages of 500 mg./day can be prescribed when indicated.	Reduction or elimination of gastric and intestinal flora. Digestive disorders are possible, though uncommon, side effects.

A dedicated word processing system was used for this project. This system did nothing but word processing. It had a primitive column development mode and was not well suited to the project. In order to produce the desired results, the first column was typed in, the number of lines it took up was calculated, and the cursor was moved up that number of lines. Next, margins were changed for the second column. The column was typed in, the number of lines was counted, and the cursor again moved up the appropriate number of lines. A final format change for the third column was made and the column was typed in.

Before the first column format could be returned to, however, the longest of the three columns had to be measured so that the next set of entries would be properly spaced in comparison to the current one. On the screen the display was an unusable jumble of words. Actual preparation of columns was a matter of time-consuming trial and error.

The purpose of this rather lengthy discussion of another word processing system is this: if Word 3.0 had been available, it would have made the entire task much simpler and would have saved many hours of time. Once a basic format was set up using Word, it could have been used for all entries no matter what their length. For this 200-page project, the savings would have been significant. Word 3.0 is currently the only version of Word that can produce multiple columns of varying width. Word 2.0 can produce newspaper-style columns of equal widths.

Newspaper-style columns are also referred to as *snake columns.* This is due to the way that the text wraps (snakes) up from the bottom of one column to the top of the next. Early word processors weren't particularly adept at this type of column: if your printer was capable of moving the paper up the page, and if your word processing program could generate the codes to move the paper up, you could type one column, calculate the line length of the column, instruct the system to move the paper back up to the top of the page, set a new format for the next column, and begin over.

Microsoft Word handles all the complicated calculations for you. It calculates the width of each column, determines where your text should appear in each column, and prints a complete line at a time, without the hassle of trying to get the paper to scroll down the proper amount each time.

The other type of column format is new to Microsoft Word and is currently available on version 3.0 only. In some ways, it is also a snaking column; however, you have the flexibility of varying the width of each column. Thus, the previous drug schedule example could be produced using three differently sized columns. A special format command in Word 3.0 tells the system to start printing each of the columns on the same line. It also can tell where to start the next set of columns or text without the hassle of figuring the length of the longest column and moving the next paragraph beyond that point.

Newspaper-style (Snake) Columns

The newspaper-style document is really very easy to prepare. In order to produce this type of document, you must perform a simple format calculation to instruct the system how you want your columns to appear.

Begin a new document called SNAKE. Type the text shown in Figure 10-14. Your text will not appear as it does in the figure. For now, don't worry about the heading above the columns. After you've typed the first paragraph, you can set Word to handle your columns.

The Snake Column

Once upon a time, not too very long ago, there was a very lonely word processor operator sitting, as it were, on the horns of a dilemma.

Needless to say, it wasn't very comfortable for the operator, nor, for that matter, for the dilemma, which didn't like people sitting on its horns.

This word processor was a great typist, was skilled at all types of word processing tasks. Justified columns were child's play. Centered text was laughably easy.

For months, everything went along fine. Things to be done would be brought in--letters, memos, manuscripts, charts: and they would go out to the originator, ready to mail.

The operator never mentioned the word processing system's limitations. Until one day it happened.

The horror assignment--the one that this operator hoped would never arrive--a newsletter.

"Sure, I can do it," this operator said, "we'll just make it like a regular letter 60 spaces wide, and drop in a masthead at the top of the page.

"No," said the voice of authority. "I want three columns."

The operator pondered the situation for a while.

"Okay, that's simple. I'll just print out one long column, and we can cut and paste it onto a single page."

"That's not how we want it," authority chimed in. "It's got to be printed on one page."

"But it can't be done that way" said the operator.

"Do it that way" the authority ordered.

While sitting uncomfortably atop the dilemma's uppermost protuberances, the operator took a backward glance at the columns that ran behind the desks in the office, and seemed to hold the ceiling up.

To immense surprise, a giant python was working its way around a column from the top to the bottom. Its body then headed toward the top of the next column and began to slither again towards the bottom. As its head reached the bottom, it headed for the top of the third column. This was ONE BIG SNAKE.

And, in a flash, the word processor operator thought that there must have been a message in all this.

Of course there was: "Call the boss, then call the zoo. While they're busy with the serpent, I can figure a way to squirm out of this project."

That didn't work. The operator looked at word processor manuals for other systems and found that they allowed you to type a column, then do a reverse backspace to get to the top of the page and begin the next column. Unfortu-nately, the reverse line feed didn't work on the printers installed in the office, and the calculation was a hassle. And they weren't using this word processor anyway.

Suddenly, the skies parted and a copy of Microsoft Word and a book dropped out of the heavens. They missed by just three inches. Boy was that close. The operator then opened **The Advanced Guide to Microsoft Word**, and found THE ANSWER.

After a minimal amount of effort, the project was completed, the authorities were delighted, and everyone (except, perhaps, the python) lived happily ever after.

Figure 10-14. SNAKE.DOC

WORD 3.0 ONLY

The method for setting up a snake column is slightly different for version 3.0 than for version 2.0. To set up a snake column, select Format Division Layout. This involves three steps and brings you to a menu similar to that shown in Figure 10-15.

WORD 2.0 ONLY

The method for setting up a snake column is slightly different for version 2.0 than for version 3.0. When you select Format Division, you are brought to a menu that allows you to select your column parameters. In both versions the commands are basically identical.

For this example, you want three columns, with 0.3 inch between them. The system automatically calculates the width of each column based on the overall margins set for the page using the Format Paragraph Menu. Thus, even though you are using multiple columns, the width of the text on your page is the same as it would be for a single column of text. To do this, you must be in the Format Division or Format Division Layout Menu, depending upon which version of Word you use. Using your keyboard or mouse, tell the system to set three columns and set the space between columns to 0.3 inch.

```
FORMAT DIVISION LAYOUT footnotes: Same-page End
        number of columns: 3        space between columns: 0.3"
            division break: Page Continuous(Column)Even Odd
Select option
P1 D1    {8}                        ?              Microsoft Word: SNAKE.DOC
```

Figure 10-15.   The Format Division Layout Menu for version 3.0 of Word

As a rule, it is generally a good idea to allow 0.5 inch of space between columns. However, since you will be putting three columns into six inches of space, you are already working with small columns. To calculate the width of each column, take the usable space (6 inches), subtract the amount of space between columns (using 0.3 inch, this would be 0.6 inch, since you have the same space between two columns), subtract the space between the columns from the usable space (6 minus 0.6 equals 5.4), and divide by the number of columns (5.4 divided by 3 equals 1.8).

If you use too much space between columns, you may reduce the size of your columns so much they are barely usable. Further, if you plan to right justify your columns (probably an excellent idea, since most newspapers justify their text), the difficulty of justifying and hyphenating text increases the smaller the column becomes. Thus, as large a column as is practical is often the best choice. When you are back inside your document (once you've set and accepted the column parameters), instruct the system to right justify your document by using the ALT-J key combination for the high-lighted paragraph or by going into the Format Character Menu.

Set Column as the division break. This allows you to tell the system to end a column at a point before it would normally end. For example, if you wanted to place a chart at the bottom of a column, you could tell the sys-

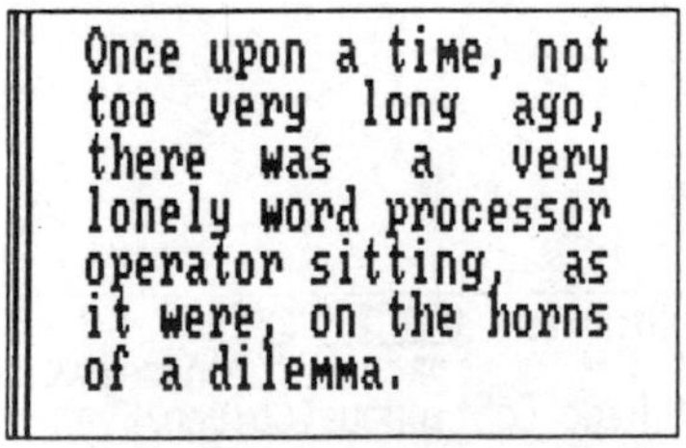

```
Once upon a time, not
too very long ago,
there was a very
lonely word processor
operator sitting, as
it were, on the horns
of a dilemma.
```

Figure 10-16.   The first paragraph in column mode

```
For      months,
everything  went
along      fine.
Things to be done
would be brought
in--letters,
memos,
manuscripts,
charts--and  they
would go out to
the   originator,
ready to mail.
```

Figure 10-17.   A justified column of type showing poor spacing between words

tem to leave space at the bottom to accommodate the chart. If you were in Page Division mode, the command would cause the page to end, while in the Column Division mode, the cursor is moved to the next column. You needn't worry about text running over on the page, since the system still automatically paginates a columnar document.

Once you have made your column settings, your screen changes. What was once a 6-inch wide paragraph has become a 1.8-inch wide paragraph. Your first paragraph should look like Figure 10-16. As you type the rest of the document, notice that the system doesn't automatically break columns for you. However, the system creates three columns when you have finished typing the page and used the PRINT REPAGINATE command.

You should also notice an excellent example of what happens when narrow columns of type are justified. The paragraph in Figure 10-17 shows lines with large spaces between words and lines that can handle only single words. If printed as is, this paragraph would look awful. If you went to two columns, the number of these awful breaks would be reduced.

There is another way to handle this. Highlight the entire document. Next, select the LIBRARY HYPHENATE command. Tell the system to confirm each hyphenation decision by selecting the Yes option and accept the setting by using the mouse or pressing RETURN. After processing the entire document, you may still note some minor glitches. For example, the word *manuscripts* is by itself in the paragraph shown in Figure 10-16. If left by itself, this line would not be justified; instead, the single word would be printed, with space left open after it.

When you run into a situation like this, you must be a bit creative. For example, in this case it is obvious that the system is looking at *charts—and* as a single word. You may try to change *charts—and* to *charts; and* and then run the Library Hyphenate function. In this case it doesn't work.

Change *charts; and* back to *charts—and*. Notice that there is a large space in the line above the word *manuscripts*. This would indicate that the line could take more text from the line below. So, hyphenate the word *manuscripts* by placing a hyphen after the *u*. Take this one step further and hyphenate the word *originator* (place the hyphen between the *i* and the *n*). When Word checks the hyphenation in columns, it doesn't hyphenate all the words where and when it should. By checking through your document and finding places where a hyphen may help improve the look of the paragraph, you can create an almost professional columnar document.

NOTE: Manually hyphenating, as was done here, can give you a good-looking paragraph. However, there's an important trade-off when you add normal hyphens to these words. The hyphen stays embedded inside the word—if you change the margins or add words to the paragraph, it is likely that the hyphenated word will no longer be at the end of a line and the word won't be broken at the hyphen. Instead, the word will print inside a line with the hyphen printed in the middle of the word. You should thus be careful to add the hyphens only before the final printout to avoid erroneous hyphens being printed in your document. ■

Adjusting Columns Now that you have typed in the entire document, you have one very long column. To create three columns, use the Print Repaginate function. On the screen you still see only one column. However, when you scroll through the document, you see a page break symbol and a number to the side of it. The break for the second column is shown in Figure 10-18.

You can quickly see that the column would take a funny break, breaking at the word *arrive*. It would be preferable to start the second column with the complete paragraph. To specify a different column break, move the cursor to the point where you want to make the break and press CTRL-RETURN. You should remember, of course, that any change you make to

Figure 10-18.   The column break symbol for the second column, shown in
the margin

this column lengthens or shortens the subsequent column. It is important
to repaginate a columnar document after you make any column breaks.

The COLUMN BREAK command is also useful if you want to add
white space to the bottom of a column. Since Word doesn't provide line
numbers, deciding on an exact position for the start of white space is something of a trial-and-error proposition: you must first print out the document and then find the line where you want to place the break. A column
break ends the printing of a column at that particular point. You then
must repaginate the document to adjust for the blank space the new
column break leaves in the document.

Doing a wraparound for an illustration inserted inside a column is also
somewhat iffy. The best way to insert white space is to print out the document and identify the space you want to designate for a graphic. Next,
figure out the length of the graphic and press RETURN six times for each
inch of space you need. Again, after inserting white space, you must repaginate to adjust the length of each column.

This particular document, as you entered it, repaginated to more than
one page. You wish to print the document on a single page. The most
obvious modification that allows you to do this is changing the page
length. Although you are still using 11-inch paper, you may be able to do
without the 1-inch top and bottom margins.

Highlight the entire document. (From the keyboard, press SHIFT-F10;
using the mouse, point to the scroll bar at the left side of the screen and
click both mouse buttons.) Next, go to the Format Division Margins Menu
and change your margins to a 0.6-inch top margin and a 0.5-inch bottom
margin. Accept the changes. Run a Print Repaginate on the document.
You will find that this isn't enough of a change—one and one-half paragraphs are still on a second page.

Return to the Format Division Margins Menu and reduce left and right margins to 0.75 inch each. Your columns are now 2 inches wide. Run another Library Hyphenate on your document and go back to fix the words that have hyphens and shouldn't (for example, *manu-scripts*). The extra 0.2 inch has made a smoother looking document—the text doesn't look as choppy as it did with the narrower column width. Repaginate the document again. The combination of changed page widths and a larger printed area does the trick.

Adding a Head to the Document   Snaking documents must be printed on their own page. If you were to try to add a head to the page, the system would try to make a page break after the head was typed, since you are going from page division format to column division format. However, if you wanted to place a title line or header above your column, you could set up such a header as a running head. Although running heads are discussed further in Chapter 12, the following instructions guide you through creation of a head for this particular document.

First, return to the beginning of the document. Now, type the running head "The Snake Column." Highlight this text, select Format Running-head, select the Top position, respond no to the Odd and Even Page prompts, and respond yes to the First Page prompt. You have told the system to print the head at the top of the first page only.

In addition, you can use the FORMAT CHARACTER and FORMAT PARAGRAPH commands to change the look of the head and have some control over its positioning. You should also remember to add a space between the running head and the first line of text; otherwise, the head prints directly above a column of text. If you've centered the head and set it up to print in bold type, the top of your page should resemble Figure 10-19.

TIP: Although this example used a standard page size, Word allows you to use other page lengths and widths. One effective method of producing high-quality columnar text is to define a wider and longer page than you normally would or to use two wider columns. Once these wider columns are printed, they can be reduced on a photocopy machine and used as camera-ready original copy. In other words, you can use different width columns and adjust them to fit after printing them out. ■

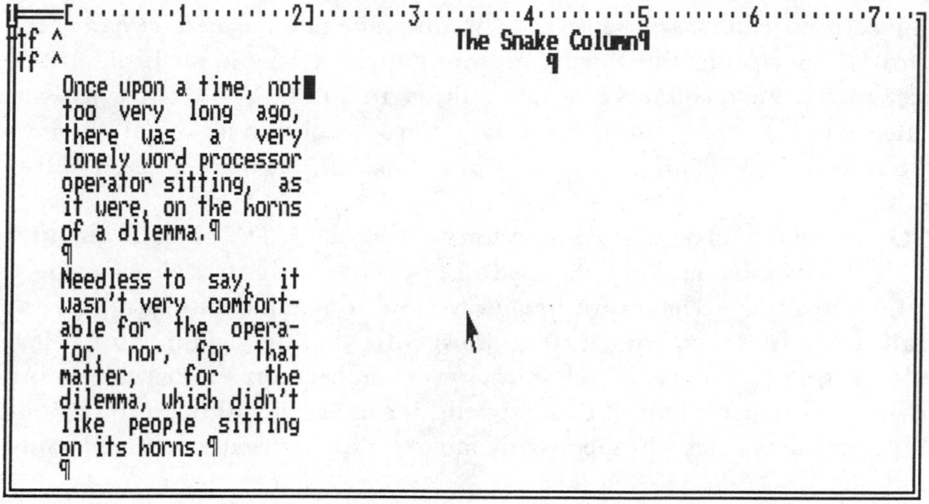

```
||──[··········1··········2]··········3··········4··········5··········6··········7···┐
║tf ^                            The Snake Column¶
║tf ^                                   ¶
║        Once upon a time, not█
║        too very long ago,
║        there was a very
║        lonely word processor
║        operator sitting, as
║        it were, on the horns
║        of a dilemma.¶
║        ¶
║        Needless to say, it
║        wasn't very comfort-
║        able for the opera-
║        tor, nor, for that              ▶
║        matter, for the
║        dilemma, which didn't
║        like people sitting
║        on its horns.¶
║        ¶
```

Figure 10-19.   A centered, boldfaced running head for SNAKE.DOC

TIP: If you do many columnar documents, it will be very valuable to save your column setup as a gallery listing. This way, once the document is typed, all you have to do to put it into correct column width is to highlight the columnar text and apply the style sheet to the text. ■

Irregular Columns: Word 3.0 Only

As can be seen here, the newspaper-style (snake) columns are fairly easy to set up and modify. Both Word 2.0 and Word 3.0 support this mode. The irregular column mode is one supported only by Word 3.0. The drug schedule example presented at the beginning of this chapter is an example of one use of the irregular column facility. Unlike the snaking column, irregular columns can be included anywhere on a page or within text.

This type of column is referred to as a *bound column* by other word processing programs. Essentially, when you prepare this type of column, you set up the left and right indents for each column. Each column has a preset width — each — usually — contains a certain type of text. (That is, one column can be a product code number; the next, a product name; the third, a description; the fourth, minimum quantities; and the fifth, unit or case price.) Each column can have a different width. Typically, when you enter data for these columns, you type in each column and then go on to the next.

NOTE: This mode is often used for numeric data. The obvious question is this: why not just use tabs instead of going to the trouble of using a columnar mode? The answer relates to how your table will be organized. Tabs work fine if *all* your listings are smaller than the width you set each tab for; that is, if none of your entries ever encroach on another tab setting or into another column. If this happens, it can become difficult to fix your table. In many cases a numbers-only table can be done extremely well using only tabs.

However, if you are also using text or if your entries may run to more than one column width, this column mode is superior. First, it automatically wraps from one line to the next *within a column*. This saves the hassle of readjusting your table each time a listing becomes too long.

Second, it allows you to vary the alignment of an entire column. For example, you may want a text column right justified, a parts number column right-aligned, and a price column aligned with a decimal tab. By creating a style sheet for each column, you can easily have your table looking *exactly* as you want it. ■

Save SNAKE.DOC and begin a new document called CATALOG. The first step in preparing this type of column is to determine the width of each column and the amount of space used to separate the columns. If you enter such things as product names, descriptions, or other one- or two-word entries, the most practical way of determining the required column width is to find the longest such entry for each column category. Adding these lengths together yields a required line width. You should also add at least two character spaces (in most cases 0.2 inch) between columns so that the text doesn't run together. At times, you may not be able to get as many columns as you need onto a line. In such cases remember that Word supports hyphenation; you can allow hyphens to be used in selected columns.

In the example provided here, four columns are used. In order to get the four different columns, you must alter the amount of indent from either side of the page. Figure 10-20 shows the document as it looks when printed.

Part #	Product Description	Qty/Pack	Price per unit
17-324	Ferganchick Fastener	24/case	1.27
17-822	Kumquat clip	144/case	.12
05-240	9x9 Static Ram	6/pack	1.073
59-080	Borkowski Bolt	1/ea.	17.24

Figure 10-20.   CATALOG.DOC as it appears when printed

Once you've defined column indents (you'll do that in a minute), you type each of your columns. By using the special paragraph command, SIDE-BY-SIDE, when it comes time to print the paragraphs, you ensure that each paragraph in a column prints alongside the others.

NOTE: Since with this type of column you normally type many different entries, it is almost mandatory that you save the setup for each column in a gallery. This way, you get consistent columns from listing to listing and don't have to bother resetting margins each time you switch from one column to the next. ■

The heading for the columns uses the same format that the columns do. The fourth column, the Price column, differs in that a decimal tab is used to align the numbers under the column head. The first column head is "Part #." A look at the data below this column shows that a maximum of six characters is used. Type Part # and then highlight the entry.

Next, go into the Format Paragraph Menu. The menu lines look like this:

```
FORMAT PARAGRAPH alignment:  [LH] Centered Right Justified
         left indent: 0"          first line: 0"        right indent: 0"
         line spacing: 1 li     space before: 0 li       space after: 0 li
         keep together: Yes(No)  keep follow: Yes(No)   side by side: Yes(No)
```

Since this is the first column, you want it to start flush with the left margin. However, since the largest entry is only 6 characters (in 10 pitch that's 0.6 inch), you must move the right indent so that it won't allow the column to print beyond the desired limit. Thus, you should set your right indent to 5.4 inches. (This is equal to 6 inches—the total width of the printed page—minus the 0.6 inch needed for the column.)

Line spacing should be kept at 1. Set a single line after the paragraph. The next critical setting is the response to the side-by-side prompt. Telling the system yes instructs it to print the other columns on the same line. This command is necessary for lining up the uneven columns.

TIP: Spacing between listings can be done a few different ways. If you are doing single-line listings, as illustrated here, you may not want to have any space between one entry and the next. In other words, each listing lines up right above the next listing. With this type of listing, you would probably only want to insert space between the column head and the first listing.

To do this, you would press RETURN before typing the text for each column. It is important to realize that each column is printed as a separate paragraph. The only real difference between these paragraphs and normal paragraphs is that they are indented differently, and all paragraphs begin printing on the same line. Thus, if you had four columns and you wanted to separate them from the listing above them (in this case, the header), you would have to insert a blank line before each of the four columns.

If, on the other hand, you wanted to have a space between each listing, you would set the column paragraph formats the same way, usually with one line before or one line after each paragraph. Failure to be consistent in the settings for each column can cause confusing formatting problems when it comes time to print your columns. ■

Once the parameters for the first column are accepted, your screen shows the indents for this column and you are ready to write the next column. You should, however, create a gallery entry for this column. Call this entry c1.

The second column is much wider than the first. The longest listing is the first one, Ferganchick Fastener. When you type this entry, you can see that the longest listing is 2 inches in length. Thus, if you were to set this column width to 2.4 inches, there would be plenty of space for any entries.

Highlight the "Ferganchick Fastener" line. Next, select the FORMAT PARAGRAPH command. The left margin must be indented to allow for the first column. Allow 0.2 inch beyond the end of the first column. In this case, then, the left indent must be 0.8 inch (0.6 inch used by column 1 and 0.2 inch for spacing). When you add the 2.4 inches you plan to use to allow for the second column to the 0.8 inch used by the first column, you have 3.2

inches occupied by column 2. Subtracting this from 6.0 (the width of the page) leaves you with a 2.8-inch right indent. Again, indicate that the paragraph is a side-by-side paragraph. Once you accept the setting, the entry slides to the right, and the indent brackets appear at the top of the screen. Again, save these settings in the gallery, calling the entry c2.

The next listing is eight characters wide. Allow nine characters, in case you have an entry in the 1000-unit range. Type in the column head and select Format Paragraph. The format for this requires a left indent of 3.4 inches, since the first two columns took up 3.2 inches and you wanted to have 0.2 inch between margins. This column runs to the 4.3-inch mark (3.4 plus 0.9). Thus, the right margin should be set for 1.7 inches (6.0 minus 4.3). Again, set the Side by Side prompt to yes. And, again, save this format in your style sheet as c3. This column is shown on the screen below and to the right of column 2.

The fourth column has a large heading and includes decimal numbers. Type the head, as seen in Figure 10-20, to see the actual width of the head and to make sure that it doesn't go beyond the 1.5 inches (1.7 minus 0.2 inch of space between columns) that you have available. Next, highlight the line and set the format for this column.

In this case the left indent is 4.5 inches, with a 0-inch right indent. And, of course, the Side by Side prompt is answered yes. In addition to establishing this setting, you also want to insert a decimal tab at about 5.4 inches from the left margin. This can be done easily using the FORMAT TAB SET command. Again, create a gallery listing for this entry and tab setting and call the listing c4.

Now that you have four sets of columnar indents set and stored in the gallery, go back and change the second header from "Ferganchick Fastener" to "Product Description." In this case, to assure consistency, the author went back into each paragraph and applied the style for each type of column. The first four lines of the heading look like Figure 10-21.

Now add a space after the last header entry and type the rest of the table, remembering to use the style sheet listing for each column and to tab for

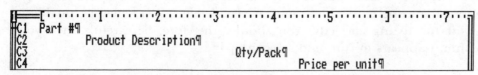

Figure 10-21.   The header paragraph with styles attached

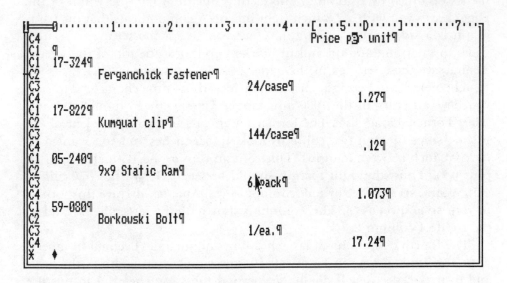

Figure 10-22. The completed entries for CATALOG.DOC

the decimal entry in the fourth column. The completed entries for the table, including attached styles, should look like Figure 10-22.

You could also have chosen to make the unit entries right aligned. However, in its present condition, the table should print correctly and without error, resembling Figure 10-20. Again, it is important to set the width of your columns using the indents available, so that there is adequate space between columns. It is also critical to define each paragraph as side by side.

You can type many lines of text within any of the columns. When you finish the last column, the system automatically adjusts spacing so that the first line of the next entry is spaced after any other columnar entries. The only other possible exception is the case in which one or more of the columns ends a page and carries over onto the next. In this case Word may have difficulty determining where to begin the next entry. In addition, if more than one entry flows onto a second page, Word may be unable to print the listing correctly. You should, therefore, be careful when your column appears to run onto a second page.

OUTLINING

Outlining is one of the the most recent additions to Microsoft Word. Outlining programs are among the most important classes of software released for personal computers in the last few years. Many people who use outlining programs are shamelessly addicted to them. Most such programs allow you to develop an outline and then use that outline to help you write your document. A key advantage to outlining programs is that they allow you to make a rough outline and then modify it, changing levels of headings and reorganizing items.

In many cases outliners are perceived as thought organizers: they visually represent the organization of ideas and allow users to manipulate elements of the outline so that a more accurate model can be developed. These also can be an important tool in management: an executive who does not have enough time to draft a document can develop an outline and leave it to lower-level personnel to flesh out the text. Much like boilerplate text, standard portions of outlines can be merged from different documents to produce an accurate outline for a new document. In short, there are many uses for outliners, some of which are discussed in this chapter.

For a short period Microsoft Word 2.0 was distributed along with a copy of Ready!, the outline processor from Living Videotext, Inc. Ready! is a memory-resident outlining program that allows the user to develop an outline and then use that outline to develop a Word document. If you have Word 2.0, plus a copy of Ready!, you probably already know how to use your outline processor.

If you have Ready! files and plan to upgrade to Microsoft Word 3.0 (or have already), you are still able to use Ready!, although it is probably wise to convert your Ready! files to outlines compatible with Word 3.0. The instructions for making the conversion are straightforward and are covered in Appendix C of the Microsoft Word Reference Guide.

The outliner built into Word 3.0 is not compatible with Word 2.0—that is, files containing outlines developed using Word 3.0 cannot be accessed by a system running Word 2.0. If you transfer files between machines and not all the computers run Word 3.0, you should be aware of this limitation if you expect to use the outlining features.

THE BUILT-IN OUTLINER: WORD 3.0 ONLY

It is not the intent or purpose of this chapter to teach you how to outline. However, a few basic principles are presented. One of the most important concepts in outlining is that of levels. Essentially, you are developing categories and related subcategories when you develop an outline. For example, if you were to use Word to prepare an outline for an organizational chart, you would probably first break the organization into major divisions, such as Executive, Administrative, Support, Marketing, and Finance. The first-level breakdown would look like this:

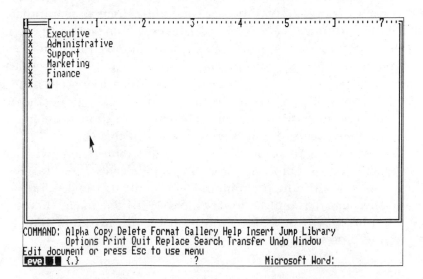

Then you would probably enter job titles in each major category. For example, working with the Executive category, you might create a secondary breakdown that looks like this:

```
╠══[·········1·········2·········3·········4·········5·········]·········7···╗
║*  Executive
║*      Chairman of the Board
║*      President
║*      Vice President
║*      Executive Vice President█
║*  Administrative
║*  Support
║*  Marketing
║*  Finance
```

Next, you might break down these categories further by entering the name of the person who holds each position. The chart with this next level of information appears in Figure 11-1.

As you continue outlining, each level should be indented further in, to make it easier for Word to distinguish one level from the next and easier for you to see the structure of your outline. Microsoft Word 3.0 allows you to build outlines up to seven levels deep. This is adequate for most purposes. The screens presented here were prepared using Microsoft Word 3.0. While in the Outline mode, Word automatically adjusts the indents to represent

```
╠══[·········1·········2·········3·········4·········5·········]·········7···╗
║*  Executive
║*      Chairman of the Board
║*          Gilbert Bates
║*      President
║*          Phillip Kain
║*      Vice President
║*          Milton M. Milton
║*      Executive Vice President
║*          Delbert Darwin
║*  Administrative█
║*  Support
║*  Marketing▶
║*  Finance
```

Figure 11-1.   An organizational chart employing three levels of headings

the level of each entry. In addition, Microsoft Word 3.0 allows you to type text inside of an outline. This is useful when you want to use your outline as the framework for your document and build your document from within the outline.

Outline Modes

Microsoft Word 3.0 has two editing modes: a regular text edit and an outline mode. It also has two outlining modes: Outline Outline mode and Outline Text (edit) mode. The best way to explain this apparent incongruity is to demonstrate how these modes work. Begin a new document called OUTLINE1. Type the first line (*Executive*) of the outline shown in Figure 11-1. Press RETURN to bring the cursor down to the second line. Your screen should look like Figure 11-2.

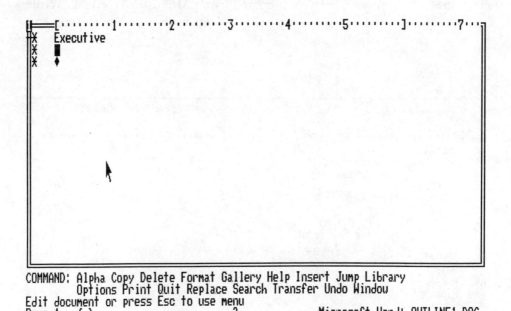

Figure 11-2.   The beginning of an outline in standard text edit mode

```
COMMAND: Alpha Copy Delete Format Gallery Help Insert Jump Library
         Options Print Quit Replace Search Transfer Undo Window
Edit document or press Esc to use menu
Level 1 {·}                        ?            Microsoft Word: OUTLINE1.DOC
```

Figure 11-3.   The outline prepared in outline mode, with the "Level 1"
indicator in the bottom left corner of the screen

At the bottom left corner of the screen, the message "Page 1" appears.
Now go into Outline mode. To get into Outline mode,

Type: SHIFT-F2

The message at the bottom of the screen changes to indicate you are in
Outline mode. The message "Level 1" indicates the level of your current
entry in the outline. This message can be seen in Figure 11-3. Now type in
the rest of the level 1 entries: Administrative, Support, Marketing, and
Finance. Your screen should look like Figure 11-4.

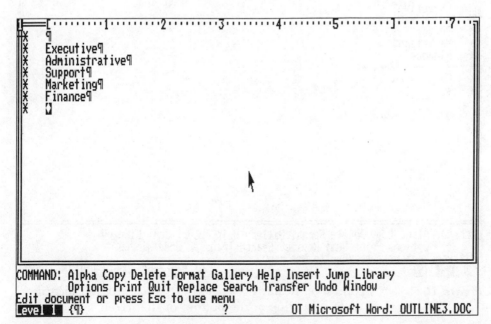

Figure 11-4.   The outline with level 1 headings only

You can now enter second-level entries. Do them only for the Executive category in this exercise, although in actual practice you would complete entries for all categories. To move one level down, position the cursor at the beginning of the line that follows the insertion. In this case place the cursor on the *A* in *Administrative*. To move down one level,

Type: ALT-0 (This uses the 0 at the top of the keyboard, not the number on the numeric keypad.)

Note that *Administrative* is indented and the message at the bottom of the screen indicates you are in level 2, as shown in Figure 11-5.

You don't want *Administrative* to be a second-level heading. However, you want to insert a second-level heading at this position. Press RETURN, adding a space between *Executive* and *Administrative*. Now move the cursor to the *A* in *Administrative*. To raise this heading one level,

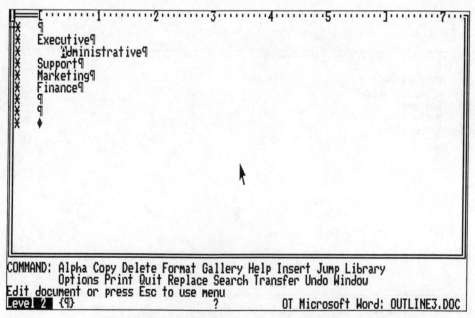

Figure 11-5.   A second-level heading automatically indented and identified as a level 2 heading at the bottom of the screen

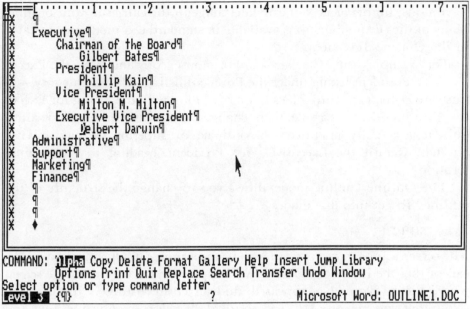

Figure 11-6.   The outline as it appears when level 3 headings are entered

Type: ALT-9 (Use the 9 on top of your keyboard and not on the numeric keypad.)

This brings *Administrative* back to level 1.

Next, move back to the blank line on level 2.

TIP: You can achieve the same result by highlighting the word *Adminis-trative* and pressing RETURN. This places a space between *Executive* and *Administrative*. Next, you can backspace to the new line above *Administra-tive* and assign it to a new level by typing ALT-0. Both methods have the same result — use the method that is most comfortable for you. ■

Type in the second-level categories as shown in Figure 11-1 (Chairman of the Board, President, Vice President, Executive Vice President). When you go from line to line, the level doesn't change.

Add another level for each division and type in the names of each officer, being careful to assign each person to level 3. The screen should look like Figure 11-6. The outline mode you are currently in is the Outline

Text mode. In this mode you can enter and edit the entries in your outline. Many of the editing functions available in standard text mode are available in the Outline Text mode.

For example, using your keyboard or mouse, copy and move the Executive Vice President listing under the President listing. The subcategory—in this case Delbert Darwin—does not move along with the listing for Executive Vice President. As a rule, then, changes made while in this mode affect only text actually modified—subordinate or superior listings are not affected. Return the Executive Vice President heading to its original location.

The Outline Outline mode allows you to change the structure of the outline. To get into this mode,

Type: SHIFT-F5

The screen's appearance is similar to its appearance in Outline Text mode, except that the indicator "OUTLINE" appears at the bottom of the screen where the level number appeared, and an entire listing is highlighted. (Note that you may use SHIFT-F5 to toggle between the Outline Text and the Outline Outline modes.) Maneuvering in this mode differs from standard editing with Word. Pressing UP ARROW or DOWN ARROW moves the cursor from listing to listing in the same level. Pressing RIGHT ARROW or LEFT ARROW moves the cursor up or down a row, regardless of level.

To demonstrate this,

Type: HOME

You should now be at the top of the outline. The word *Executive* should be highlighted. Now, press DOWN ARROW to move to the other level 1 entries—Administrative, Support, Marketing, and Finance. Pressing UP ARROW or DOWN ARROW moves the cursor only to listings in the same level.

Pressing HOME doesn't bring you to the beginning of the outline; it only brings you to the top level of your current division. Thus, you were able to get to the Executive listing from one of the sublevels, but only because you were in a level subordinate to the main Executive listing.

Press UP ARROW to return to the top of the outline. Now,

Type: END

The highlight extends to the bottom listing for the next level—in this case the Executive Vice President listing. In this screen any changes you make to one level also affect all subordinate listings within that level.

To demonstrate this, move the Executive Vice President listing so it appears below the President listing. Highlight the Executive Vice President listing. Your screen should look like Figure 11-7. Delete the listing. The Executive Vice President listing and its subordinate listing, Delbert Darwin, are both deleted. The contents of both lines appear in the scrap. The highlight moves down to the next line, Administrative.

Now insert the data currently in the scrap into its appropriate position in the lines above. Remember that pressing UP ARROW and DOWN ARROW can only move the cursor to listings on the same level. To get to a listing in a different level, press RIGHT ARROW or LEFT ARROW. You may press RIGHT ARROW to move down one line or LEFT ARROW to move up one line. If you use a mouse, you may select any position on the outline by pointing and selecting, using the left mouse button.

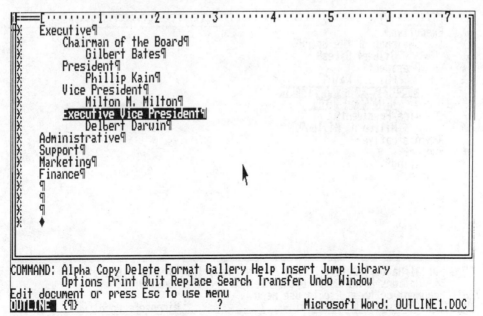

Figure 11-7. The highlighted Executive Vce President listing

Press LEFT ARROW to move up to highlight the Vice President listing. This is the point where you want to insert the Executive Vice President listing.

Type: INS

or select it by using the mouse. The contents from the scrap are inserted and highlighted. Your screen should now look like Figure 11-8.

Expanding and Contracting Listings

In many outlines the listings can become quite lengthy. In the example you are currently editing, the organizational chart would obviously be much longer if it were completely filled in. While such an extended outline can provide a great deal of structure for documents, it may also become somewhat unwieldy. To quote a much overused phrase, you may not be able to see the forest for the trees.

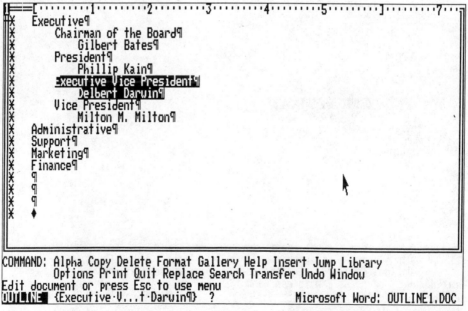

Figure 11-8. A listing highlighted when it is inserted into a new position

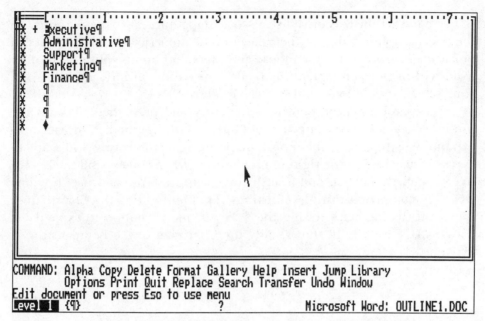

Figure 11-9.   The outline as it appears when subordinate listings for Chairman of the Board are contracted

Thus, it is often desirable to contract your outline—reduce the number of levels shown on the screen. Expansion and contraction is really quite simple. The basic steps work equally well in either the Outline Outline or Outline Text mode.

Assume for now that you want to shrink your outline to show only level 1 and level 2 headings. To contract a listing, press the − key on the numeric keypad. (The hyphen on the keyboard does not work.) In either Outline Text or Outline Outline mode, select the first line at level 2— Chairman of the Board. Now press the − key on the numeric keypad. The subordinate listing, the chairman's name, has disappeared from the screen, and the rest of the outline has moved up. Using the mouse in Outline Outline mode, you can also contract all subordinate listings by pointing to Chairman of the Board and clicking the left and right mouse buttons simultaneously. This combination contracts all levels below the one chosen. In the left margin a plus sign (+) appears, indicating that there are listings below this level. Your screen should look like Figure 11-9.

To contract the Executive listing to a single line, move the highlight to the Executive line and press the − key (on the numeric keypad). Or you can point to *Executive* with the mouse and press both mouse buttons at once, from within the Outline Outline mode. The entire category closes up, and your screen should look something like Figure 11-9.

To expand an entry, highlight the entry and press the + key on the numeric keypad. If you are in the Outline Outline mode, you can also expand a listing using the mouse by pointing at the listing you want to expand and pressing the right mouse button. When you expand the Executive listing, the four second-level listings reappear. You can use the same technique to retrieve third-level listings. Try highlighting the Chairman of the Board listing and pressing the + key or mouse button to expand the listing. As Figure 11-10 shows, only the Chairman of the Board listing is expanded.

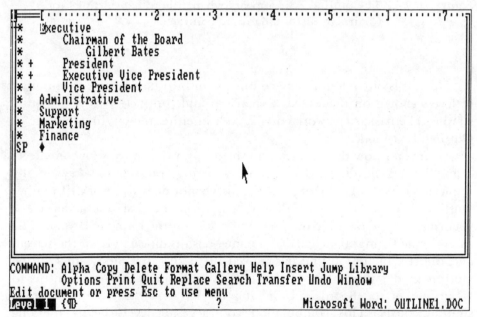

Figure 11-10.   The outline as it appears when subordinate listings for only one heading are expanded

To expand all levels below a certain listing, Microsoft Word 3.0 has provided another method. Since you want to see the Executive level fully expanded, highlight the Executive line. Now, press the * key on the numeric keypad. This expands the entire listing for Executive. The +, −, and * keys on the numeric keypad work in either the Outline Outline or Outline Text mode, while the mouse commands work only from within the Outline Outline mode.

Numbering

Microsoft Word 3.0 can automatically number an outline, whether or not it is in a contracted or expanded form. Word also gives you several numbering options. The first option is referred to as Roman numbering. The sequence takes the form IA1a and so on.

To number your document, select Library Number. The system lists two options at the bottom of the screen: Update and Remove. The Library Number Menu looks like this:

```
LIBRARY NUMBER: Update Remove          restart sequence:(Yes)No
Select option
```

Accept the Update option, and the system numbers all the sections in the outline. Your outlined document should look like Figure 11-11.

Word automatically numbers based on the format you set up. It looks for numbering and extends that scheme. For example, you can tell the system to apply the second option, legal numbering, simply by numbering the first item on the first level. Before doing this, you must first remove all the Roman numbers from your outline. To do this, again go into the Library Number Menu and select Remove. The system strips off all level numbering.

Next, tell the system you want to use legal numbering. To do this, move your cursor to the first heading, Executive, and

Type: 1.SPACE

Don't forget to put a period and a space after the number. The period and space tell the system you are numbering your entry. Your screen should look like Figure 11-12. Use the Library Number Update function to

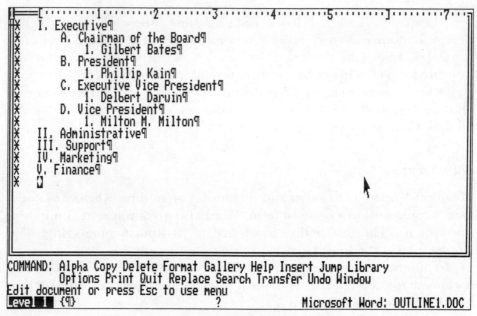

Figure 11-11.   The outline automatically numbered with Roman numerals and letters

renumber your outline. Your screen should look like Figure 11-13.

Although Roman and legal numbering are probably the most widely used numbering schemes, you can instruct the system to mix styles. The system evaluates the number or letter used at a particular level and assigns subordinate levels new numbers or letters consistent with that scheme.

To demonstrate this, again remove the numbers from your outline. Assign the Executive category the number 1. (Type 1. SPACE.) Next, assign Chairman of the Board the letter *A*. (Type A. SPACE.) Once this is done, renumber the outline. The screen now looks like Figure 11-14, an odd hybrid mix of legal and Roman numbering styles.

NOTE: When automatically numbering an outline, be careful to remove numbering from your outline each time you renumber. If you don't do this, you will end up with incorrect numbers carrying over from an earlier numbering session. For example, you may have numbered your outline before a current revision. During your revision, you've moved some sections from one part of the outline to another; you've deleted some parts and added others. If you were to stick with the current numbers, the outline

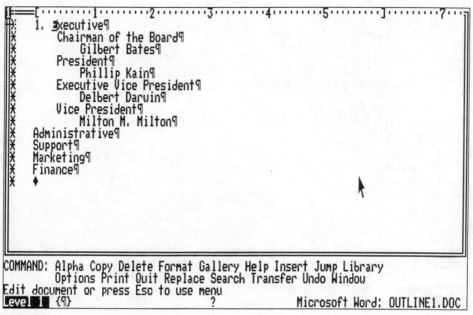

Figure 11-12.   The outline with legal numbering set up, before automatic numbering

would be numbered out of order.

Although you can have the system automatically resequence your numbering, attempting to correct any changes in order, using the LIBRARY NUMBER RESTART SEQUENCE command, you are still trusting the system to renumber accurately. Especially when mixed formats are used, the system may not be able to number correctly a complete, greatly modified outline. It is always best to start with a clean outline before renumbering.

You can automatically number an outline even if it is compressed. The system ignores any compression when it is renumbering—after you expand the outline, you will see all the numbers as they should appear. ■

Incorporating Body Text

Since the usual goal of outlining with Word is to provide a structure you can build your written documents around, there will come a time when you want to get back into regular text edit mode and start writing. To do this,

Type: SHIFT-F2

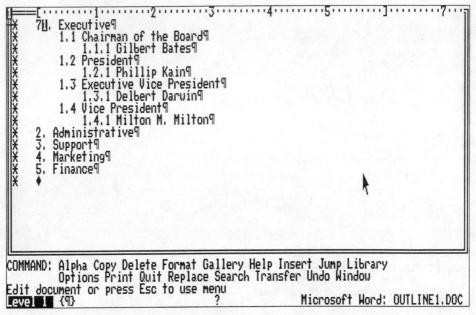

Figure 11-13.   The outline automatically numbered with legal numbers

Your outline appears on the screen completely expanded and loses its special formatting, as shown in Figure 11-15.

If you aren't comfortable with the appearance of this outline (and you probably shouldn't be), you can attach the style sheet called OUT-LINE.STY to this document and the appearance will be greatly improved. To do this, select the entire document by using the mouse or keyboard. Next, select the Format Style Sheet Menu and apply OUTLINE.STY to the document. Once this is done, your document should look like Figure 11-16.

Now that your outline looks good in both modes, you are ready to type in some text. Move the cursor under the Support heading and begin typing the text shown in Figure 11-17. A text format, T1, is applied to this text. The style sheet OUTLINE.STY provides for up to seven levels of text—each level refers to the level of the outline section under which the text falls.

```
|[ · · · · · · · · 1 · · · · · · · 2 · · · · · · · · 3 · · · · · · · · 4 · · · · · · · · 5 · · · · · · · · ] · · · · · · · · 7 · · · ]
|X  1. Executive¶
|X     A. Chairman of the Board¶
|X        1.1.1 Gilbert Bates¶
|X     B. President¶
|X        1.1.1 Phillip Kain¶
|X     C. Executive Vice President¶
|X        1.1.1 Delbert Darwin¶
|X     D. Vice President¶
|X        1.1.1 Milton M. Milton¶
|X  2. Administrative¶
|X  3. Support¶
|X  4. Marketing¶
|X  5. Finance¶
|X  ◆
```

```
COMMAND: Alpha Copy Delete Format Gallery Help Insert Jump Library
         Options Print Quit Replace Search Transfer Undo Window
Edit document or press Esc to use menu
Level 1  {¶}                        ?            Microsoft Word: OUTLINE1.DOC
```

Figure 11-14.   The outline automatically numbered with a hybrid mix of
Roman and legal numbering

```
|[ · · · · · · · · 1 · · · · · · · 2 · · · · · · · · 3 · · · · · · · · 4 · · · · · · · · 5 · · · · · · · · ] · · · · · · · · 7 · · · ]
|X  1. Executive¶
|X  A. Chairman of the Board¶
|X  1.1.1 Gilbert Bates¶
|X  B. President¶
|X  1.1.1 Phillip Kain¶
|X  C. Executive Vice President¶
|X  1.1.1 Delbert Darwin¶
|X  D. Vice President¶
|X  1.1.1 Milton M. Milton¶
|X  2. Administrative¶
|X  3. Support¶
|X  4. Marketing¶
|X  5. Finance¶
|X  ◆
```

Figure 11-15.   The outline in standard text edit mode, minus special
formatting

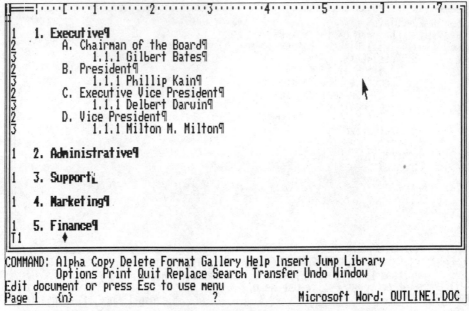

Figure 11-16. The outline in standard text edit mode with the style sheet
OUTLINE.STY attached

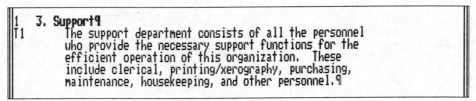

Figure 11-17. Body text with a text format, T1, applied to indicate the level
of the heading under which it falls

As a rule, any text that is not a part of the actual outline becomes body
text. When you enter outline mode, text is indicated by a *T* in the margin.
Also, in the Outline Text mode, the message "TEXT" replaces the level
number in the lower left corner of the screen. If you haven't applied the
style sheet, your outline text will be indicated with a *T* in the margin of
any areas of text. With this style sheet the outline mode lists in the margin

```
|0....|....[......2..........3..........4..........5..........].........7...|
|1    1. Executive
|2        1. Chairman of the Board
|3            1.1.1 Gilbert Bates
|2        B. President
|3            1.1.1 Phillip Kain
|2        C. Executive Vice President
|3            1.1.1 Delbert Darwin
|2        D. Vice President
|3            1.1.1 Milton M. Milton
|1    2. Administrative
|1    3. Support
|T1T      The support department consists of all the personnel
|         who provide the necessary support functions for the
|         efficient operation of this organization.  These
|         include clerical, printing/xerography, purchasing,
|         maintenance, housekeeping, and other personnel.
|1    4. Marketing
|1    5. Finance
|T1       ♦
```

COMMAND: Alpha Copy Delete Format Gallery Help Insert Jump Library
         Options Print Quit Replace Search Transfer Undo Window
Edit document or press Esc to use menu.
Level 2 {1}   ?   Microsoft Word: OUTLINE1.DOC

Figure 11-18.   Text entered in outline mode, with T1T in the margin to
                   indicate the style attached (T1) and the formatting for body
                   text (T)

the attached style, followed by the letter *T*. In this case T1T appears in the
margin, as shown in Figure 11-18.

As you build your document, the text you type spaces the outline sections further and further apart. In order to close up your outline (and hide
the body text), move to the level above your body text and

Type: SHIFT-— (using the — key on the numeric keypad)

The text is then collapsed for that level.

To again bring body text into view, move to the level where body text is
collapsed (this is indicated by a *t* in the margin) and

Type: SHIFT-+ (using the + key on the numeric keypad)

The body text is now restored. Within Outline mode the body text lacks
any formatting that may be applied to it in text edit mode. However, when
you return to the Text Edit mode, all appropriate formatting again appears
on screen and is applied to your document.

TIP: There may be times when your body text is treated by the system as part of an outline. This happens most often when you type notes or messages under an outline heading. Many people build outlines and flesh in major points so that they know what they will write about when they go into full text mode. These notes are treated as outline text unless the operator indicates to the system that they are intended as body text.

Although it makes little difference at print time whether or not these notes are part of an outline or part of text, it can make a great deal of difference when you rearrange or examine your outline. By designating these sections as body text, you can easily collapse your outline, hiding all body text. Thus you can rapidly change a fifty-page document back into a two-page outline with just a few keystrokes.

To designate text as body text, highlight the appropriate text and

Type: ALT-P (or ALT-X-P if you are using a style sheet)

The highlighted area is then treated as body text and can be collapsed or expanded, when desired. If you make a mistake and designate part of an outline as body text, this is easily repaired. Highlight the text "determine the desired level" and

Type: ALT-*level number* (or ALT-X-*level number* if you are using a style sheet)

For example, to designate a level 3 entry, you would type ALT-3. This would remove the text mark from the margin and replace it with the correct level indicator. Alternatively, you could use the ALT-9 and ALT-0 key combinations to move the heading to its appropriate position in your outline.

To expand or contract all the text in your outline, highlight the entire document, go into outline mode, and use the appropriate key combination (SHIFT-+ to expand the outline, SHIFT— to contract it). This key combination works *only* on body text—if your outline is contracted, these keys will not change it.

If you want to expand body text *and* your outline, highlight the entire document and

Type: * (on the numeric keypad)

Similarly, you can expand or contract *only outline levels* by highlighting the entire document and pressing the — and + keys on the numeric keypad. The — key contracts your document—outline and body text—while the + key expands only the outline, leaving body text unchanged. ∎

Text is attached to the outline heading that precedes it. If, for example, you wanted to reorganize your document, you could easily move all text by going into the Outline Outline mode and making your changes. All the text attached to your outline heading moves with it.

You should be careful not to try to make changes in the Outline Text mode: rearranging an outline in this mode does not move related text. Thus, you may have apparently reorganized your outline only to discover that none of the related text or sublevels has been moved. You should, therefore, be careful to look for the "OUTLINE" indicator in the lower left corner of the screen before moving any sections of your outline. (You should recall that SHIFT-F5 toggles between the two outline modes.)

ADDITIONAL APPLICATIONS: WORD 3.0 ONLY

Oultine mode can be used for a wide range of applications. The first and most obvious is to provide order to your document. When you print your document, the outline text also prints. You may not want all your documents to print as an expanded outline; you can prepare your outline without printing it.

This method, to be discussed in some detail in Chapter 12, uses Word's hidden text feature. *Hidden text* can be made visible or hidden within your document. It is used for such things as entering nonprinting notes inside of a document or setting up search fields for Word's automatic table of contents or automatic indexing feature. An ideal application is for hidden outlines.

The first step for setting up hidden text is to set up the Window option to allow you to see hidden text. Go to the Window Options Menu and answer yes to the Show Hidden Text prompt. Next, expand the outline. Highlight the text you want to hide (everything but body text) and

Type: ALT-E (or ALT-X-E if you are using a style sheet)

Depending on the mode your system is in (graphics or character), the hidden text is either shown in a different color or with a series of dots underlining it. In this example the outline text is marked as hidden, with the body text left as text that prints. This can be seen in Figure 11-19.

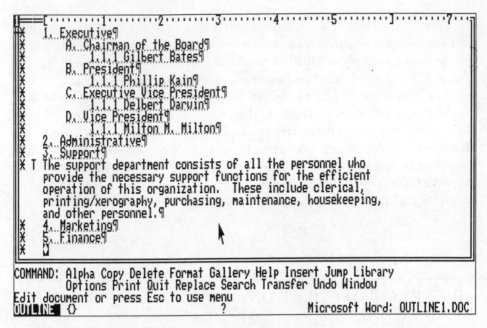

Figure 11-19.   The outline with a hidden text (underlined by dots) displayed
on the screen

TIP: If you use style sheets, it is a good idea to modify OUTLINE.STY
and develop a sheet with hidden character formats for the outline styles.
Then save this modified style sheet with a different name, such as OUT-
LINEH.STY (for outline hidden) or HOUTLINE.STY (for hidden outline). This way, you can create an outline and quickly switch from hidden
to unhidden outlines just by applying a new style sheet.

Of course, you can also toggle on and off the Show Hidden Text option
in the Window Options Menu, but if you are using other types of hidden
text, this unwanted text will also print. ■

NOTE: Unless you use a special style sheet, you must be careful to
expand and highlight all outline text you want to hide. If your outline is
compressed and you highlight only top-level headings, any changes made
to these headings will not apply to lower levels. To change the entire outline, you must highlight the entire outline. ■

To demonstrate how the hidden text works, get back into the Window Options Menu and answer no to the Show Hidden Text prompt. Once this is accepted, the screen looks like Figure 11-20. The double arrows indicate hidden text. When you print out your document, these areas are ignored — the space occupied by this text is not printed. Thus, even though in this example it looks as if part of the screen for this page is occupied by space, text prints on the first line of the page.

Navigating Through a Document

Using an outline can be more than a means of organizing your thoughts. It also allows you to move large amounts of text just by moving the outline headings to which they are attached. A logical extension of this is the ability to copy large sections from one document to another just by copying the sections of outline where the text is attached.

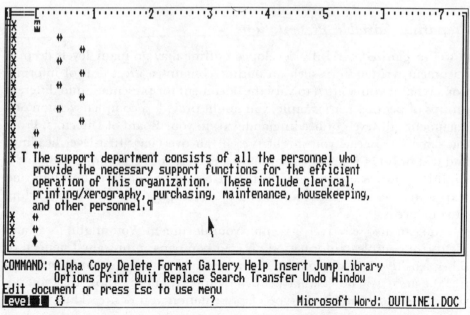

Figure 11-20.   The outline with hidden text (indicated by double arrows) not displayed on the screen

Another benefit is the ability to move quickly to a specific location in a document. In a large document it is not always convenient (or efficient) to search for a particular section of that document. Although you can use the Jump Page or Search functions or the scroll bar, these are still either approximate or too slow.

However, if you go into outline mode and compress your body text, you can quickly select the specific section where your text is located. Once this section is selected, you can go back into standard edit mode and quickly find your desired text. Using an outline in this way is probably the fastest method of navigating through your document.

Using Windows When Outlining

If you were to use two windows—one in outline view and the other in text view—you would quickly see where you were in an outline, in addition to being able to work on your text. In this case a vertical split in the screen might be desirable. Using a split-screen view would remind you where you were and where you were going while inside a document.

Preparing Variable Presentations

A well-organized, carefully developed outline may go many levels deep. A document written from such an outline contains a great deal of information. What if you wanted to vary the document for presentation to different groups of people? For example, you might provide a complete version of a document (all levels of heading and text) to your Board of Directors. From the same document, you might present an overview (first-level headings and text only) of your organization to a high school economics class and a slightly more detailed summary (the first- and second-level headings and text) to new employees. You can contract or expand the outline according to your needs.

You can also selectively assemble your document. You might, for example, print complete information on your company minus any financial or other sensitive information. By going through your outline and compressing the areas you don't want printed, while expanding those that you do, you can custom tailor any type of presentation you desire. Thus, Word's ability to easily produce many different versions of the same basic document can be a tremendous time-saver. A well-planned, carefully prepared document based on a very specific outline can be adapted to many diverse users. Microsoft Word 3.0's outlining ability can go far beyond basic outlining functions. A few additional suggestions are included in the documentation that came with your program. With a little imagination, you can quickly develop a number of new applications using this system's organizational capabilities.

ADVANCED FEATURES

In previous chapters you have seen many of the basic and advanced tools provided by Microsoft Word. However, with such a full-featured package as Word, some features and some time-saving combinations of features have yet to be fully explored. In this chapter you work with many of the as yet unexplored or underexplained features of Microsoft Word. The only real exceptions are those covered in the next chapters: some special Library functions and desktop publishing using a laser printer.

THE SPECIAL REPORT

Perhaps the greatest challenge for many word processing operations is the preparation of special reports, such as papers and statistical reports. Word provides special features that make preparing these once dreaded documents almost fun.

During the course of preparing a special report, you may be required to perform a number of nonroutine formatting steps. These can test your ability to use what was already described in this book; test a word processing program's capabilities; and, in many ways, test your capability and imagination.

Superscripts and Subscripts

Depending upon the type of document, you may be required to print superscripts or subscripts. The most common type of document requiring these special characters is a scientific or engineering document, which may require chemical formulas or mathematical equations.

A *superscript* prints a number or letter above the standard line of text. A familiar example of a superscript in an equation is Einstein's theory of relativity, $E = MC^2$. A *subscript* prints a number or letter below the standard line of text. A familiar example of a subscript in an equation is the chemical formula for water, H_2O.

The ability to print either a superscript or a subscript depends primarily upon the ability of your printer to print these characters. Depending upon how your printer handles these characters, the super- or subscript may be printed the same size as a normal character, but one-half line above or below normal text; it may be printed a full line above or below text; or it may be printed as a reduced character at the top half or bottom half of the standard line. You must be aware of the possibility of a subscript or superscript printing in the line above or below — that is, if the character is raised or lowered one-half line, the top or bottom of that character may spill onto the line above or below it.

The best way to see how your printer handles superscripts or subscripts is to try printing some. Setting up a superscript or subscript is easy. Type the equation and highlight the character you want to superscript or subscript. Next, you have two basic choices. The first is to go to the Format Character Menu and select Superscript or Subscript in the Position Menu. The highlighted character is given the selected attribute.

The second choice is to use the quick format command for superscript or subscript. To quick format a superscript once you have highlighted the character,

Type: ALT-+ (or ALT-=; this is the + or = key on the keyboard)

If you have attached a style sheet, you must type ALT-X plus the + or = key. To quick format a subscript once you have highlighted the text to be subscripted,

Type: ALT− (ALT-minus)

Again, if you have a style sheet attached, type ALT-X=−.

NOTE: Quick formatting superscripts or subscripts is an odd exception to the normal rules in some cases. You may have to type the quick format code twice in order to set the superscript or subscript. In addition, you may have to type ALT-SPACE twice to remove super- or subscripting from a highlight or to return to regular format mode. ■

When a character is super- or subscripted, its appearance on screen should change. If you are in a graphics mode, the superscript and subscript appear as shown in Figure 12-1. If you are editing in the character mode, the super- or subscripted text appears on the screen in a different color, if you have a color monitor, or at a slightly different intensity if you have a monochrome monitor.

NOTE: Microsoft Word handles single-level superscripts or subscripts very well. It cannot handle multilevel super- or subscripts. A multilevel super- or subscript may be needed when preparing complicated mathematical formulas—for example, cubing a squared quantity. Present versions of Word are unable to provide this level of utility.

This can be partially accommodated for using a trial-and-error method. This method places the first level super- or subscript in its normal position. Next, you move the cursor to its appropriate position in the line above or below the desired super- or subscript. By typing in characters, you can move the cursor to the desired position for your next numeric entry. Once the super- or subscript is entered, go back and overtype (press F5 to turn on overtype) all the characters leading up to the super- or subscript, replacing each of the letters with required, nonprinting spaces by pressing CTRL-SPACE. Although it may sound confusing, it really isn't. An example of such a setup is shown in Figure 12-2. ■

Other Special Formatting

Although character formatting was discussed in Chapter 5, it is useful to remind you briefly of the variety of character formats available. A look at the Format Character Menu gives you a quick look at the variety of ways

Figure 12-1.   Superscripts and subscripts added to text in graphics mode

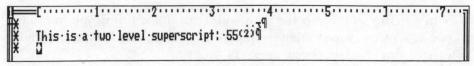

Figure 12-2.   Setup for a two-level superscript, showing the required spaces preceding the superscript

Word can potentially change the look of your text. These capabilities are referred to as *potential* because Word's character-formatting abilities are directly related to your printer's capabilities. Refer to the printer guide that came with your copy of Word to determine which special formatting features your printer supports.

By now you should be aware of the two ways that character formatting can affect a document. If you change the format of highlighted text, only that text is affected; once a change is made, any text you type retains the same format it had before you changed highlighted text. If, on the other hand, you make character format changes with only one character or space highlighted, everything you type from that point on carries the newly set format until you change back to your original format or to another type of format.

The combination of ALT, or ALT-X, plus a second letter can be used to speed format any of the attributes listed in the Format Character Menu. For the most part these important letters are easy to remember. For example, to indicate that text should be struck through (that is, a hyphen typed over the highlighted text to indicate it has been deleted from a document but was present in an earlier draft), type ALT-S (for strike through). Similarly, press ALT-D for double underline, ALT-U for underline, ALT-K for small caps, and ALT-B for bold.

These special characters appear as formatted if you are in the graphics mode. If you are in the character mode, most of the characters appear in a different color (or different intensity on a monochrome monitor), with the exception of the Bold function, which will print characters in highlighted text (brighter than the other characters).

Another formatting variable that hasn't been completely discussed is changing type size or style within a document. This is very closely related to—in fact, is dependent upon—the ability of your printer to print different styles and sizes and the method your printer uses to produce characters.

The first two options on the bottom line of the Format Character Menu relate to type style. To see which styles your printer is able to produce (or rather, that your printer can produce or that Word lists for your printer), select the Font Name field and press RIGHT ARROW or the right mouse button. The screen shows the type styles that Word identifies as those your printer can produce.

NOTE: If your printer uses a daisy wheel or print thimble to change type styles, you must have the style that you select in order to print that style. Although this may seem obvious, it is surprising how often an unavailable style can be selected. Also, if you choose to italicize some passages, you must have an italic type wheel or thimble. At print time the system automatically stops the printer so you can change print elements, so that jumping from one style to another is relatively foolproof.

In addition, it is possible that with some laser printers or other printers using font cartridges or disk-based fonts, you may select a font you don't yet have for your system. Be careful to select font styles and sizes you know you have. You can sometimes get away with substituting a font you do have for a different one you selected, but this doesn't always work properly. ■

Once you've seen the listing of fonts available for your printer, you should probably also check the available font sizes. To do this, move to the Font Size field by pressing TAB or by using the mouse pointer. To see the sizes available, press RIGHT ARROW or the right button on the mouse. Select the desired type size by moving the highlight to the size desired.

NOTE: With some printers you may have a range of font sizes available. You should be careful about selecting sizes greater than 12 picas. This is because a 12-pica character is roughly the height of a normal printed line. Selecting a larger font while working on a single-spaced document results in type that is bigger than the line it is printed on and can result in a barely readable jumble.

For this reason, you should be careful to make sure that your line spacing is larger than the size of your characters. Microsoft Word can automatically adjust the space between lines of text to accommodate for any over- or undersized lines of text. To select this, go into the Format Paragraph Menu and answer the Line Spacing prompt with the Auto selection. ■

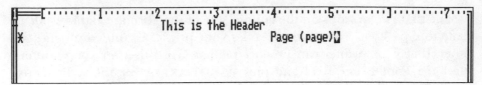

Figure 12-3.   Header text

By carefully mixing type styles or sizes, you can achieve some very striking effects. The keyword here is *carefully*. If you get carried away by the new capabilities of Word, you can easily come up with text that looks awful. As a general rule, you should use a maximum of three different fonts within any document. Few magazines use more than one or two fonts for an entire magazine—there is little reason for you to use more than a magazine.

RUNNING HEADERS AND FOOTERS

When you prepare a multiple-page document, whether it is a large document or just a letter, you often want to number each page. Microsoft Word has the capability to number pages automatically, in addition to printing selected text at the top and bottom of each page. Headers and footers are very simple to set up. You can set your system to print either or both. For this example, set up your document to print a header on even-numbered pages and a footer on odd-numbered pages.

If you don't already have a clear window, create one now. You should specify a header or footer at the beginning of a document. Type in the header as it appears in Figure 12-3. Note that the top line is centered. In the second line the text was tabbed to the 4-inch mark. The second word *page,* enclosed in parentheses, is an instruction to the system to print the number of the page in that location automatically.

The first word *Page* on this line prints every time this header prints. Thus, if you were printing page 2, the second line would print as Page 2. The method for telling the system to print the page number automatically is simply to

Type: **page** F3

The system's Glossary function converts the word *page* into an instruction to print the page number automatically.

In addition to page number, the system can also print the date and time you are preparing a document or the date and time a document is actually printed. To print the current time, type time and press F3. To print the current date, type date and press F3. To tell the system to print the date or time your document is actually printed, type dateprint or timeprint (whichever is appropriate) and press F3. The system is then prepared to print the correct date or time when the document is printed. (Of course, this depends on the time and date settings loaded into the computer when it is turned on. If you have an automatic clock/calendar, this should not be a problem.)

You must next set up the text as a header. Highlight the header lines. Now tell the system that the highlighted text is a running head. To do this, select Format Running Head, using the keyboard or mouse. Your page should look like Figure 12-4. The first prompt, Position, asks if you want

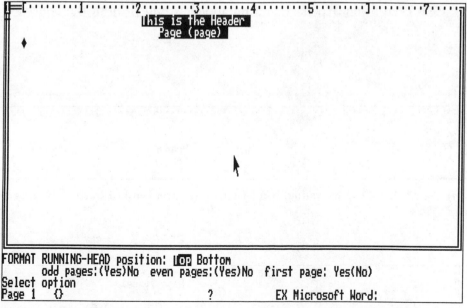

Figure 12-4.   Running head text highlighted, with the Format Running Head Menu at the bottom of the screen

this highlighted text to be a header or footer. Tell the system you want this to be a header (to print at the top of the page). If you printed at the bottom of the page, the text would be a footer.

The next prompt, Odd Pages, asks if you want the header or footer to print on odd pages. In this case tell the system no. The next prompt, Even Pages, asks if you want the header to print on even-numbered pages. Set the answer to yes. Finally, the First Page prompt asks if you want the header or footer to print on the first page. Leave this setting at no. Save these settings.

A caret symbol (^) is then printed in the left margin, and your header text may move toward the right side of the screen. The screen should look like Figure 12-5.

Next, prepare your footer text, as shown in Figure 12-6. Highlight the Footer text, and go to the Format Running Head Menu. The first item prompts you to specify the position of the running "head." In this case you are actually formatting a running footer. Tell the system this "header" prints on the bottom of the page. Also tell the system to print only on odd pages—and to skip the first page.

Your screen with the header and footer should look like Figure 12-7. If you were to go on and enter a document, the header would print at the top of each even-numbered page and the footer would print at the bottom of

Figure 12-5. The formatted header with the caret symbol in the left margin

Figure 12-6. Footer text

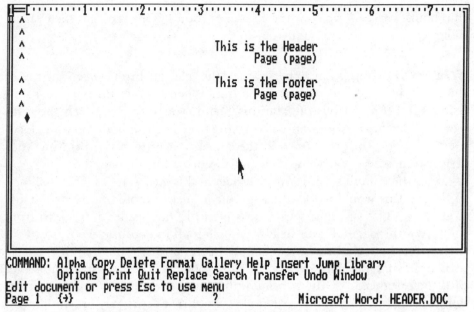

Figure 12-7.   The formatted header and footer

each odd-numbered page. In this example no header or footer would print on the first page.

As already stated, Microsoft Word allows you to print a header, a footer, both, or none on each page. In some applications you may desire a header and a footer on each page, with different text in each. Word makes this very easy to set up using the Format Running Head Menu parameters.

You can also change your running header or footer inside the body of the document or begin using a header or footer while already into the document. To do this, paginate your finished document and then move to the page where you want to add (or delete) a header or footer. Simply type in the text for your new header or footer and apply the parameters you desire, using the Format Running Head Menu. You should answer no to the First Page prompt (since you are already in the middle of your document and can't get back to page 1 anyway). If you want to stop using a running head, highlight a blank line or press RETURN at the point where you want to stop printing your running header or footer, and tell the system to print that blank space as the running header or footer. This replaces the header/footer that you were previously using.

NOTE: It is important to be aware of the relationship between the size of the running head and the page margins. When you set up page margins, using the Format Division Margins Menu, you told the system how far from each margin you wanted to begin printing the body of your document. In addition, you also told the system where to begin printing your header and where you wanted to end the print for your footer.

If, in the default settings, your header and footer were less than 0.5 inch in height, this would work, although the header or footer might print close to the text. The standard setup starts printing the header at 0.5 inch from the top of the page. If your header was 0.5 inch in depth, it would run to 1 inch from the top of the page—at about the position of your first line of text. A similar problem occurs with the footer. If the height of the footer plus the distance from the bottom of the page were greater than the bottom margin for text, your footer either would not print correctly or would print over the last line(s) of text. Thus, you should be careful to adjust your page margins and the distance from the top or bottom of your page to accommodate headers and footers. ■

TIP: If you don't have a letterhead, you can use Word to print letterhead text as a running head. In this case you may want to use a larger type size or bold font for the running head. Once you design the head, you should tell the system to print it about 0.1 inch from the top of the page. This also gives you 0.9 inch to work with in designing your letterhead.

Once this is prepared, you can tell the system to print this running head only on the first page of your document by specifying this in the Format Running Head Menu. Once this is done, highlight the complete running head and save it in your glossary, giving it an easy name, such as lh (for letterhead).

One additional step is required: you must change the standard division in your style sheet (the style sheet you use for letters) to reflect the new position of the running head. Once this is done, you are set to add the letterhead to all your letters. It's as easy as typing lh and then pressing F3. This method can also be used for a standard footer—for example, a return address line printed at the bottom of every page. Setup is similarly simple. Standard headers and footers can be saved in the glossary and called up using normal glossary commands. ■

Error Recovery for Headers And Footers

What happens when you have set up a running header or footer that you no longer want? Or, worse still, what happens if you make a mistake, as the author did, and set up an entire chapter as a running header? Since a header prints at the top of a page, it won't print as body text. Also, if your entire document is designated as a header, it probably won't even print at the top of a page. There is no obvious way to remove the caret symbols from a header — in effect, to stop the header from being a header. But there is a less obvious way to change a header back to regular text. To do this, select the text you want to change back. Next, go into the Format Running Head Menu and answer no to all three items: you don't want the header to print on odd pages; you don't want it to print on even pages; and you don't want it to print on the first page. The system interprets these responses as meaning that you don't want the text to be a header or footer at all and removes the carets.

Automatic Page Numbering

There may be times when you don't want to bother with running headers or footers, but you do want to number pages. Alternatively, you may want to start numbering a document at a number other than 1 or to use numbers other than Arabic numerals.

For example, you might be writing a book. Although you might store each chapter as a separate file, when you print the book, you naturally want the pages consecutively numbered. Thus, if the last page of Chapter 1 was page 35, the first page of Chapter 2 should be page 36. With Microsoft Word you could tell the system to begin numbering that chapter at page 36. In the introductory section of the book, you might want to number each page using lowercase Roman numerals. In this case, then, you would need to tell the system what numbering style to use. Again, Word makes this very easy.

To print numbers, but not running headers or footers, you must set these numbering defaults from the Format Division Page Numbers Menu. You get to this screen by jumping through three menus: the Main Command Menu, the Format Menu, and finally the Format Division Menu. The Format Division Page Numbers Menu is shown in Figure 12-8.

The first prompt on the top line asks where you want to place the page numbers. If you aren't using your running header or footer to insert page

```
FORMAT DIVISION PAGE-NUMBERS: Yes No    from top: 0.5"    from left: 7.25"
                numbering:(Continuous)Start    at:            number format:(1)I i A a
Select option
```

Figure 12-8.   The Format Division Page Numbers Menu

numbers, you will respond yes to the first prompt. This tells the system to print the page numbers.

The next two fields ask where you want the page number to be printed. These locations refer to the size of your page, not the already established margins. Thus, if you use 8 1/2-by-11-inch paper, the page number prints 0.5 inch from the top of the page and 1.25 inches (8.5 minus 7.25) from the right margin, or 0.5 inch above the standard right margin. If you prefer to have the numbering in a different position, you can type in the location you want. For example, if you prefer to have the number at the lower left corner of the page, telling the system to print the number 10.5 inches from the top of the page and 1.25 inches from the left will print the number at the left margin, 0.5 inch from the bottom of a standard 8 1/2-by-11-inch page.

As another example, assume that the placement of the numbers is being handled by a header or footer. However, in the case of your book, you want Chapter 2 to begin at page 36. The second line of the menu is the one you want to modify. The Numbering option presents two choices. Continuous numbering numbers each page, starting at 1. When you select Start, you are telling the system to begin numbering at the number you enter in the next field, At. In this case, then, select Start, move to the field, At, and type 36. This tells the system to begin numbering at page 36.

In the final example, the introductory text paginated with Roman numerals, you probably want the numbering to be done continuously. In most cases you will probably have an alternating footer—with the footer printing the page number at the lower right corner of odd-numbered pages and the lower left corner of even-numbered pages. Therefore, you don't want the automatic numbering feature activated.

You want the numbering to be continuous. The major modification involved here is the selection of the numbering method. As you have seen in Figure 12-8, you have a choice of number formats. Move to the Number Format field, and select i as the number format. When you print your introduction, the first page is numbered i, the second, ii, and so forth.

Word's page-numbering flexibility can help to give a professional touch to nearly everything you produce.

FOOTNOTES

Footnotes have been called the curse of the researcher. Added to the problems of formatting and tracking them, there are two different ways of printing them: at the bottom of the page on which they appear or at the end of a document. With typewriters or word processors, they are often very difficult to keep track of and to format.

Not so with Word. Word provides you with the option of printing the footnote at the end of a document or at the bottom of a page. You can't do both, and you can't mix the formats within a document (that is, put footnotes at the bottom of the page in one part of your document and at the end of a section for the rest of your document), but you probably wouldn't ever want to do this anyway. Before you record your first footnote, you should tell the system how you want footnotes printed. To do this, go to the Format Division Layout Menu shown in Figure 12-9. The first line on this menu is used for instructions regarding footnotes.

If you select Same-page, your footnotes will be printed at the bottom of the page they fall on: choosing End will print all the footnotes at the end of the document. Go back into your header document, leaving the footnote layout set to Same-page.

One other tool is also valuable with footnotes—the footnote window. Using the footnote window, you can see what footnote number was used last, review what format was used for preparing the footnote, and scan to see if you've already used a particular reference. To display the footnote window, select Window Split. The menu gives you three choices: Horizontal, Vertical, or Footnote. Choose Footnote.

```
FORMAT DIVISION LAYOUT footnotes: Same-page End
        number of columns: 1        space between columns: 0.5"
            division break:(Page)Continuous Column Even Odd
Select option
```

Figure 12-9.   The Format Division Layout Menu, which is used to select footnote print options

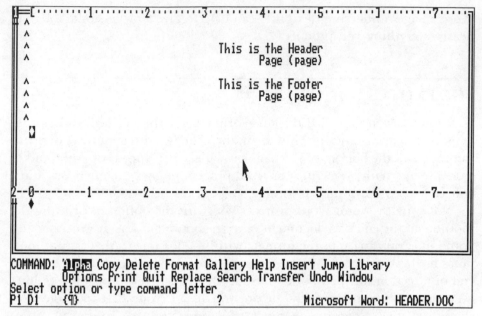

Figure 12-10.   The split screen with the footnote window at the bottom

Next, tell the system that you want the split at line 15, to give you enough room to see what you're editing in Window 1, the main document window. (How to increase the available space at the bottom of your screen is discussed further in "The Options Menu" in this chapter.) Once the selection is made, a second window, the footnote window, appears. This one looks different from any other window, since the ruler at the top is made up of dashes rather than dots. The screen, with the footnote window, should look like Figure 12-10.

Now that your footnote window is in place and you have told the system where to print your footnotes, type in the following lines:

The nerd phenomenon was one that was slow to be recognized. Although there have probably been nerds throughout history, it wasn't until the late 1970s that the word, and the nerd, were really noticed.

Place your first footnote at the end of the first sentence. Move the cursor to the space after the period. To tell the system you want to insert a footnote here, select Format Footnote. The system prompts, "reference mark." Your screen should look like Figure 12-11.

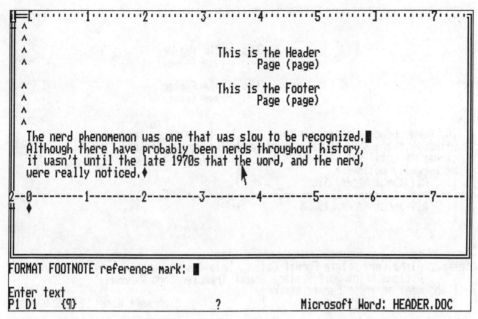

Figure 12-11.   The Format Footnote Menu with the cursor marking the position of the footnote in the text

If you enter a number or text in this position, the number or text will be printed where the highlight appears on the page. Leaving this position blank tells the system to update the footnote number, incrementing it by one. For now, leave this selection blank.

Once you make this selection, the system puts the number 1 in the highlighted space. Since you are at the bottom of the page (and the end of your document), the system puts the number at the bottom of the page. The cursor has moved into the footnote window to enable you to type the text of the footnote.

Type the text for the footnote as shown in Figure 12-12. As you type, the text for the footnote appears both in the footnote window and at the bottom of your page. If you desire, you can change the format of the footnotes so that they print in a different type size or style—for example, a footnote at the bottom of the page is often printed in italics, to further differentiate it from body text. Although Word inserts a ruled line at the bottom of the page to separate footnotes from body text, it may also be appropriate to change the type style for footnotes.

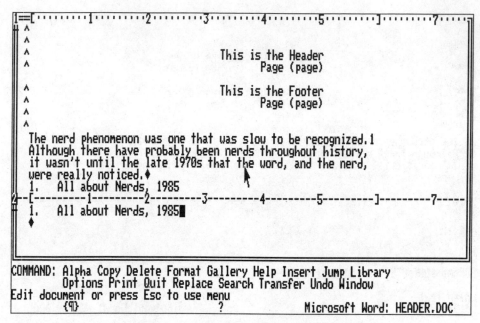

Figure 12-12.　　Footnote text entered in the footnote window

The cursor is still in the footnote window. If you were putting footnotes at the end of your document, this could be a problem: how would you quickly get back to the position of your footnote in text? You don't want to have to do a reverse search. To return to the point where you inserted the footnote, use the JUMP FOOTNOTE command. To do this, select Jump on the command line and then select Footnote to return to the text. Now add another footnote, this time at the end of the paragraph. Once you have done this, your screen should look like Figure 12-13.

Word automatically updates numbers. To demonstrate this, you can delete the first footnote. Move the cursor back to the first footnote (the number 1), highlight it, and delete it, using the mouse or keyboard. Once this is done, the numbers are readjusted, as shown in Figure 12-14.

The deleted footnote is currently in the scrap. If you change your mind about deleting the footnote, you can reinsert it back into your text. You can also move the footnote. In the example shown in Figure 12-15, the footnote has been moved past the new number 1 footnote and inserted below it. A

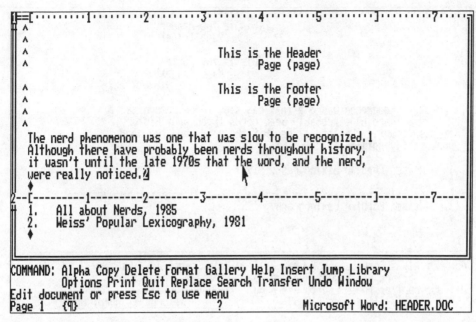

Figure 12-13.   The document with two footnotes entered in the footnote window

comma separates the footnotes. When INS was pressed to reinsert the footnote, the text was again placed in the footnote window and at the bottom of the page. The footnote was renumbered.

AUTOMATIC INDEX AND TABLE OF CONTENTS

Microsoft Word provides you with the ability to index text automatically and to prepare tables of contents or other tables. The information you want to put into your table is prepared along with the normal text. When you print your document, you can instruct Word to go through the document and search for this special text, creating a special table of contents or index. The index and table items are created using hidden text.

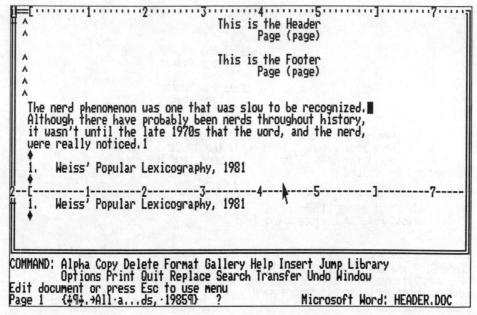

Figure 12-14.   Text showing automatic renumbering of footnotes when a footnote is removed

Hidden Text

Hidden text is text specially handled by the system. This type of text appears differently on different monitors. Hidden text is underlined by dots in graphics mode or given a different color or intensity in character mode. You have the option of leaving the text hidden or making it visible. When it is visible, it is included in any pagination processes and is also printed during a print operation. However, when it is hidden, the text does not print and pagination occurs as if the hidden text does not exist. Make the choice to hide or reveal hidden text in the Window Options Menu. For now, set the system to reveal hidden text.

When you create tables of contents or indexes, the system searches for a specific character sequence: it is .i. for an index, and it is usually .c. for a table of contents. Any text between the sequence and the end of a paragraph, the end of a division, or a hidden semicolon becomes part of the table or index listing.

```
█═[·······1·······2·······3·······4·······5·······]·······7·····┐
 ║ ^
 ║ ^                    This is the Header
 ║                        Page (page)
 ║ ^
 ║ ^                    This is the Footer
 ║ ^                      Page (page)
 ║ ^
 ║
 ║ The nerd phenomenon was one that was slow to be recognized.
 ║ Although there have probably been nerds throughout history,
 ║ it wasn't until the late 1970s that the word, and the nerd,
 ║ were really noticed.1,2█
 ║ ♦
 ║   1.   Weiss' Popular Lexicography, 1981
 ║   2.   All about Nerds, 1985
2--[---------1---------2---------3---------4---▲----5---------]--------7-----
 ║   1.   Weiss' Popular Lexicography, 1981
 ║   2.   All about Nerds, 1985
 ║ ♦
 ║
 ║
 ║
 └──────────────────────────────────────────────────────────────┘
COMMAND: Alpha Copy Delete Format Gallery Help Insert Jump Library
         Options Print Quit Replace Search Transfer Undo Window
Edit document or press Esc to use menu
Page 1   {#¶#.→All·a...ds,·1985¶}    ?            Microsoft Word: HEADER.DOC
```

Figure 12-15.   A footnote reinserted at the end of a paragraph

Index Entries

Microsoft Word does a great job of index preparation: it locates all words you indicate you want indexed, and it can also find subentries for your index. The system alphabetizes your entries, determines page numbers for each listing, and creates a table. Word can also handle multiple documents — for example, it can handle a book made up of many separate chapters (each a separate document).

You must know in advance what text you want to index — the system can create an index only from the text you tell it to index. That is, even though indexing is automatic, you still have to tell the system what you want indexed.

Setting up index entries is easy. When you come to text you want indexed, turn on Hidden Character mode and type .i. to designate an entry. To turn on hidden text, the ALT-E, or ALT-X-E, command is used. You can also set up a style on your sheet that sets ALT-E to hidden text. You also can set up a glossary listing to type a hidden .i. character sequence. To do this, type a hidden .i. character sequence, highlight it, and save it to your glossary — you may want to call it i. Then, when you have an index entry, you can type i and press F3, and the hidden .i. replaces the i.

Once you've entered the hidden .i., by whatever method, remember that whatever text appears after the .i. and before a paragraph end (hard return), division end, or semicolon becomes part of the index listing. If possible, it is a good idea to put each index item on its own hidden line just above the use of the indexed term. For example, if you wanted an index entry for *nerds,* you could type the hidden entry as it appears in Figure 12-16. If, on the other hand, you wanted to index the word *nerds* inside of the paragraph, you would put the .i. in front of the word when it appeared in the paragraph and place a hidden semicolon after the word to signal the end of the index listing.

You can also prepare index listings up to four levels deep. That is, you can have subentries for first-level index items. To separate the main listing from the secondary listing, a colon is used. Such a listing looks like this:

.i. Nerds: throughout history;

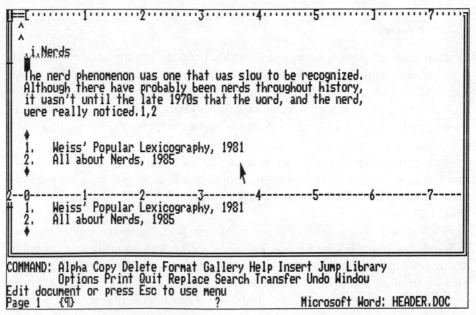

Figure 12-16. A hidden index entry, nerds, entered on its own hidden line

```
LIBRARY INDEX entry/page # separated by: ███    cap main entries:(Yes)No
             indent each level: 0.2"              use style sheet: Yes(No)
Enter text
```

Figure 12-17.   The Library Index Menu

The listing after the colon is the secondary listing, and the semicolon signals the end of the listing. When Word goes through the document and sets
up the index, it is able to handle these secondary listings and also to handle
duplicate entries for the same indexed item, printing the item and the page
number(s) where they can be found.

For items that contain quotation marks, colons, or semicolons as part of
the index item, the entire index item must be enclosed in quotation marks.
A listing for an item containing a quotation mark looks like this:

.i. ""Nerds I Have Known" by A. Hacker"

The Library Index Function   Before you can prepare an index, you should
hide the hidden text. Go to the Window Options Menu and tell the system
not to reveal hidden text. The hidden index items disappear from the
screen. (Note that you don't have to hide index text—only the .i. preceding
the entry and the colon or semicolon following the entry.)

Next, repaginate your document. The Index function scans your document and records the page number for each index item. If you don't paginate your document, the index may be incorrect.

TIP: If you want to run an index on a document made up of smaller
documents—a book made up of separately stored chapters, for example—
you can use the TRANSFER MERGE command to link the documents,
then paginate and, finally, run the index. ■

Next, go to the Library Menu. Select the Index option. The Library
Index Menu is shown in Figure 12-17. The first option, Entry/Page #
Separated By, asks how you want to separate the index entry from the page
number. The default, as suggested by the program's developers, is two
spaces. This puts two spaces between the index listing and the number. If
you prefer to tab to a certain position, you can enter the tab command by
typing ^T (using the caret created by typing SHIFT-6). If properly formatted,
all numbers in an index listing can print from the same right-aligned tab.

The next option, Cap Main Entries, asks if you want the system to capitalize the first word of each entry. This depends to some degree upon the style you prefer, and also on the nature of your index items. Many indexes capitalize the first word of an entry. The next prompt, Indent Each Level, asks how much space to indent a second-, third-, or fourth-level listing below the next higher listing. Microsoft sets the default at 0.2 inch, which seems to work well for most people.

Finally, you must tell the system if you want to use a style sheet. Unless your style sheet has special formatting codes for index listings (that is, bold-facing first-level listings, but not second-, third-, or fourth-level listings), you should answer no to this prompt.

Once you have set the desired parameters, accept them by pressing ENTER or, with the mouse, by pointing to Library and pressing the right mouse button. The system scans through the document, looking for index items and recording the number of the page for each item. The system then alphabetizes the listings, checks for duplicates, and arranges an index, which it places at the end of your document.

The Library Table Function

The Library Table function works very much like the Library Index function. The basic difference is in the organization of the table. When Word creates a table, it goes through a document from front to back, looking for the hidden text used to create the table. When the entire document has been scanned, the system creates a table that reflects the page order of your listings rather than an alphabetical list, as the Index function does.

This type of table is valuable for tracking sections of a document as they appear in the document. The system doesn't check for duplicate sections or duplicate listings: whatever it picks up as table material is printed in your table. If you write your document from an outline, creating a table of contents from your outline is an excellent idea. Your outline, as with most documents, has different levels of headings. Word allows you to set up different levels of table headings, with each lower level indented when the table is printed.

Setting up the hidden table listings is very much like setting up index listings. For a table of contents, you would use the hidden .c. to mark table items. The system recognizes the semicolon, division mark, or paragraph end mark as the end of a listing. In most cases, however, each new table item is on its own line. Putting the .c. at the beginning of the line with the

```
LIBRARY TABLE index on: █     entry/page # separated by: ^t
     indent each level: 0.4"          use style sheet: Yes(No)
Enter a letter
```

Figure 12-18.   The Library Table Menu

table entry places the entire line in the table—when you end the line, you also end the table listing.

Second-, third-, and fourth-level listings are easily differentiated. A first-level entry uses .c. only. A second-level entry adds a colon (.c.:). A third-level entry uses two colons (.c.::). Similarly, a fourth-level entry uses three colons (.c.:::).

To instruct the system to create your table, go to the Library Menu and select Table. The Library Table Menu looks like Figure 12-18. The first option asks what letter to index on; the default is C. When you select this default, the system looks for all occurrences of a hidden .c. and creates a table for all those listings.

TIP: Besides the basic table of contents, you can create other tables using this feature. For example, during the writing of this book, a table of figures was created. This was done using a hidden .f. to indicate each figure. When it was time to have the system make the table of figures, the system was told to index on *F*.

Any letter can be used to index on; however, you should not use the letter *i*, since the system uses that letter to create an index. With 25 other available letters, there should be little reason ever to use *i* to index a table.

This can be especially useful for creating a table of authorities. Indexing on the letter *a*, an indexing mark can be placed before each new authority. Again, it is useful to remember that your table can contain complete paragraphs. To end a table entry within a paragraph, and before the paragraph mark, use a hidden semicolon to indicate the end of the listing. ■

The rule for formatting entries containing enclosed quotations also applies here: for any table listing that includes quotation marks, a pair of quotation marks must surround the listing (but not enclose the hidden .c.).

The next option, Entry/Page # Separated By, asks how you want the system to separate the entry from the page number. The default sets a tab, which helps to ensure that all the numbers line up one above the other.

(This only works if you have a single tab in your table format line. Since table entries are bound to be different lengths, multiple tabs would result in the number appearing at different tab stops, depending upon the length of the table entry.) You can also use spaces, dots, or some other device to separate the entry from the number. It should be noted, however, that the tab works very well in most cases.

TIP: If you are creating a table that doesn't require numbering—such as an unnumbered table of contents—you can use this field to make it easy to search for and delete numbers. To do this, enter a separator string that is unlikely ever to appear in your table—a string such as SPACEzzzz would probably work well. Once the table is made, a search for a string such as zzzz brings you to the beginning of each number. Highlighting the word and then deleting it easily removes the number from the table. ∎

The next prompt, Indent Each Level, asks how you want to handle second-level, third-level, and other level entries. The default indents each new level entry 0.4 inch to the right of the entry at the preceding level. Thus, a second-level entry begins 0.4 inch from the left margin; a third-level entry begins 0.8 inch from the margin. In most cases this is a useful amount of space: it is greater than that for an index (and so makes it easier to distinguish an index from a table), and it is superior to a tab, since you may have problems separating your entry from its number if you use other tabs in your table.

The final prompt, Use Style Sheet, asks if you are using a style sheet that can work with the table. If so, the style sheet controls spacing between levels, in addition to character formats. For example, one style may be to have primary headings printed bold, with all other headings in normal type. The two previous settings are overridden if you use a style sheet. Thus, if you are using a style sheet for your table, the only responses the system acts on are the one telling it what to index on (in most cases, the letter *c*), and the one telling it to use a style sheet to format your table.

Once your selections are made, the system finds each table entry. At the end of the document, it creates a table. It is important to remember to repaginate your document with hidden characters hidden. This way, your table will be correctly numbered and will correspond to your printed text.

Although the text here suggests that the entries for your index or table should be set into your document as you write it, this isn't necessarily the case. You can just as easily create your document and then go back and enter the index or table information. You may choose whichever method works best for your particular style.

A few more brief points about automatic indexes and automatic tables are in order. First, when the system creates a table or index, it puts each table or index on its own page at the end of the document. If you wish, you can renumber the page of your index, using the Format Division Page Numbers Menu, print it, and then move it to the beginning of your document.

Also, there will undoubtedly be times when you have to create an index or table for a document that already has a table or index. When you attempt to do this, the system will ask if you want to replace the previous table or index. Since you have probably changed your text and performed a repagination on your document, you will probably always want to replace the old table or index with your new one. Deleting an old table or index is a good idea: this way you don't have to figure out which table or index is the current and correct one and which is obsolete.

LEADER CHARACTERS FOR TABS

Although the various types of tabs have been covered previously, there is another aspect that hasn't yet been discussed in enough detail: the tab leader characters. These are especially useful for tables and indexes, because they make it easy to see which number corresponds to which table listing. This setting prints a selected character (or blank) between the point at which you pressed TAB and the point at which you filled in your tabular information (the point to which pressing TAB moved the cursor). You have actually been using this all along—the character you have been printing between those two points is a blank.

For example, you may be preparing a table with chapter titles flush left, page numbers flush right, and the space between titles and page numbers left blank. It may become difficult for many readers to be able to tell which number belongs to which item. Since, in most cases, you or the system types the text for your listing and then tabs over to insert the number, the solution to this problem is simple: change the character separating the text and the number (the leader character) from a blank to a different character. If your table has already been prepared, you want to change the leader character for the numeric tab.

To do this, first highlight your table. Next, go to the Format Tabs Set Menu. This should display the tabs as they are currently set. Select the tab just above the numbers. (If you don't find a tab above the numbers, create one. In most cases you want the numbers right aligned, so that the numbers end at the same point — this makes numbers of any size align correctly.)

Next, decide on the leader character you want to use. You have four choices: a blank character, a period, a hyphen, or an underline. When you use the period, a line of dots connects your text to the numbers. A hyphen produces a line of dashes that connects the two. The underline character prints a solid underline between the two; if used in conjunction with underlined text and numbers, this character makes each listing appear as a separate entry on its own line. In most cases you will probably prefer the dot as a leader character. Once this setting is selected, all the entries have the selected leader. If you don't go overboard, you will have a very professional-looking, easily read table.

If you haven't yet prepared your table, you can set up your tabs to have the appropriate leader character. In some cases you may want to use two tabs between your text and numbers. The first tab is the one with the leader characters. The second tab is the right-aligned or decimal tab that prints the numbers. The two tabs are located close together.

The advantage to this type of arrangement — for example, a leader tab at the 5-inch mark and a right-aligned tab for the numbers at 5.5 inches — is that all the dot leaders end at the same position. They don't actually run into the numbers. This type of setup often looks better and is more read-able than one in which the leader runs into the numbers.

TIP: If you plan to prepare many tables, you can create a special style that automatically applies the proper format for entries using this type of tab and leader character. That way you can apply it to a table the system prepares or use it to automatically format your tabular text as you enter it. Having styles with your particular leader characters ready can save some time and assure consistency from one document to the next. ■

SPECIAL CHARACTERS

Microsoft Word doesn't limit you to just the characters that appear on the keyboard. The computer you use is probably capable of producing up to 128 other characters. These include foreign characters, certain special symbols, and lines and boxes. Word allows you to include these characters in your documents. These may be especially useful if you plan on doing international correspondence — the ability to print foreign characters may make your communications more readable, in addition to impressing the recipient.

The use of these special characters is dependent on your printer's ability to print them. Your printer manual may tell you which of the characters it can print. As a rule, if the manual indicates that the printer supports the IBM Graphic Character Set, you should be able to produce all the characters available to you. These characters are listed in the *Reference to Microsoft Word*, Appendix A, and are those characters numbered 128 and above. For example, the mathematical symbol beta (β) is one that normally isn't printed. Its numeric code is 225.

To enter a special character, hold down ALT and type in the numeric value of the character *on the numeric keypad*. When you have entered the number, release ALT. The character appears on the screen.

Figure 12-19 contains the complete set of extra characters. Note that the set starts with number 127. Although 127 is technically not an extended character, it is a character not accessible from the keyboard. The entire figure was created using the key combination of ALT plus a number.

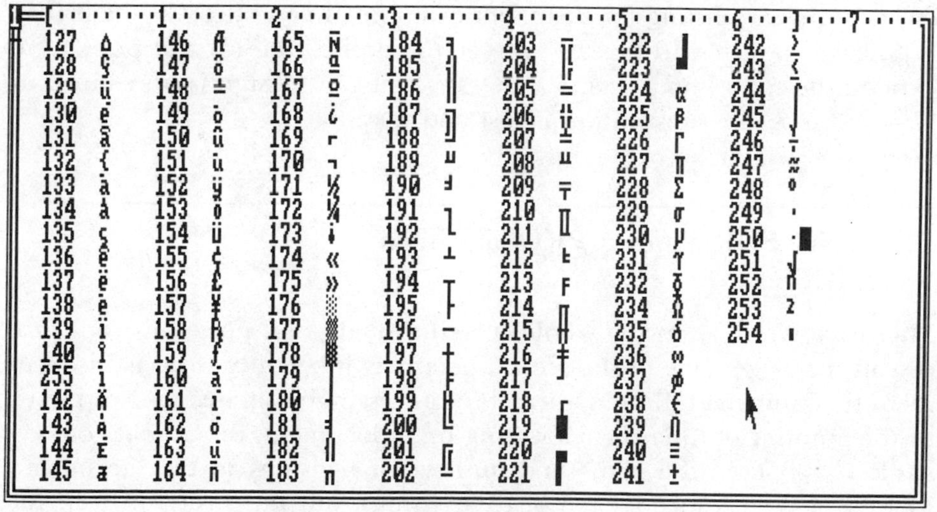

Figure 12-19.   The extended character set

NOTE: The way the table was created may be of interest. Although it would have been possible to figure out how many lines could be printed in a column, and the table filled in row by row (that is, by entering the code for 127, then 146, then 165, and so on), this wasn't the method used. Similarly, the column mode wasn't used. This table was created one column at a time. The first column, with entries one above the other, ran from character 127 through character 145. Once that row was completed, the cursor was brought up to the end of the listing for 127.

Since there was a RETURN at the end of each line, inserting the next row after the listing for 127 wouldn't have worked — it would have inserted 146 between 127 and 128. Instead, when the new column was to be typed in, the mode was changed from the normal Insert mode, to Overtype mode (by pressing F5). In this mode, whatever is typed replaces the text it types over. Since the new text was being typed in blank space, this process worked.

At the end of each entry, DOWN ARROW was pressed. This brought the cursor to the end of the last listing on the line below. For example, after 146 was entered, pressing DOWN ARROW brought the cursor to the end of 128. Pressing RETURN would have inserted a space between the entry and the next line and wouldn't have worked properly. However, use of the cursor movement keys and Overtype mode produced this well-formatted, readable figure. ■

If there are special characters you regularly use, you should probably create a glossary listing for them. For example, if you often use the British pound symbol, it will be easy to type the dollar sign ($) and press F3 to expand the entry into a pound sign. Once the pound sign is stored in your glossary as $, the substitution is fast and easy.

BILLING FOR WORD PROCESSING SERVICES

Microsoft Word is, on the whole, a well-thought-out, powerful word processing package. One of the areas where it is inherently weak is in document tracking and billing. Other word processing programs can keep track of the amount of time spent working on a document, the number of keystrokes, and even the name and number of revisions to that document. Microsoft Word can do some of these things, but not easily. In fact, the ability to use Microsoft Word to keep track of time and keystrokes hasn't been covered in any other book or documentation.

Billing for services is an important aspect of many word processing operations. The corporate word processing department often charges the departments for which work is performed. Independent word processing companies charge their customers for services. Although you can charge by the page, often this is not the most accurate or fair method of billing: a simple memorandum may take no time at all, while a one-page scientific table may take many times as long to produce. Statistical typing takes longer than text typing—in many cases time, rather than pages, may be a better basis for billing. There are a few ways to prepare your billing: by keystroke, by character, by word, by printed page, and by hour. You can arrive at numbers for most of these parameters.

Word Count Billing

Microsoft Word has included a utility, Word Count, that can count the number of words in any of your documents. The Word Count program is accessed through the Library Run Menu. To count the number of words in the document you called STEIGER.DOC, first select the Library Run Menu. The screen prompts you for the DOS command that you want to run. (Library Run is covered in more detail in Chapter 13.)

Type: **wcSPACE**

The system next must be told the name and drive location (if in a directory or on a disk drive other than the default system disk and directory).

Type: **steiger.doc** RETURN

Your screen goes blank while Word Count counts the words in the document. After a pause the system tells you how many words were counted in the document. This feature is also useful for writers who get paid by the word.

You can count the words in any document, even one you are currently editing. When you make up a bill, you can type the name of the document you are billing for and then use Word Count to get an accurate number of words in the document.

Character/Keystroke Billing

Characters and keystrokes are not equivalent. The number of keystrokes will normally be greater than the number of characters in a document. This is because such things as backspaces and control codes are often counted as keystrokes. Since a character count accurately represents all the usable data in a document, this number is usually used for billing. A problem arises, however, when you edit a document: if you were to count characters, you might end up with fewer characters after you edited a document than you had before you edited it (due to deletions made during editing).

Therefore, character billing is not always appropriate for anything other than original input. To count characters, all you have to do is perform a Transfer Save on your document. When the system finishes saving it, you get a report on the number of characters saved. Write this down or copy it to your billing window, and you should have little problem billing on total characters in a document.

Page Billing

Billing by page is extremely simple. When you run a Print Repaginate, the system automatically calculates the number of pages in a document. Objections to this are similar to those to character billing: changes made during editing aren't necessarily reflected by the final page count. Additionally, you may be billing both for prepared page and printed page. To be able to track both figures accurately, you must keep a separate listing for each version of a document.

Time Billing

Time billing is probably the best way to bill for word processing services. Although there is the potential for "fudging" your time records (for example, leaving a job on the screen while you go to lunch or changing the time and date on your system clock), in actual practice this usually isn't worth the trouble. Safeguards can be incorporated into time billing. For example, a rough relationship between number of characters and time can be determined. If this ratio is too far out of line, it may indicate some "creative" time reporting.

One method for time recording requires a small amount of diligence, since you must record each time you start or stop work on your document.

However, this method attaches start and stop times to your document, and you can print the times out in tabular form any time you need a record. This method uses the Hidden Character mode, and a set of glossary macros. Remember that a macro is a string of text or instructions that can be easily called up using one or a few characters.

The following command stores your starting time:

.b. date time

To make this work, you must press F3 after you type in the date and time macros. For example, when you press F3 after the word *date,* the day's date appears on the screen. When you press F3 after the word *time,* the current time is put on the screen. Saving this entire date and time line as hidden text allows you to keep track of starting time for your work session. (Note that .b. was used here since it is an easy mnemonic—*b* for *billing.*)

To end time recording, use a similar macro:

.b.: date time

Again, you must press F3 after date and time so that the current date and time are stamped. You added the colon to the hidden character .b. so that the ending time would be indented when your table printed.

Saving both start and finish sequences as macros—for example, bs for billing start and bf for billing finish—makes it easy to record the start and end time for your editing sessions. Using the Library Table function, you can have the system sort on B and create a summary table of all start and stop times for each document. There is still another minor problem: although you have start and stop times, the actual time worked on a document has to be calculated. This is probably best done from outside Microsoft Word. Word's math capabilities make it easy to calculate charges, if they are put in terms of decimal hours or decimal rates. Again, it may be easiest to use a mathematics program, a desktop calculator, or even good old pencil and paper.

CUSTOMIZING WORD

Throughout this book you've seen only a few variations in the standard format. You've seen style bars turned on and off; rulers turned on and off; and hidden text turned on and off. There's more to Word than just these

```
OPTIONS visible: None Partial Complete  printer display: Yes(No) menu:(Yes)No
   default tab width: 0.5"    measure:(In)Cm P10 P12 Pt          mute: Yes(No)
Select option
```

Figure 12-20.   The Options Menu

options. This section discusses how you can customize the way text, symbols, and command lines appear on the screen.

The Options Menu

The Options Menu, shown in Figure 12-20, lets you make a number of choices about how you want to use Word. The first option, Visible, relates to how much information the system puts on the screen. With the option set at None, none of the special characters are visible on the screen. Characters such as tab symbols, paragraph marks, and spaces between words are hidden. This mode most closely approximates the appearance of the printed page. However, it is not useful when you are just getting a feel for Word or when you are trying to develop a table.

Being able to see some of the characters used by the system can be of value to you. It is recommended that, at least for the period you are learning Word, you use the Partial setting, which shows you more of the characters you use. Your paragraph end mark is the one you'll probably see the most. In addition, the paragraph mark moves along with the end-of-text mark.

Choosing the Complete option results in a screen that conveys much more about your text. It is very valuable when making up tables or lists, since all tabs and spaces are displayed. It is much simpler to line up text if you can count tabs than it is without this ability. In many cases, however, this display may give you more information than you really want.

Your response to the next option, Printer Display, tells the system how you want to see your text. If you answer yes, you will see line breaks and hyphens as they will appear when printed. As a rule, the line on your screen is wider than when you select no printer display. This can give you a feel for where each line will break when printed, but it can be something of a nuisance if used for regular editing. In order to navigate from one side of the line to the other, you must press SCROLL LOCK and cursor movement keys in combination or use the mouse. Also, there are times when lining up a table with the printer display on produces a printed table that isn't lined up. Lining up tables with Word is not especially easy; however, the largest chance of success is with the system in the text display rather than the printer display mode.

The next item, Menu, is a very important one. Responding yes to this option leaves the Main Command Menu displayed at the bottom of your screen. If you turn it off by selecting no, your menu will not be seen on the screen until you press ESC or move the mouse pointer out of the editing window and press a button. At that point the system recognizes that you want to enter a command, and the menu reappears.

With a relatively small system screen, you will probably appreciate the extra four lines much more than you do a menu that you probably don't need to refer to frequently. Once you become comfortable with Word, you will seldom need to refer to the Command Menu—and it's still only a keystroke away. It is recommended that you try running the program with the menu hidden.

The Default Tab Width option was already briefly discussed in Chapter 1. However, the system automatically sets tabs separated by the default width unless you load a different style or change the tab settings. If you want your tabs to be different from the default setting, you can enter the preferred tab increment.

The Measure prompt asks how you want to measure the text and spacing in your documents. If you are comfortable with the metric system, for example, you may be more at home with the measure set for centimeters rather than inches. The ruler at the top of the screen is then converted from inches to centimeters. If you are an experienced typesetter, you may appreciate the control that Pt (for point) gives you: using this measure you can format text in 1/72-inch increments. Line and character spacing are automatically converted into the measure that you select. Thus, a 1-inch indent becomes a 2.54-centimeter indent.

Finally, the Mute option tells the system whether or not you want it to beep when you make a mistake or when you must provide a response. Since you are probably getting better and better at Word, it is probably a good idea to leave this option on—you won't be hearing many beeps anyway.

The Window Options Menu

Window options can apply as well to one window as they do to many windows. The Window Options Menu is shown in Figure 12-21. The first option, Window Number, tells the system which window your changes will affect. The number of each window appears in the top left corner of the window. The Outline option tells the system whether or not you want to

```
WINDOW OPTIONS window number: 1█  outline: Yes(No) show hidden text: Yes(No)
                background color: 0   style bar: Yes(No)              ruler:(Yes)No
Enter number
```

Figure 12-21.   The Window Options Menu

show the window in outline view — that is, as if you pressed ALT-F2 to go into Outline mode. The standard default is to answer no to this item, especially since it is easy to switch from outline to normal views.

The next option, Show Hidden Text, allows you to display or hide hidden text. If you are creating tables or other hidden text annotations, you probably want to show hidden text while you work. However, unless you set this feature to no, hidden text is included in repagination and is printed at print time. Thus, you should probably show hidden text while editing but hide it before printing or repaginating. Even when hidden, the codes for tables and indexes are found by the system when it creates tables and indexes.

If you are using many windows at once, the Background Color option allows you to to apply a different background color to each one. This way, you can avoid confusion about which window has which generation of text in it. In addition, if you get tired of white characters on a black screen and have a color monitor, you can drop a background color into your text window. Subjectively, white characters against a blue background seem very readable and easy on the eyes.

This option only functions in character mode, although the graphics mode may support color if you are fortunate enough to have an EGA monitor and EGA card. To see which colors are available, move to this option, and press RIGHT ARROW or the right mouse button. The screen clears, and you can see the available colors. Select a color by using the mouse or by typing in the number you prefer.

The next option, Style Bar, asks if you want to be able to see the code for the styles you are using. This is of value if you are preparing a document that requires many format changes. With the style bar displayed, you can tell at a glance which glossary style has been selected for each paragraph. If you have not selected a style, an asterisk appears in the style bar area. Since this option does not reduce the amount of space for normal text nor slow down the system, you should probably display the style bar.

Finally, you can use the Ruler option instead of the mouse to display or hide the ruler. If you don't have a mouse, the Ruler option is especially important. When the ruler line is displayed, you can tell where indents are, where tabs should be set, and where margins are set. In addition, when you are indenting a paragraph, you can see how far from the left margin the indent is. The ruler conveys valuable information.

The ruler is displayed or hidden by answering yes or no to this prompt. To display the ruler using the mouse, point at the top right margin of the window and click the right mouse button. To hide the ruler using the mouse, point at the top right margin of the window and click both mouse buttons at the same time. The standard top line replaces the ruler.

THE JUMP FUNCTION

The Jump function has already been briefly discussed in the footnote section of this chapter. This command has two uses. In a paginated document you can quickly go to any numbered page. To do this, select Jump and then select Page. The system prompts, "Jump Page number." In response, type the number of the page to which you want to jump.

To some extent this involves printing the document so that you can identify a page when you want to jump to it. However, it is much faster and more accurate than the Search function or the somewhat inaccurate pointer at the side of the screen. Also, it is the best way to jump around a document without using the mouse. The Jump Footnote function has been discussed in "Footnotes" in this chapter. Using this option you can jump from a specific footnote in the footnote window to the corresponding body text.

FORMATTING

Although formatting has been discussed in Chapter 5, it is further summarized here, since many Word users are either intimidated by the system or unaware of the flexibility built into the system. Formatting changes are easy.

To set up page margins, go into the Format Division Margins Menu. In this menu you must tell the system the size of the paper you are printing on and the margins you want established. For example, if you wanted to print

6 inches of text on a standard 8 1/2-by-11-inch page, you would set a left and right margin of 1.25 inches. The default margins are probably adequate for most print jobs.

When you change from letter-sized to legal-sized paper, the only change you must make is in page length — your margins remain the same. If you plan to use headers or footers, you may want the margins to be less than 0.5 inch from top or bottom, in the event they exceed 0.5 inch in length. Other than that, the division margins seldom require changing.

Next, you may want to change paragraph format. For most purposes, a left-aligned paragraph with no indents is the usual setting. Line spacing can be changed from inside this menu. Also, if it fits your style, you can have the system insert an extra space between paragraphs, saving you the trouble of pressing RETURN twice to separate paragraphs of text. Perhaps the most difficult thing to get a handle on is the indented paragraph. If you remember that the left indent indents text from the second line down, and that the first line begins printing at the sum of the left indent and the first line indent, you should have little trouble with this setting.

An example of one such use is the following development of a table:

Figure 12-9   Format Division Layout menu, note that this is used to select Footnote print options.

The text for the table is indented 1.5 inches, while the title of the figure is printed at the margin. To set this up, you set the left indent to 1.5 inches and the first line indent to −1.5 inches. The sum of the two (−1.5 plus 1.5), zero, indicates that the first line of text prints at the left margin.

Finally, character format is also easy. To set character format, select the character or block of text you want to format. It is easiest to make changes using the quick format keys; however, these keys can't be used to change type sizes or styles.

The Format Character Menu lets you select a number of attributes for characters, in addition to changing the font and type size. Once you have selected the formats you desire, you should create a style sheet using these settings. That way, whenever you want to change character, paragraph, or division formats, the change is just a few easy keystrokes away. Using style sheets and Word's formatting flexibility, you can create documents that should meet most, if not all, of your needs.

GETTING THE MOST OUT OF
MICROSOFT WORD

This chapter has touched on many of the advanced functions built into Microsoft Word. Microsoft Word is a very powerful program that takes practice to master. This chapter does not provide everything you will ever need to know to get the most out of Word. Rather, it gives some suggestions for techniques, outlines some options, and instructs you on how to perform certain advanced functions. However, the system is flexible enough to fit your needs very well. Since the only person who best knows your needs and work style is you, you must experiment on your own to determine how best to use Word.

You are encouraged to experiment with different options. Try out many of the advanced features covered in earlier chapters, in addition to those yet to come. There is little that you can do that can damage the program or the computer. When you have some time, experiment, innovate—take a chance. Even though most of the main features of Word can be found in this book, the program is very flexible, and there may be some features, tricks, or techniques you can discover for yourself.

Aspiring screenwriters, for example, can use Word as the basis of a full-featured, automatic screenplay formatter. Using styles and the glossary, a screenwriter can easily set Word to indent character names automatically, to give a different indentation to dialogue, and so forth. With the addition of a product called Scriptor, from Screenplay Systems, the computer can produce scripts ready for production. In fact, many screenwriters swear by the combination of Scriptor and Word.

Few users have fully explored all of Word's capabilities. You'll probably find Word able to do things you didn't think were possible. With a bit of imagination, you may be able to get Word to do practically everything you need.

LIBRARY FUNCTIONS

Most of the library functions have been presented in a number of different chapters in this book. However, several functions deserve more attention.

THE LIBRARY AUTOSORT FUNCTION

The Library Autosort function sorts columns of text, data in a merge data file, entries in an outline, or paragraphs in a document. This feature works in combination with the Library Number functions. There are two basic types of sorts: numeric and alphanumeric. A *numeric sort* sorts only on numbers, with a few exceptions. The characters $, %, − (the minus key on the numeric keypad, not the hyphen), c (comma), and . (period) can be sorted by the system during a numeric sort when included in a numeric sort field. Any other characters that appear in a numeric field would be interpreted by the system as the end of that sort field. Thus, if you wanted to sort by Social Security number, a numeric sort would only sort the first three numbers. When the system found the first hyphen, it would stop the sort.

Any non-numeric sort, or sort of numbers that also contain other symbols, is considered an *alphanumeric sort*. When performing an alphanumeric sort, the system sorts the following, in order: symbols, numbers, uppercase letters, and lowercase letters. Thus, #345 is sorted above 3456, which is considered greater than 345A, which is greater than 345a. Understanding this order can simplify the task of designing a sort and eliminate any confusion about the order of the sorted materials.

In addition, Word can sort in ascending or descending order. Using the numbers listed previously, a descending sort would produce the following ordered list: 345a, 345A, 3456, #345. If you were doing an alphabetic sort, an ascending sort would order letters from A through Z, and a descending sort would order letters from Z through A.

The Library Autosort command lines are shown in Figure 13-1. After you've selected ascending or descending sorts, the next option is Case. Answering yes to this option tells the system to sort uppercase listings above lowercase listings—that is, a listing of Z9 would be above a1. The final setting, Column Only, tells the system whether or not you want to change the order of the rows that a column is attached to, or just the column itself. This is clarified in the next section.

Sorting Tables

Call up the document called TABLE 1. If you don't have the document on disk, refer to Chapter 9 and create it now. There should be two tables in that file. The one you are sorting is the second of the two. Using Word's column mode, highlight the Fleet Price column.

To do this, move the cursor to the tab before the number 698.99.

Figure 13-1.   The Library Autosort command lines

Figure 13-2.   A highlighted column before sorting

```
LIBRARY AUTOSORT by: Alphanumeric Numeric   sequence:(Ascending)Descending
                case: Yes(No)               column only: Yes(No)
Select option
Page 1   {}                     ?                Microsoft Word: TABLE1.DOC
```

Figure 13-3. The command lines as they appear when a numeric sort is specified

```
Item→→    →    →    →    Fleet·Price→    →    List·Price¶
Brakes→   →    →    →    $→ 195.00→→     →    $→ 249.99↓
Wheels→   →    →    →    $→ 349.98→→     →    $→ 349.99↓
Windshield→    →    →    $→ 597.45→→     →    $→ 599.99↓
Tires→    →    →    →    $→ 698.99→→     →    $→ 699.99↓
Lighting·Package→   →    $→3749.99→→     →    $→4500.00↓
Total→    →    →    →    $→5591.41···········$→6399.96············↓
↓
```

Figure 13-4. The Fleet Price column sorted in ascending numeric order, with related columns and entries moved

Type: SHIFT-F6

Now, using the mouse or the cursor movement keys, move the highlight to the end of the column (the wheels entry), the number 349.98. The screen should look like Figure 13-2. Tell the system that you want to do an ascending numeric sort and be sure to set the Column Only setting to no. When these parameters are correct, the command lines look like Figure 13-3.

Once the column is sorted, the table looks like Figure 13-4. It should be clear that the item names for the rows the sorted columns were attached to were also moved during sorting, as were the values in the List Price column. The underline below the prices for wheels was also moved along with the numbers. To make this table look right, you would have to delete the underline below the wheels prices and move it under the lighting package figures.

Since you will demonstrate more sorts, you should restore the table to its previous state (before sorting). To do this, select the Undo function.

NOTE: You must select Undo immediately after carrying out an action you want to change. If you make any later deletions or other editing changes after an autosort, you may not be able to undo your sort easily. You can also use the UNDO command to flip back and forth to see the table before it was sorted and after it was sorted. The UNDO command toggles from one view to the other. ■

Undo the sort, and your screen should again look like Figure 13-2.

Next, highlight the names of the items in the Item column and do an ascending alphanumeric sort, again leaving Column Only set to no. You should also specify Case as yes (although in this instance it doesn't matter, since all entries are in uppercase). The sorted columns now look like Figure 13-5.

Undo this sort so that you can see how the Column Only option works. With the row labels still highlighted, again select an alphanumeric sort, but this time with Column Only set to yes. Only the entries in the highlighted (sorted) column change. The contents of the other columns stay as they were. This is shown in Figure 13-6. Undo those changes to return the table to its original state.

Sorting Text

If you have ever wished that you could easily rearrange the paragraphs of a document, your wish has been answered. There may be times when you've put together a document or paper and realize that it may read better if organized slightly differently. Or, if you are doing word processing, you may be presented with a first draft that has insertions marked and also has paragraphs numbered. If you were using most other word processors, you would have to select the paragraphs in order and then move them to their new positions.

Item	Fleet Price	List Price
Brakes	$ 195.00	$ 249.99
Lighting Package	$3749.99	$4500.00
Tires	$ 698.99	$ 699.99
Wheels	$ 349.98	$ 349.99
Windshield	$ 597.45	$ 599.99
Total	$5591.41	$6399.96

Figure 13-5. Columns sorted alphanumerically by item name

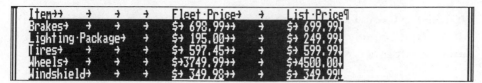

Figure 13-6. Column sorted with Column Only turned off

Using Microsoft Word, however, reorganizing a document is easy. When Word sorts your document, it puts all numbered paragraphs in order. If, for example, you had a paragraph numbered 1 at the beginning of your document and one marked 2 at the end, the Autosort function would move paragraph number 2 directly below number 1.

While this may seem rather obvious, what it means is that you must number every paragraph highlighted during a sort. If paragraphs have been renumbered only in certain parts of your document, it is best to perform the autosort on those isolated areas. *All* numbered paragraphs are moved before any unnumbered paragraphs. If any unnumbered paragraphs fall between numbered paragraphs to be sorted, and if those paragraphs are highlighted when the Autosort feature is selected, they will appear after numbered paragraphs when the sort is complete.

Unless you want the numbers to print, they should be deleted after the document is sorted. You can either do this manually or use the Library Number facility to remove the numbers. Again, this can be done automatically by the program. Unfortunately, Word is unable to number paragraphs automatically.

Sorting Outlines

Outline numbering has already been discussed in Chapter 10. However, there may be times when you want to reorganize an outline. To do this, assign new numbers to the first-level listings. Be sure that you are in the Outline Outline mode, not the Outline Text mode, so that all subheadings are moved along with the first-level headings.

Once this is done, perform an ascending numeric or alphanumeric sort, depending upon the outline style you used. All subheadings and subentries and all related body text are then put into the new order. After this is done, however, the numbers at secondary and lower levels may not be correct. You should next use Library Number to update numbers and to restart the numbering sequence to place the numbers for all the headings and sub-headings in order.

Sorting Data Lists

When you prepare lists for repetitive letters or envelopes, it is often important to be able to sort your mailing list by ZIP code. For convenience, it is also a good idea to be able to sort lists alphabetically and then by ZIP code. Unfortunately, Word was designed to allow you to sort only one field at a time—that is, you can sort ZIP codes, but you can't sort by last name.

There is a way around this, however. When Word sorts data fields, it only sorts the *first* field in the data file. Thus, if the first field were Zip, the system would sort ZIP codes. If the first field were Last Name, then the system would sort last names.

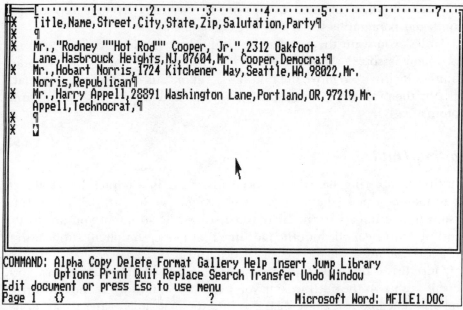

Figure 13-7.   MFILE1.DOC before sorting

Telling the system to sort a data field is very easy. Just go into the data document and select the sort parameters. To demonstrate this, call up the MFILE1.DOC, shown in Figure 13-7. As you can see, a sort on this data would be meaningless, since the first field is Title, and all the titles in the document are Mr. It would be much more meaningful to be able to sort by last name and by ZIP code.

TIP: When you want to sort by two fields, a primary and a secondary, a precise order is required. In this example the primary field is Zip. The secondary field is Name. The order that must be followed to make this sort work is as follows: sort on the secondary field and then sort on the primary field. This would give you a field that is in order, both by ZIP code and by last name.

In this example, however, that still would not work properly, since the Name field includes first and last names. The system would sort by first name, since it appears first in the file. To produce an accurate sort by last name would require modifying the file. A better alternative would have been to design the file to meet the potential requirement for use of a last name. ■

Since this file is short, a new field can be created, one called Last Name. Modifying the data file requires inserting this new name into its appropriate location in the header and inserting a comma between the first and last names. In order to reorganize the data, you should first prepare it so that you can easily move entire columns. You must first replace commas with tabs. Highlight the entire data file and perform an automatic replace to accomplish this. The command line for this replacement should look like Figure 13-8.

```
REPLACE text: ,                          with text: ^t█
     confirm:(Yes)No  case: Yes(No) whole word: Yes(No)
Enter text
Page 1   {,}                    ?              Microsoft Word: MFILE1.DOC
```

Figure 13-8.   The command lines as they appear when commas in the data field are replaced by tabs, represented by ^t instead of the tab symbol

This gives you a confused-looking display. In order to make this work, you first have to change your margins. Tell the system that your paper is 22 inches wide (the maximum width Word allows). You should also reset your division left and right margins to 0 inches, to allow for maximum width. This spreads out your data fields so that each one is on a separate line.

You still haven't set up your system to make it easy to select and move a column. To do this, you must reset tabs. With the entire document still selected, select Options Default Tabs and set the default to 2.2 inches. To make the entry work, you must delete, Jr." from the Cooper entry. You must also add the quotation mark (") after "Hot Rod" in the Name field. Quotation marks must be balanced in this type of document.

Next, using column mode, delete and move the Last Name field to the front of the list. The beginning of the list should now look like Figure 13-9. Now you can sort the last names in the document in alphabetical order. (Be careful not to select the field name, or it will be included in the

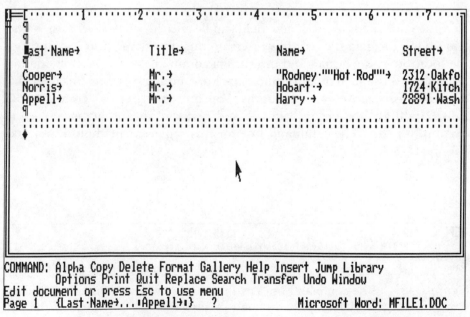

Figure 13-9.   The data document with Last Name as the first field

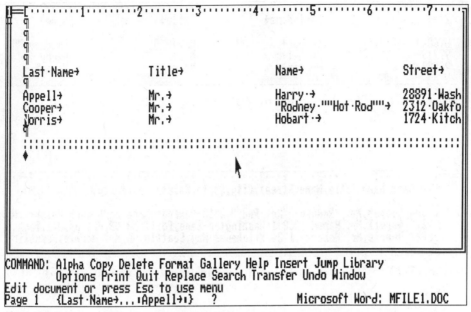

Figure 13-10.   The list sorted alphabetically

sort.) The sorted list looks like Figure 13-10.

Next, select Zip and move it to the front of the list. The list, sorted by ZIP code and then alphabetically, looks like Figure 13-11. With a large list you could more easily see that this sort is in the order you want. If you want to return your list to its previous state, with commas as delimiters instead of tabs, do a global replace, with the system replacing $^\wedge$t with a comma. The reordered list, with comma delimiters, now looks like Figure 13-12. Finally, reset the division defaults and the default tabs, and you can print the letter.

THE LIBRARY SPELL AND LIBRARY RUN FUNCTIONS

The Library Spell function has already been discussed. However, Word comes with a set of tools that can be used to help in the preparation of your document.

```
[········1·········2·········3·········4·········5·········6·········7····
Zip→                    Last·Name→           Title→              Name→
¶
07604→                  Cooper→              Mr.→                "Rodney·""
97219→                  Appell→              Mr.→                Harry·→
98022→                  Norris→              Mr.→                Hobart·→
```

Figure 13-11.   The list sorted by ZIP code and alphabetically

```
[········1·········2·········3·········4·········5·········6·········7··
Zip,Last·Name,Title,Name,Street,City,State,Salutation,Party¶

07604,Cooper,Mr.,"Rodney·""""Hot·Rod""",2312·Oakfoot·Lane,Hasbrouck·Heights,N
97219,Appell,Mr.,Harry·,28891·Washington·Lane,Portland,OR,Mr.·Appell,Techn
98022,Norris,Mr.,Hobart·,1724·Kitchener·Way,Seattle,WA,Mr.·Norris,Republic
¶
```

Figure 13-12.   The list with comma delimiters reinstated in place of tabs

Spelling Checking a Single Word

If you wanted to check the spelling of a single word or get a suggested
spelling, the Lookup program would help you do this. In order to use
Lookup, you must select Library Run. The Library Run prompt asks you
to enter the name of the program you want to run. In essence, Library Run
allows you to run other programs while you are still doing word processing
with Word. To load this program,

Type: **Lookup**

Next, type a space and then type your guess at the spelling of the word
you want to look up. For example, to see if *mispelled* should be *misspelled,*

Type: **Lookup mispelled**

The system checks for the word and prints the correct spelling, if it can find
a word that matches it phonetically. Lookup can't look up every word, but

it is helpful for many words if you can provide an approximate spelling of the word.

Running a Word Count

The Word Count program was already discussed in Chapter 12. It is useful when you want to determine the word length of a particular document. You can use this program to count the words in a document you are currently editing or in a previously edited document stored on disk.

To run the program, select Library Run and

Type: **WC**

Next, type the name of the document you want word counted. If the document has an extension other than .DOC, type in the extension after the name of the document. Press RETURN or point to the LIBRARY RUN command and press the right mouse button, and Word Count counts the number of words in your document.

Checking Word Frequency

The Word Frequency program is also activated when you run a spelling check. It gives you the total number of words (just as the Word Count program does), the number of unique words (as Library Proof option does), and the number of words appearing once. This program can be of some use in assessing the size of your vocabulary and can be an indication of the complexity of your document.

To run this program, select Library Run and

Type: **wordfreq** SPACE*filename*

where *filename* is the name of the file you want checked. If the document has an extension other than .DOC, type in the extension after the name of the document.

You can also see a list of the words in a document. When WordFrequency counts the words in a document, it creates a frequency file, which counts the number of times each word is used. To view the list, select Transfer Load and type the name of the file, including the .FRQ extension. This list can be viewed and edited like any other Word document.

Using Word Find and Anagram

The Word Find and Anagram recreational programs can be used to make word games somewhat easier. Word Find can look for words that match a particular pattern. For example, if you were doing a crossword puzzle and you only knew two of the letters, you could type the letters that you knew and a question mark for those that you didn't. For example, a six-letter word with a *z* at the third and fourth position could be entered like this: ??zz??.

From Library Run,

Type: **wordfind**

The system prompts you for a word pattern to search for.

Type: **??zz??**

The system then searches the dictionary to find possible matches.

Anagram creates words from the letters you type in. It can also make words from letters and wild card characters. A wild card character can be any letter in the alphabet. It is signified using a question mark (?) or asterisk (*). To run Anagram, go to Library Run and

Type: **Anagram** RETURN

The system then asks for the anagram pattern that you want to use. After you type the pattern and press RETURN, the system checks the dictionary for possible matches using the letters and wild card characters you entered.

Note that the Library Run programs discussed here can also be run from DOS. However, the ability to run these programs while still in Word can be of some value.

Running Other Programs

Microsoft Word can, in some cases, run other programs or DOS commands while still in Word. For example, you can format a disk without leaving the word processing program. This is useful if you attempt to save a document to a disk and get a "Disk Full" error message. In this case you can take a blank disk, go into Library Run mode, and type Format A:(or B:). The system then formats your new disk in the A:(or B:) drive. You can then save your file to your newly formatted disk.

In some cases, however, the system may prompt you to insert the "full" disk in the drive. This is because it may have to read parts of the file on the first disk that it hasn't stored in memory. After some disk swapping, you should be able to store your file onto a newly formatted disk. There are some limitations, however. In order to use DOS commands, your word disk or your hard disk must have the COMMAND.COM file, which instructs the system how to come back up.

The syntax for telling the system to run a program is as follows:

drive:directory \program.ext

where *drive* is the drive letter, *directory* is the subdirectory, and *program* is the name of the program. If the program is on the directory from which you are running Word, you do not have to enter the drive or directory information.

You are limited to the amount of memory available on your system. Since the Word program uses more than half of the 640K bytes of memory on a fully configured system, only small programs can be library run from Word. The ability to run a program on another directory is also somewhat hit-and-miss. Not every program can be accessed or run using Library Run. However, for the important things—quick spelling utilities, disk formatting, and so on—this ability to jump briefly to DOS can be quite beneficial.

FILE CONVERSIONS AND TELECOMMUNICATIONS

If Microsoft Word were the only word processing system in use in corporate America, anyone at any computer in the country could take anyone else's document disks and read, edit, and print Word documents. Theoretically, you could send disks instead of paper. This would allow the recipient to read and print an *exact* replica of your original correspondence. If you were in a hurry, you would be able to transfer your document over the phone lines, from one part of the country to another — or even across the street.

The world is not perfect. Many companies are standardized on a variety of different word processing systems and formats. Some aren't standardized at all, resulting in many different types of word processing formats. Of the "standard" word processing programs for IBM-compatible computers, Microsoft Word, MultiMate, DisplayWrite, WordStar, and WordPerfect are among the most widely used. Each system stores text on a disk in a somewhat different manner. For most purposes a standard document prepared on any of these systems is not compatible with any other system. Thus, if you wanted to view, edit, or print any of these other documents using Word, or if someone with another word processing program wanted to view your Word files, there would be a problem.

In addition, it would be difficult to use the data from a spreadsheet inside a Word document — perhaps to move a few columns of data — or to use a database program to feed in an address list for a repetitive letter, because these also are not directly compatible. If you wanted to send a Word file over a telephone, using a modem, you would normally have to modify it, since it uses more characters than a standard transmission can handle. (Methods for getting around this difficulty are discussed in "Telecommunicating Data Files" in this chapter.) Thus, although it is very convenient when your company has standardized on Word, you may still run across occasions when you need to be able to translate files into Word format and from Word format into a format that can be read by other computers or other programs.

HOW FILES ARE TRANSMITTED BY TELECOMMUNICATIONS

Possibly the simplest area for converting files is that of telecommunications. Essentially, telecommunications transmits a copy of your file, using telephone lines and a modem, to another computer and modem at the other end of the line. Standard telecommunications deal with what are referred to as ASCII (American Standard Code for Information Interchange) code. The portion of the code normally transmitted is the first 128 characters.

In terms of computer information, each character has its own, unique code—it shouldn't matter which computer you are sending to or receiving from, if the ASCII standard is observed. That there are 128 characters is significant: since data is transmitted as on/off tones, each character is made up of a unique combination of seven on/off signals (2^7 equals 128). These seven signals are known as *bits* (binary digits, or on or off pulses). An eighth bit is called a *parity bit* and is used as a basic form of error checking.

Microsoft Word and most other word processors use more than 128 bits to produce their documents. The ASCII characters from 129 through 256 mean different things to different word processors. These characters are referred to as *high-bit characters*. A high-bit *b* might mean *bold* to one word processor and be meaningless to others.

When computer users first began using modems for telecommunications, they were somewhat limited in their ability to transmit files. Since the basic format was ASCII, and the eighth data bit was used as an error checker, any 8-bit characters could not be sent, or worse, might have caused the telecommunications system to stop completely. This meant that all 8-bit characters had to be stripped off a document, thus removing all special formatting instructions. To transmit a Word file from one computer to another would normally mean losing formatting information.

CONVERTING FILES TO OR FROM OTHER WORD PROGRAMS

Assume for now that you want to send a Word file to another computer that also uses Word. Obviously, you want to be able to send a complete file, with all formatting intact. This can be done easily, using XMODEM or other so-called error-free transmission protocols. XMODEM is included on many, if not all, telecommunications software packages. It is also available in public domain or "shareware" programs available at low or no charge from many computer bulletin boards.

XMODEM is useful for sending 8-bit files over telephone lines or wired connections between computers. It sends or receives an exact image of your file to or from another computer using XMODEM. If both computers use Word, it is simple to recreate a file exactly, using XMODEM or another protocol at both ends. You should note, however, that you may also have to transmit the style sheet you applied to your document, so that the system at the other end can accurately format it. Since it is possible that the style sheet you send may have the same name as a style sheet at the other end, you should rename it before sending it, to avoid the possibility of your transmitted style sheet overwriting the one at the receiving end.

If you or the party at the other end of your telecommunications session does not have XMODEM (this is unlikely), you can also send or receive text in ASCII. (This is discussed in "ASCII conversion" in this chapter.) However, this is not as efficient as an XMODEM transfer of an entire file, which includes formatting.

CONVERTING FILES TO OR FROM OTHER WORD PROCESSORS

Using the XMODEM or other protocol described previously, you can transmit your Word file to another computer. In some cases the system used by the party at the other end is able to convert to or from Word. If this is so, the party at the other end can receive your files *exactly* as they appear on your system and can convert them to work with his or her word processor, or the party can convert his or her documents into a Microsoft Word format.

Again, XMODEM is faster than straight ASCII transfers and reduces the chance of transmission or reception error. If at all possible, an error-free transfer is the best way to move a file between two computers (other than shipping copies of your disks). Ideally, the files you receive are converted to a Word format, and the system at the other end can convert from Word into its word processing program. This is not always the case. If you can't make a direct conversion, you may have to work with a straight ASCII file or with an intermediate conversion. For example, Word gives you the ability to convert a WordStar document into a Word document.

WordStar Conversion

WordStar uses an 8-bit format for many of its print attributes and other features. These 8-bit characters have different meanings to Microsoft Word. A utility included with Word can convert the 8-bit formatting instructions into equivalent Word copy. Figure 14-1 shows an example of a WordStar document as it appears on a WordStar screen.

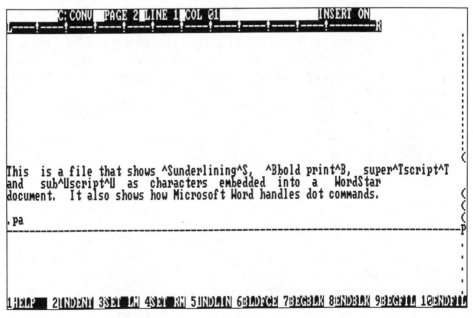

Figure 14-1.   A WordStar document before conversion

To convert a WordStar file into Microsoft Word, insert your utility disk in the A: drive, or check that you have the file CONVWS.EXE on your Word drive, and

Type: **convws** RETURN

The screen should look like Figure 14-2. In Figure 14-3 the name of the WordStar document and the name of the converted file are entered. Note that in most cases you can use the same name for source and target (providing, of course, that your files are in different directories or on different drives), but you should be careful not to use names that may already be in use. If you are using a floppy disk system, you should insert your WordStar document disk in the selected drive and your Word target disk in its appropriate drive. The system prompts you for the line width of your WordStar document. Normally, the default of 65 is acceptable, unless your WordStar document is wider than the 65-character default.

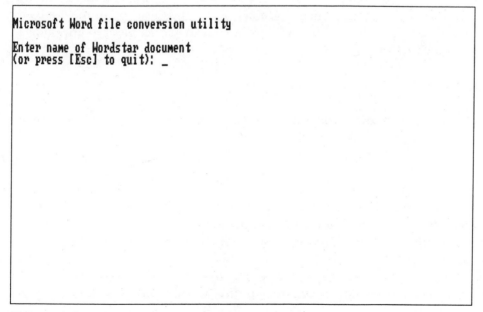

```
Microsoft Word file conversion utility

Enter name of Wordstar document
(or press [Esc] to quit): _
```

Figure 14-2.   A WordStar-to-Word conversion screen

```
Microsoft Word file conversion utility

Enter name of Wordstar document
(or press [Esc] to quit): conv

Enter Microsoft Word file name
(or press [Esc] to quit): wstest_
```

Figure 14-3.   WordStar parameters for source and target documents

The WordStar document converted for this example looks like Figure 14-4 when loaded into Word using the text mode. Bold, underlined, and superscript text appears on screen as they were formatted in WordStar. Also note that, since WordStar normally tries to justify text, extra spaces have been inserted between some words. In addition, the subscript command is not supported.

Note also what Word does with the WordStar dot commands. Since it can't carry out the dot command, it places three asterisks in front of the command. This makes it easy to use Word's search capabilities to find the location of each dot command. Knowledge of the meaning of the dot commands can make it easy to modify your converted document to appear as it did in WordStar.

ASCII Conversion

You can also convert your file to ASCII form, which strips off all formatting and produces a pure text file. In the following example this is done with the converted WordStar document, minus the dot command.

There are actually a few ways to convert to ASCII using Word. One method places RETURNs only at the end of a paragraph, the other places a RETURN and a line feed at the end of each line. For telecommunications or transfer of files, the first method is probably best, since it spares the person at the other end from having to strip off RETURNs when the document is loaded into another word processor.

In order to make the first type of conversion, select the Transfer Save Menu. Rename the document (in this case, from WSTEST.DOC to

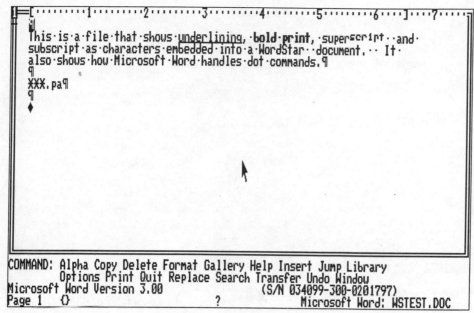

Figure 14-4.   Document converted from WordStar as it appears on the Word
screen

WSTEST.ASC). Next, tell the system you want to make an unformatted
save. The system prompts you to confirm this decision, as shown in Figure
14-5.

When you reload the ASCII file, you get a document that looks like
Figure 14-6. The spaces between words and the characters are all intact, but
special formatting has been removed. You should note that any ASCII file
can be read into Word and will appear without formatting.

TIP: Chapter 1 describes a process worth mentioning again here. If you
want to prepare a system file or batch file for your computer (such as
AUTOEXEC.BAT or **CONFIG.SYS**), you can write them using Word and
save them as unformatted ASCII files. Using this method allows you to
format your files easily and is much simpler than using **EDLIN**, which
comes with your operating system. ■

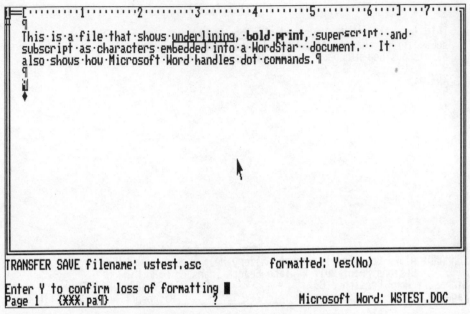

Figure 14-5.   The Transfer Save Menu as it appears for an unformatted save
for ASCII conversion

TIP: To a great degree, you can also transfer character formats using ASCII. This involves substituting ASCII characters for the formatting codes in your files. For example, if you wanted bold text, you could mark the beginning and end of the bold text with a code you would normally never use—something like BBBB or xbx. Similarly, underlines would be marked UUUU or xux, italics would be IIII or xix, and so on. If you received a file with this formatting, you would search for each occurrence of each code, highlight the text between the codes, apply the format to them, and then delete the ASCII formatting codes.

If you sent such a document, the recipient would use his or her word processor's search function to locate the format codes and replace your ASCII code with the code appropriate to his or her word processor. This method, while it takes time, is extremely useful, especially when special formatting is important. ■

The other method of creating an ASCII code requires printing your document to a file. From within your document, select the Print Options

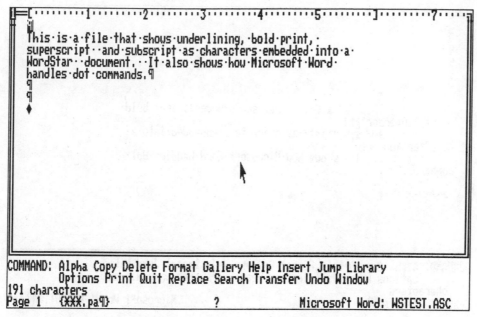

Figure 14-6.   The unformatted ASCII document

Menu. Insert your printer disk and press RIGHT ARROW if you are using a floppy disk system or just press RIGHT ARROW if you are using a hard disk system. You should see a list of printer drivers. Alternatively, you can designate the driver you want just by typing the name. In either case select the printer driver called Plain.

This driver prints ASCII text, with no formatting and line endings marked by RETURNs and line feeds. Once this option is accepted, select the PRINT FILE command. The system prompts you for a file name. Give your file a new name and press RETURN (or point to Print File and press the right mouse button).

When you reload this document, it looks like Figure 14-7. Note that there are spaces added to indent the first line of each "paragraph" (this wasn't visible before), and a hard return at the end of each line. To produce a correctly centered document, format the document with 0-inch margins. Adjusting the page width also changes the number of characters in a line of ASCII text.

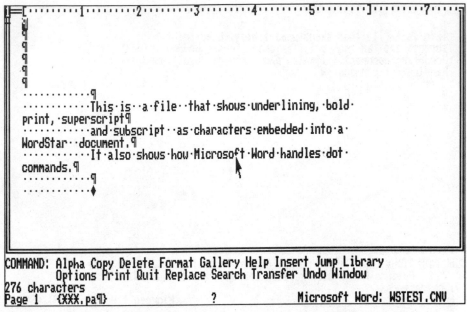

Figure 14-7.   The ASCII document produced using the Plain printer driver

With 0-inch margins, your document should look like Figure 14-8. Although the lines are longer, each line ends as a paragraph and extra spaces are inserted between words.

CONVERTING FILES TO OR FROM DISPLAYWRITE/DCA

The Document Content Architecture (DCA) is a format developed by IBM and currently used on such products as DisplayWrite 2 and DisplayWrite 3, as well as the IBM-dedicated word processor, DisplayWriter. Formatting and other information is stored much differently in this architecture than it is in Word or most other word processing systems. Since DisplayWrite 3 is one of a few corporate "standards" for word processing, and since it is widely used, it may be important to be able to transfer documents between Word and DisplayWrite or other packages that use DCA. Specifically, Word can convert documents to or from what is called Revisable Form DCA (RFDCA). This format allows you to make changes in line width and other parameters.

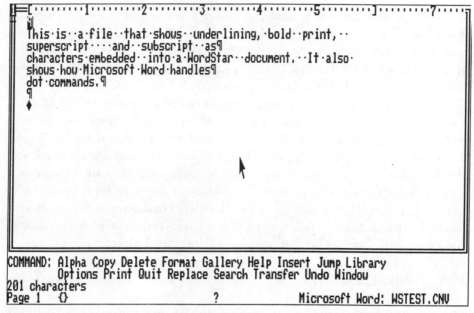

Figure 14-8.   The converted document with 0-inch margins

Converting From Word to RFDCA

The utility included with Word supports the transfer of text from Word to Revisable Form DCA. In your documents you may also have more than just text. For example, you may have applied a style sheet. Word doesn't automatically transfer style sheet information. However, you can lock the style sheet data into your document (save your original document before doing this) using the following sequence of commands.

Highlight the entire document by pressing SHIFT-F10 or by using the mouse. Next, select Format Character. Answer no to the Uppercase prompt. Accept the settings. With the entire document still highlighted, select Format Paragraph. Answer no to the Keep Together prompt. Accepting this screen produces a document that has the proper styles attached.

This document currently shows the formats selected and doesn't require a style sheet. If you prefer the flexibility of changing your styles on the style sheet, save this new version of your document under another name. Thus, you will have two versions of your document: the one that you just created with the style formats locked into the text, and the second, original version of the document, which can be modified by changing styles or style sheets.

Multiple columns also can't be directly converted. In this case you should first save your original columnar document and then prepare a version for transfer to DCA. To prepare for the transfer, select the entire document and select the Format Division Layout Menu. Next, set the Number of Cols field to 1. The document is converted as a single column.

Merge data is treated as regular text. Therefore, you can't easily transfer a merge document from Word to DCA format. Also, fonts are not converted. Instead, the system changes the font to an equivalent DCA font. Running headers and footers are also not directly transferable. Instead, this text is inserted at the beginning or end of each page of your document.

Finally, it is actually quite easy to convert from Word documents to Revisable Form DCA. Insert a copy of the utility disk in one floppy drive if you are using a floppy disk system. If your convert utilities are on a hard disk, you only have to be sure you are in the Word directory.

Type: **wordtorf** RETURN

The system prompts you for the name and drive designator of the Word file to be copied. It next prompts you for the name you want to give the DCA document. Don't forget to enter drive and directory information if the converted document is going anywhere other than the Word directory.

When you have entered the required information,

Type: RETURN

and your document is converted to DCA format. If you want to stop a conversion while the system is still converting, press CTRL-BREAK. The DCA document will be only partly converted. The amount converted depends upon the amount of time you allowed the system to work before ending the conversion process.

If you do not stop the conversion, the system prompts you to indicate whether you want to make another conversion. If you do, answer *y* and fill in the required information. If not, answer *n*.

Converting From RFDCA to Word

Word also provides you with the ability to convert a Revisable Form DCA document into a Word document. As with the conversion in the other direction, not everything in a DCA document is automatically converted.

Document comments stored in the document as comments (rather than as text) are not included in your Word document. If you want comments to pass through to Word, you must type them as text. It may be of value to surround the documents by a unique code, such as xcomx, which can be used in Word to indicate comments. Once in your Word document, you can locate these areas, highlight the affected text, and hide the comments. Lines and boxes drawn in DCA are also deleted from your converted file.

To make the conversion from Revisable Form DCA to Word, insert the utilities disk in the floppy drive if you are using a floppy disk system, or make sure you are in your system directory on a hard disk system.

Type: **rftoword** RETURN

The system then prompts you for the name of the DCA file to be converted (be sure to include the drive and subdirectory, if appropriate), and for the name and location to which you want the Word document copied.

Once the parameters are set,

Type: RETURN

to start the conversion. If you want to stop the conversion while it is in progress, press CTRL-BREAK. This gives you an incomplete Word document.

The text conversion programs described previously can also be run using your Library Run utilities. The only restriction is that you can't convert a document you are currently editing.

CONVERTING FILES THROUGH INTERMEDIATE FORMATS

Intermediate formats were mentioned earlier but not explained. Since Word can only convert to ASCII or DCA formats for text, and from ASCII, DCA, or WordStar format, you only have a few document types that you can convert to or from. If you wanted to convert to or from MultiMate or Word Perfect, this couldn't be done directly. You would have to convert your files to a "language" that both programs understand.

For example, Word Perfect can convert to or from Revisable Form DCA or WordStar (in addition to other formats). Since Word Perfect documents can also be converted to RFDCA or WordStar, you can pass documents between the two word processing systems by converting to and from DCA or WordStar. Similarly, since MultiMate can also convert to and from DCA, you can use DCA as an intermediate format for conversion from MultiMate to Word, and vice versa. Although ASCII conversions may be easier than using intermediate formats, retaining formatting instructions is also quite important and certainly worth the trouble.

TRANSFERRING DATA

Data conversion—moving information from spreadsheets or data bases into or out of Word—is supported by Word. The basic conversion uses the program called Convert. Since there are many different formats and a wide range of parameters that you may apply to your data, it is probably best not to try to list any specific instructions. Rather, the information in the *Reference to Microsoft Word* provides instruction for a variety of formats and is a good reference.

Convertd asks you to define the format and style of the data you are converting from, and the format and style of the data that you are converting to. By completing the fairly lengthy setup screens, you can instruct this utility to produce accurate, usable transfers of data into and out of Word.

Telecommunicating Data Files

Data files may be either 7-bit or 8-bit files. Normally 8-bit files can't be telecommunicated. However, using XMODEM and other error-free protocols, you can easily (and usually without error) transfer any data file from one system to another.

As stated earlier, the XMODEM protocol is a standard feature on most telecommunications packages. These packages can run anywhere from $35 and up. You can also try communication packages such as "shareware," obtainable off many bulletin board systems. One of the best is *Procomm*.

Since Word is only one of many commonly used word processors (and should gain ground fast), you may occasionally (or frequently) need to transform a document in one format to one in another. Word provides you with the capability to perform a few of these transfers. In addition, with the use of transfer capabilities built into other word processors, and ASCII as a last resort, there should be few, if any, word processors that can't transfer files to or from Word. The transfer of data from databases and spreadsheets is relatively simple, although you must be specific about the formats for the transferred data. Once this is known, Word can interface with most commonly used database and spreadsheet programs.

DESKTOP PUBLISHING AND LASER PRINTERS

Microsoft Word is slightly ahead of its time. Although it competes head-to-head with other word processing programs, it isn't truly a word processor. It lacks certain features common to many other word processing programs. It doesn't provide a status line that informs you of the page, line, and column number of the cursor. The system doesn't automatically end one page and begin the next. The exact location of the cursor isn't visible while working with Word. In addition, you can't tell how many pages your document has until you repaginate it.

However, Microsoft Word is more than a word processing program. It is probably the first text processing program for the IBM PC and compatible computers. This program lets you mix varieties and qualities of type; switch from straight body type to bold, italic, or any combination of other character formats; print 24-point (1/5-inch high) letters on one line and 6-point (1/20-inch high) letters on the next; and automatically adjust spacing to provide the best-looking printed page. Word is an exceptional page or text processor, far superior to a mere word processor.

Until recently, with the advent of laser printers that print a page at a time (rather than the line at a time that most printers can handle), the advanced text-formatting features had to go virtually unused. However, with the price of laser printers dropping and availability increasing, Word is an excellent program for preparing near typeset-quality documents. Although the quality of text produced using laser printers is not as good as that produced by phototypesetting equipment, it is usually more than acceptable for internal manuals, internal corporate communications, and correspondence. The publications it is least suitable for are those with high-resolution requirements—magazines and books, for example.

In this chapter Word is explored as the page development system that it is, with particular emphasis on the Hewlett-Packard Laserjet printer and the Cordata laser printer. These two printers are currently among the most popular (and capable) laser printers. In addition, general instructions are given for other laser printers, as well as for the Qume LaserTen Plus printer. Combining Word with a well-designed laser printer can give your organization an acceptable desktop publishing system.

TYPESETTING PRINCIPLES FOR LASER PRINTERS

The field of typesetting evolved from hand-carved type to typed characters made out of lead, placed into a frame, and printed. Next, printing plates were made from these framed pages of text and the metal plates were used to print from. In the last decade or two, computer technology has been called on to set type using mechanical type pullers and placers and, more recently, to print an image of a character onto a sheet of photosensitive paper and make a metal plate from that printed photographic image.

Most recently, desktop systems have been developed that use the laser printer to print an image of each character onto a page. However, the laser printers, for the most part, haven't been able to produce the quality customarily expected of set type. Automation, however, has not eliminated the artistic aspect of typesetting. Instead of worrying about manually placing spaces between characters, words, or lines, the typesetter can instruct the automated system to insert a specified amount of space. Instead of moving text to fit around a graphic, the typesetter can instruct the system to leave space for a graphic. The choice of type sizes and styles is still (for the most part) made by the typesetter or by the person(s) commissioning the typesetting work. Page layout is still an art. And although Microsoft Word doesn't provide you with the same degree of flexibility in font selection or spacing that the computerized typesetters provide, you still can make a wide range of choices affecting the look of your finished document. Finally, the vocabulary of typesetting can also be used, to some degree, when working with Word.

Selecting Fonts

A *font* is a style of type. Old typewriters used to be able to print a single font, either Pica or Elite. There are only minor differences between the two. The first difference is the character width; Pica characters print 10 letters per inch and Elite characters print 12 letters per inch. The next major difference is that the characters look different — without measuring a character's width, it is easy to tell a Pica document from an Elite document. Both character types are about the same height, since they print on the same size line (1/6 inch). Finally, both types are known as type faces or fonts.

Depending upon the laser printer you use, you may have a wide variety of fonts to choose from. Figure 15-1 shows a list of the fonts that Word 3.0 supports for the Cordata laser printer. The Cordata laser printer works somewhat differently from the Hewlett-Packard Laserjet. The Cordata printer comes with a circuit board that is installed inside your computer system. This board acts as the interface between the computer and the printer. When you select a font, the instructions related to printing that font are read from your system disk and translated on the board, and the print instructions are sent to the printer.

The Laserjet printers work in a different way. These printers use a standard printer interface: the same serial or parallel interface you would connect to any other printer. Instead of using a board installed into the

```
COURR9 (modern a)        COURR10 (modern c)
GOTH6W (modern e)        GOTH9M (modern f)
GOTH9MR (modern g)       PC7 (modern h)
PCSS7 (modern i)         PCSS7R (modern j)
MX7 (modern k)           MX9 (modern l)
MX9M (modern m)          MX9W (modern o)
MX10 (roman a)           BKMAN9P (roman b)
BKMAN12P (roman e)       BKMAN18P (roman h)
BKMAN18T (roman i)       TAYL9 (roman j)
TAYL10 (roman l)         CASL10 (roman n)
SWIS10 (roman o)         SWIS12 (roman p)
SWIS14 (script a)        SWIS18B (script b)
SWIS180 (script c)       SWIS20D (script d)
BANK10 (script e)        PI10 (symbol a)
```

Figure 15-1.   The fonts that Word 3.0 supports for the Cordata laser printer

computer, the intelligence that produces the print is built into the printer itself. For this reason, you can easily hook one printer into more than one machine. However, in order to change fonts, you must use a special cartridge with the font data recorded onto it, or you must download the fonts from your computer into the printer. (Note that the standard Laserjet printer does not accept downloaded fonts. This printer only accepts font cartridges.)

Microsoft Word has included printer drivers for all the font cartridges available at the time Word was released. Each cartridge has special features — for example, proportional fonts only, line drawing characters, or different character sets. (Character sets may vary — for example, one set may support international characters, while a different set doesn't.)

When you are working with laser printers, you must be aware of font families. For example, the Cordata printer uses a family called Bookman, and the Laserjet uses one called Times Roman. In essence, one member of a family looks like any other member of the family except for special attributes. The most common attributes are size (these may range from around 6 points to 24 or more), weight (these may include normal weight or bold), slant (italic or regular), and spacing (some may be proportional, while others are standard spacing).

Each particular combination of attributes is often referred to as a separate font, although each is from the same family. Thus, a 12-point Bookman normal font is a separate font from a 12-point Bookman bold font. As far as your system is concerned, these are two distinct fonts.

NOTE: Microsoft Word allows you to use a variety of fonts within your document. This is useful if you want to make section or page headings stand out, or if you want to make a specific portion of text stand out from the rest. With this flexibility it may be somewhat tempting to mix a number of fonts. However, it is usually best only to use a single family of fonts within a page. That is, don't jump from Times Roman to Helvetica to Courier; it is better to use different-sized Times Roman than to make drastic changes in the look of your document.

Some experts suggest you use no more than three different fonts on a page. Although font mixing is tempting, if you overdo it, the results look awful. Feel free to experiment with mixing fonts — Microsoft Word lets you do this with relative ease — but always keep in mind that you want the end result to be attractive, professional looking, and easy to read. ■

Changing Fonts

If you use a Cordata laser printer, font changes are extremely simple. Once you have told the system you use a Cordata printer, the printer driver tells the system which fonts are available for you to use. The printer driver used for the Cordata printer is called CORONA.PRD. This file is included on your utility disk. It is probably easiest to copy the file from your disk onto the Word disk directory.

From the Print Options Menu, you can select the Corona printer driver. When you want to change a format for text, simply highlight the text you want changed and go to the Format Character Menu. At the bottom of the menu is the Font Name prompt. To see the available fonts, press RIGHT ARROW, or if you use the mouse, point to the Font Name prompt and press the right mouse button. The system then displays the menu of available fonts.

With the Cordata printer the size and quality of the font are already built into the font name. To enter the correct size information once you've selected a font, tab to the Font Size field and press RIGHT ARROW or, using the mouse, point to this field and press the right mouse button to see the size of your selected font. Next, press RETURN (or point to Format Character and press the right mouse button) to accept the format.

If you own a Laserjet printer, however, the situation is somewhat different. In this case each cartridge has its own printer definition file. Thus, to select a particular cartridge, you must know its number. Installing the appropriate printer driver for each cartridge loads the information needed to print using that file. For example, using the HPDWNSFP file, you can load all Portrait soft fonts. (Portrait and Landscape modes are explained in "Landscape and Portrait Modes" in this chapter.) When this printer driver is selected, you have three font families to select from, as shown in Figure 15-2. A number of sizes may be available for each family. Thus, when you

```
Courier (modern a)                         HELV (modern i)
TMSRMN (roman i)
```

Figure 15-2.   The three font families available when the HPDWNSFP file for the Laserjet printer is selected

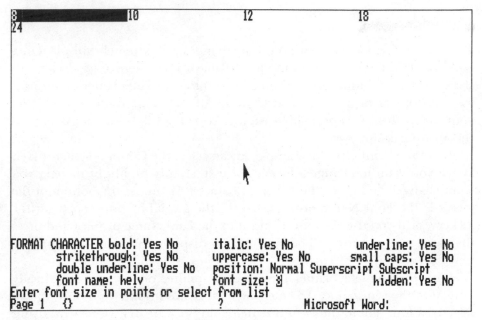

```
8      10              12              18
24




                        ▲




FORMAT CHARACTER bold: Yes No    italic: Yes No          underline: Yes No
     strikethrough: Yes No       uppercase: Yes No       small caps: Yes No
     double underline: Yes No    position: Normal Superscript Subscript
     font name: helv             font size: 8            hidden: Yes No
Enter font size in points or select from list
Page 1   {}                      ?               Microsoft Word:
```

Figure 15-3.   The range of sizes available when you select the HELV (modern i) font family

select HELV (modern i), for example, you have a range of choices for font size, as shown in Figure 15-3.

It should be noted here that Word will accept your codes for attributes that may not be available. For example, if you specify a 24-point Helvetica Bold, Word will allow you to make that selection. However, at print time the system may find that there is no font driver for that particular font. In that case the system will print 24-point Helvetica regular characters.

Microsoft Word allows you to use only one cartridge at a time when you are working with a document. This makes sense, since the Laserjet printer only uses one cartridge at a time. Thus, you must work within the limits of your selected cartridge when you are preparing a document to be printed using a Laserjet printer.

Specifying Line Spacing

With the wide range of font sizes available, you could specify a font taller than the normal height between lines. The system normally allows 12 points per line, so that a font larger than 12 points may actually be larger than the space between lines. Thus, it is a good practice to set the line spacing for any such lines to auto and to allow the system to adjust the spacing for any nonstandard height lines.

If you prefer, however, your line height can be specified in terms of points. Word uses the convention of 72 points per inch. Thus, if you wanted 1/4-inch spacing between lines, you would tell the system that your line spacing should be 18 points. These changes are made in the Format Paragraph Menu. This provides you with the flexibility of defining your line height to the nearest 72nd of an inch (or smaller, since the system also accepts decimal portions of a point). In fact, the resolution that Word allows is finer than that which most laser printers can produce.

Print Resolution

Most current generation laser printers can produce print made up of 300 dots per inch. That is, to fill a 1-inch square area, the laser printer prints 300 times 300 (90,000) dots. Characters are built from this matrix.

If you are able to merge graphics with text, the graphics will also be printed at 300 dots per inch. This resolution is better for smaller characters than for large ones. This is because as a character gets larger, it requires more dots to create its borders. As the number of dots increases, curves appear less smooth. Future printers may provide higher resolution than the current models. Using those printers, you may be able to prepare documents that look even better than those prepared on the current 300-dots-per-inch laser printers.

Landscape and Portrait Modes

If you already have a laser printer, you have undoubtedly run across the terms *landscape* and *portrait*. These relate to the orientation of text on the page. In Portrait mode text is printed with a normal page orientation. That is, the page is longer than it is wide. On an 8 1/2-by-11-inch sheet of paper, the text is printed on the narrow dimension. This orientation is similar to that used for portraits, which are often taller than they are wide.

In Landscape mode text is rotated 90 degrees. The printed page has the orientation of a landscape, with the page wider than it is high. Landscape mode is useful for printing envelopes. Most laser printers are unable to feed envelopes automatically; trying to stack envelopes into a printer's feed bin only results in jamming the printer. For this reason you must use the manual sheet feeder. For the same reason you must place the standard envelope sideways (butting it against the left side of the single sheet feeder). Thus, since the envelope goes in sideways, the address information must be printed vertically, not horizontally, employing the Landscape mode.

A second possible use for the Landscape mode is printing wide documents or spreadsheets. You can set Word to give you a wide page by going into the Format Division Menu. Before you print, however, you must tell the system that it should go into Landscape mode.

If you are using a Hewlett-Packard Laserjet printer, the system will automatically send the codes for Landscape mode when you select a Landscape font. However, with a Cordata printer, you must begin your document with the code for Landscape mode.

SENDING PRINTER CODES

The system conveys instructions to laser printers by means of special codes. The Laserjet printer, for example, uses what are known as *escape codes*. It is as if you pressed ESC and typed in special codes. The Cordata printer has a somewhat different format, using codes that you can easily enter from the keyboard.

Entering Codes for the Cordata Printer

The Cordata laser printer makes it very easy to instruct the system. The manual that came with your system provides you with all the required codes. As an example, you can demonstrate how to get the system to print multiple copies of your page(s) and how to put the system into Landscape mode. The command to print n copies of a page is @CC n; (where n is the number of copies you want printed). The system watches for the @ and ; key combination—it recognizes the code typed between the two symbols and carries out the instruction.

To enter the command to place the system into Landscape mode, type **@land;**. This is used with fonts whose driver numbers end with the letter r (for rotated).

As mentioned, these commands can be placed directly into your files, although it is best to place them at the beginning of a page or document. It is important to remember that (1) if you include these commands within a line of normal text, the system will execute the command but leave the line short because the space used for the command will not print, and (2) your system continues to carry out these commands until it is reset or a command is given to undo your change.

Word automatically handles most, if not all, text-formatting commands. It does not, however, send Landscape mode or multiple copy commands. If you want the system to print in either mode, you should place these commands at the beginning of the page where you want the attribute to take effect. Remember, however, that the line you use to type your commands will print as a blank line. If you don't want to change the spacing of your page and aren't changing your parameters after page one, it may be a good idea to place these commands into a header that prints only on the first page. This allows you to use a different header for all subsequent pages and forces the system to print with your selected attributes throughout the entire document.

Your printer manual also carries the commands necessary to draw lines and boxes. Using these commands, you may create boxes around your text, design special forms, or print borders around your pages. These line- and box-drawing commands should be placed at the top of the page, at the beginning of the document, at the end of a paragraph (where they won't affect the format of your text), or on their own line at the point where you want the box drawn. (Note that you can specify the boundaries of your box from anywhere on the page—the top of the page is as good a place as any.)

Entering Laserjet Commands

Laserjet commands are considerably different from those for the Cordata printer. In this case, you must send an escape code, followed by the appropriate codes necessary for your desired action. To send these characters to the printer, however, you must type in the ASCII equivalent of each code by pressing ALT and the appropriate number on the numeric keypad. For example, to send the code for ESC (ASCII 027), you would

Type: **ALT-027**

holding down ALT while typing in the numbers. This would place a left-facing arrow on your screen.

At print time the code for ESC would be sent to the printer and interpreted as if you just pressed ESC. The characters that follow the ESC character must also be entered in their ASCII form; press ALT and the keys on the numeric keypad. For example, the code for printing envelopes, ESC&l3h10, must be typed as follows (all codes entered with ALT held down): ALT-027 ALT-038 ALT-108 ALT-051 ALT-104 ALT-049 ALT-079. For convenience, you can enter this once and save it to your glossary.

To print multiple copies of the same page, use the code ESC&lnX, where *n* is the ASCII representation of the number of copies of the same page that you want printed. The code to be entered to tell the system to print 3 copies (3 is ASCII 051), is this: ALT-027 ALT-038 ALT-108 ALT-051 ALT-088. The *X* (ALT-088) tells the system that you are finished entering commands. Your Laserjet manual contains the codes needed to instruct your system to perform special functions.

TIP: If you save your command strings in the glossary, you will only have to enter them once — the first time you use them. Unlike the codes for the Cordata printer, you can place these codes for the Laserjet printer anywhere on the page, if you print or save them as hidden characters. If the laser printer commands are saved as hidden characters, the codes will be passed through to the laser printer even if you have set your system to hide hidden characters. Thus, you can insert your control codes within lines (or even between letters in a word, although this isn't advisable), and you will get normal printed text, as long as you reformat your page with the hidden characters hidden. ■

Printing Envelopes

Envelopes can be one of the more challenging types of documents to create using a laser printer. These are something of a challenge because you have to rotate the text and print it in a Landscape mode. Your company probably already has a printed return address. What you have to do, then, is figure out where on the page to start printing the address lines and type the codes to select the proper font and rotation.

The following procedure works well for the Cordata laser printer (and is the result of a fair amount of trial and error). Begin the envelope document. At the top of the document, type **@land;**RETURN. This shifts the system into Landscape mode. If you want to type a return address, space down 30 lines and begin typing the return address using the NEW LINE command (SHIFT-RETURN) to skip to the next line of the return address.

Once the return address is completed, move down approximately 12 more lines, to approximately 44 lines from the top of the page. Now, type in the address (or transfer it from another document). It is also best to use the NEW LINE command at the end of each line in the address. Highlight the address block, select Format Paragraph, and give the address line a 3.5-inch left margin.

Next, highlight the entire document (SHIFT-F10) and select Format Division Margins. Make the following settings: top and bottom margins, 1 inch; left margin, 6.2 inches; right margin, 0.1 inch; page length, 12 inches; page width, 16 inches. In the Format Character Menu, select Goth9MR as the type face. Although you also could have gone with PCSS7R, this is a 7-point font and too small for envelopes.

This should produce a satisfactory printed envelope. Unfortunately, there is no easy way to set up this format for a merged document; thus, if you have many letters to address, the best you can do is to split your window, with the envelope format in one window and the list of addressees in the other. Copying from the list of addressees and reformatting the address paragraph can produce a file that can be used for addressing envelopes. It is also useful to save your basic envelope format so that you can call it back onto the system whenever you need to address an envelope.

Printing envelopes with the Laserjet printer is relatively simple. After you've typed in the Laserjet escape codes given earlier for envelopes, and with your page still set to standard margins, enter enough RETURNs to bring the cursor down 35 lines. (This instruction assumes that you are not typing a return address.) Next, set a tab 5 inches from the left margin. Begin typing the address, tabbing to the 5-inch mark for each line. (If you prefer, you can type the address and then format the paragraph to use a 5-inch indent. Alternatively, you can add this paragraph to your style sheet and apply the style to the paragraph.) Also, apply a Landscape font to the entire envelope.

With either printer, you must use a single sheet feeder, located at the back of the printer. On the Cordata pull the paper tray out a few inches, enough to disengage the tray from its slot. This puts the system into manual feed mode. With the Laserjet printer put the printer into manual feed mode. For both printers, tell the system in the Print Options Menu that you are doing manual feed.

Tell the system to print your document. Insert your envelope into the manual feed tray at the back of the printer. To do this correctly, reach over the printer and slide the envelope so that the bottom of the envelope touches the left side of the feed slot. Push the envelope toward you until it stops. The flap of the envelope should be on the right side and facing down. You can, of course, go behind the printer to feed the envelopes, although it is usually more practical to lean over the machine. The printer then takes the envelope, prints it, and feeds the printed envelope out through the front of the printer.

USING OTHER PRINTERS

Microsoft Word supports a variety of laser printers. Generally, Word can produce all the required codes for page setup, formatting, and font selection. If you have downloadable fonts, it will also handle the downloading of these fonts to the printer. In general, if you have to send escape codes to the printer, these must be entered using the ALT-number key combination. An ASCII table can be found in Appendix B of this book. The required codes should be listed in the documentation that came with your printer.

Some laser printers come with *emulation* modes—that is, they act on the codes that normally control a different type of printer. For example, the Qume LaserTenPlus printer has a variety of emulation modules available. One such module, a Hewlett-Packard Laserjet emulation interface, accepts codes as if it were actually a Laserjet printer. Unfortunately, although it will accept formatting codes, it cannot upload Laserjet fonts, and font cartridges are not compatible with this printer. It is possible that some of the Qume font cartridges are compatible with the instructions for Laserjet fonts.

Another emulation option is the Qume11 emulation interface. In essence, you can use the Qume11 printer driver and operate this printer as if it were a Qume11. However, you would still need font cartridges to allow you to change fonts, and you would not have the control over character height and fine formatting within reach of most laser printers. At the time of this writing, there was no special printer driver for the Laser10 or Laser-TenPlus, and the existing interfaces didn't take full advantage of the printer's potential.

Other laser printers may fare approximately as well. Emulation of dot matrix or daisy wheel printers allows you to use the printer with standard printer drivers. However, special printer drivers are necessary to get full benefit from your printer.

A program included with Word, MAKEPRD.EXE, can be used to update or create printer drivers. However, the process is complicated and requires a great deal of patience and some trial and error. You should check with your software dealer or the dealer who sold you your printer to see if a printer driver has been written to support your laser printer. If not, a book explaining how to make a printer driver is available at no cost from Microsoft. Writing a printer driver should not be attempted by the faint-hearted—however, a well-written driver can increase the capability of your printer and the overall appearance of your documents.

PRINTING GRAPHICS WITH THE LASER PRINTER

One of the major advantages of using a laser printer, aside from the fast production of high-quality text, is the ability to merge text with graphics. Microsoft Word, in its current version, is not specifically designed to merge text and graphics. However, products under development will support the merger of print and graphics. One such program, Inset, from American Programmers Guild, allows you to capture any screen graphic, adjust its size, select any portion of the graphic, and merge the graphic into text. The program can print the graphic in Portrait or Landscape mode on Laserjet printers, in Epson mode on the Cordata printer (although the Cordata printer is not fully compatible with Inset), and in many other standard printer modes.

After a graphic has been captured and the name of the desired graphic typed onto your document and enclosed in brackets, a simple two-key combination tells you the size of your graphic and draws in the boundaries for the graphic. Thus, with little effort, you can merge graphics and text into your documents.

Slightly more difficult is a two-step process, where the graphic is printed first and measured. The document is then created with the necessary open "window," printed, and the graphic pasted to the page. Obviously, merging print and graphics in a single pass is more convenient.

PAGE DESCRIPTION LANGUAGES

With the increase in numbers and types of laser printers, it has become important to develop a standard way of describing a printed page. This description takes into account text formats, page formatting, and printed graphics. Two such "standards" are receiving a fair amount of attention.

They are called PageMaker and PostScript. Add-on boards are being marketed to make the Laserjet printer compatible with PageMaker commands.

It is probable that Microsoft Word may support one or both page description languages. In addition, PageMaker can already accept documents developed using Word. It is not clear whether it can accept merely ASCII characters or also can preserve much of the formatting and font information. Standards for page preparation are still being developed, and within the next few years, one or the other will become predominant.

While the laser printers do a good job, and undoubtedly, will do better print jobs, approaching typeset quality, they do not yet challenge the phototypesetter for print quality. The emerging standard page description languages can be made to interface with many of the most popular typesetting systems. Thus, moving a document from Word to a page description program can be a shortcut to producing true typeset documents.

A PRD file included with Word can be used by experienced programmers to develop an interface to a particular phototypesetter. This file is called MSPRINT. Using the MAKEPRD program, a programmer can modify MSPRINT to generate many of the codes required for addressing a phototypesetter.

Word will not replace phototypesetters for some time, since Word currently lacks the ability to make the very fine adjustments of space between words and letters (em and en spaces) that phototypesetters can do. Even without these capabilities, however, such a document should still look very professional.

NOTE: There is one final consideration. You must decide if you really want your letters to look typeset. This may not always be appropriate for a particular mailing. The author ran into this problem years ago, when he owned a word processing service bureau. The equipment then being used was able to print right-justified text and could produce letter-quality print that included special features such as bold print, shadow printing, and double underlines. At the time it was felt that such letters looked professional.

In some cases, however, these slick-looking letters were not received well. People expected to receive letters that looked typed rather than word processed. The fancy formatting modifications possible with a word processor marked those letters as somewhat different, and they weren't always treated with the same interest or respect as the old ragged margin page produced by a typewriter.

Today, using Word and a laser printer, you are capable of producing excellent-looking letters. However, people may still be used to receiving typed letters. In fact, with so much computer-generated junk mail floating around, a letter that looks as if it were actually typed (using a Letter Gothic or Courier font) may actually be looked on as more important than one carefully prepared using Word and a laser printer.

Before you apply the full formatting power of Word to your documents, you should be careful to evaluate which format would be best received by the recipient of your mailing. In the example given here, letters may be most effective if prepared unjustified, lacking special fonts and font characteristics (other than underline and super- or subscripts, which are available on a typewriter), and in a typewriter-like font. For company documentation — news, prospectuses, special reports, and so on — the full power of Microsoft Word is most appropriate. ■

LASER PRINTER UTILITIES AND EXTRA FONTS

With the development of relatively inexpensive laser printers, a new industry has sprung up to support these capable, flexible devices. This industry has improved performance and made it easier to communicate with the printers or to add more printable fonts to those provided by the printer manufacturers.

Cordata Utilities

The Cordata laser printer is in some ways more capable than the Laserjet printer. This is particularly so in the area of font selection. With the Cordata printer, you must specify the name of the font you want to use; the system finds the font characteristics and sends them to the printer. This is much faster than the similar process for the Laserjet, which takes a few minutes to send a downloadable font to the printer. You can, for instance, print a page with many different fonts much more rapidly on a Cordata printer than on a Laserjet printer.

It is perhaps for this reason that the only enhancement products currently available for the Cordata printer are additional fonts. Cordata and other companies currently have a wide range of fonts available for printing with the Cordata printer. The Cordata-supplied fonts include Text, a font that resembles Times Roman; Swiss, a more complete family than that provided with the printer, resembling Helvetica; Karena; and Momento. Each set of fonts carries a list price of $95 and is available from many dealers and from Cordata.

In addition, VideoSoft Software sells over 200 fonts for the Cordata printer. Its address is 2101 S. Broadway, Little Rock, AK 72206. Another company, Micro Prind-X, has 178 fonts available. Its address is P.O. Box 581, Ballinger, TX 76821. Cordata's technical reference department may be able to provide you with a current list of names of font vendors. Currently, one disadvantage to using these fonts with Word is that in many cases you must write your own PRD file to describe the fonts to your system.

Utilities for Laserjet and Other Printers

Fancy Word, from SoftCraft, is a program designed to work specifically with Microsoft Word. Using this program, you can create special print effects, print special fonts, print logos, and adjust kerning (the space between adjacent letters).

Even with the standard Laserjet printer, you can print these special fonts. The system sends the data to produce each letter dot by dot. A document prepared and printed using Fancy Word will more closely approximate typeset quality than one prepared without it. This is available for the Hewlett-Packard Laserjet, Laserjet PLUS, and Laserjet 500 printers, the Canon laser printers, the NCR laser printer, and other printers with download font capabilities, although it works best on Laserjet printers.

Another program, EFONT, allows you to create your own font characters or special characters. This may be useful for creating logos or for a unique type style that enhances company identity. Fancy Font, also available for those printers listed previously (except the Laserjet, which doesn't accept downloadable fonts), is a selection of additional fonts for the Laserjet printer and Word. These fonts come with a printer definition file, making it easy to select the driver for these fonts and use the fonts for creating documents. In addition, SoftCraft has a wide range of other fonts available for purchase. SoftCraft's address is 222 State Street, Madison, WI 53703.

USING WORD ON A NETWORK

Networks are seeing increasing use in many offices. They provide a number of advantages to the user. One of the primary advantages is cost savings. Using a network, any computer connected to the network can share devices that may otherwise be prohibitively expensive. For example, many users can share the resources of a high-capacity hard disk unit. Expensive laser printers can be pushed to maximum capacity when they are shared between users on a network. Thus, the cost of devices that increase the performance or power of a main system can be divided among all the users on a network.

Another advantage is the ability to communicate between network users. Depending upon the network, it may be possible for a person on one node (a unit in a network) to communicate with any other user. This may save a great deal of disk swapping and running around in an office. In addition, if a large storage device is shared among users, any user can have access to a main database (if this is permitted by the network administrator).

NETWORK ARCHITECTURE

Networks have been developed in many different topologies. However, certain features are common to all networks. One system is usually dedicated to controlling the operation of the network. This unit often acts as a traffic cop, coordinating communication between itself and all the other units in the network. This central unit is referred to as the *server*. The person who controls the unit is sometimes referred to as the *network administrator*. This person often decides how the server is to be implemented: who can get access to which files and directories. This person controls much of the functioning of the network.

The units connected to the server are called *nodes*. In the past these nodes were occupied by separate terminals—in effect, a monitor and keyboard, with little or no intelligence attached to them. However, more recently PCs and IBM-compatible computers have been implemented as nodes. These computers can use their onboard intelligence and storage capacity in addition to acting as a node on the network.

A number of features are often optional on most networks. File locking is a process whereby a file can only be accessed by one node at a time. In other words, if one person is working on a particular document, nobody on any of the other nodes can have access to that file until the operator working on it is finished.

This has its advantages and disadvantages. Although it protects a file from being changed by more than one person at a time (and reduces the possibility of someone undoing editing changes as soon as they are done), there may be times when you want to have more than one person working on the same file. For example, if you have a rush deadline to edit and print a large document, it may be valuable to split that document into smaller parts and assign parts of that document to people on many different nodes. Thus, the effort of four or five people on the same document may result in a document completed in one-fifth the amount of time.

Controlled access is another common feature. It allows private subdirectories to be placed on the server disk (or the node disk). The files in these private directories can only be accessed from the node to which they belong. In effect, these files are protected from intrusion by others on the network. In some cases a password may be required to gain access to these protected files.

WORD ON A NETWORK

You should not use the standard version of Microsoft Word on a network. First, this violates your license from Microsoft for a single copy of Word. Second, Word automatically saves certain configuration information each time you quit a Word session. Such information as the name of the last document edited, the colors you set up on the screen, the default style sheets and glossary, and other items are stored when you exit the system and reloaded when you reenter the system. Thus, with multiple users, each having varied requirements, the customization that fitted the program to the user would probably be lost.

Special versions of Word for use on networks are available for Microsoft Word versions 2.0 and 3.0. These versions are compatible with any network that supports the functions of DOS 3.1 or later. Specific implementations depend to a large degree on the way the network administrator sets up the network.

The networked version is slightly different from the single-user version. In the networked version the main program resides on the server, while the configuration (or customization) files are located on each node's unique subdirectory. Thus, any time a user on a particular node enters or exits the system, the program is set to suit that user's needs and settings. The effect for the node user is somewhat obvious: Word on a network then behaves almost exactly like the single-user version.

Although the two versions (2.0 and 3.0) are marketed slightly differently, their performance on networks is almost as good as that of single-user systems. The main limitations may be a result of the networks themselves: such things as memory limits can limit system functionality; demand on the server may slow system response; and other network settings may reduce access to other files. However, the cost savings that can result from sharing of peripherals and storage devices and the potential benefits of being able to share files from other nodes can make the use of Word on a network very worthwhile.

USING WORD WITH MICROSOFT WINDOWS

Microsoft Word is just one of many programs available from Microsoft. Another program gaining increasing popularity is Microsoft Windows. Windows is a program that acts as an interface between the computer user and the operating system. Using Windows, you can select a variety of programs you want to run, and Windows will automatically load them. In some applications you may be able to have many windows working on screen at once. Using Windows, you can jump from application to application and even copy the contents of one window into another.

As it is implemented on a standard PC-compatible computer, however, Windows uses a lot of memory and functions rather slowly. These limitations prevent you from using many large programs at the same time. If you have a memory expansion device, you may be able to load Windows and Word from a RAM disk. After transferring your program files to the RAM disk (actually an area of memory), you can run the programs from the RAM disk. This speeds up the performance of Word and Windows.

If you have an accelerator card, this may also speed up the performance of Windows. The Mach10 board, available from Microsoft, improves the system's handling of graphics and makes Windows perform considerably faster. If you have a so-called Turbo computer, you may also enjoy more rapid response from Windows. Finally, if you have an AT or AT-compatible computer, Windows runs faster, due to this computer's faster clock.

A program may or may not be compatible with Windows. A program compatible with Windows can occupy a window on the screen — it can be opened and closed or saved in an area at the bottom of the screen. In general, a compatible program can take advantage of many or all of the features of Windows. Microsoft Word is not compatible with Windows. Instead, you can run Word as a stand-alone program, just as it would run if you had typed the normal WORD command to load it. This program takes control of the entire screen. Only after you exit from Word can you return to Windows. Thus, there are few advantages to loading Word from Windows.

In fact, there are some disadvantages. First, if your system isn't fully loaded (to 640 kilobytes of memory), you may run dangerously close to the upper limits of memory when you load Word from Windows. The more memory you have available, the faster the system will respond when you are using Word. Second, when you load Word from Windows, the system normally loads the program with the standard default settings and brings you into graphics mode. If you wanted character or Hercules mode, you would have to change the PIF program that loads Word.

The PIF program is used to load Word (or any other software package). This program carries information about the name of the program you want to load, the location on your directory or subdirectory, and other configuration information. Although you can alter your PIF to instruct the system to load Word with a somewhat different configuration, this still is an inflexible way of getting into and out of Word. To load Word using Windows, select the PIF option on your screen. Next, move the mouse pointer to WORD or WORDEGA, depending upon your computer's graphics capabilities, and click the right mouse button.

The ALT-TAB combination can be used to move from Word to Windows and back, but this is not always satisfactory. For example, if you are using Word in a character mode, you can jump to Windows. When you go back to Word, your screen may appear garbled or unreadable, since you may have been editing in one mode and then returned to the program in another graphics mode. In general, then, although you can use Word when running Windows, it is probably best to run Word from the DOS level.

ASCII AND EXTENDED
ASCII CHARACTER SETS

LETTER CODES

Code	Character	Code	Character	Code	Character	Code	Character
0	(null)	15	✳	30	▲	45	-
1	☺	16	▶	31	(reserved)	46	.
2	☻	17	◀	32	(space)	47	/
3	♥	18	↕	33	!	48	0
4	♦	19	‼	34	"	49	1
5	♣	20	¶	35	#	50	2
6	♠	21	§	36	$	51	3
7	•	22	▪	37	%	52	4
8	◘	23	↨	38	&	53	5
9	(tab)	24	↑	39	'	54	6
10	(paragraph)	25	↓	40	(	55	7
11	(new line)	26	→	41	)	56	8
12	(new page)	27	←	42	*	57	9
13	(reserved)	28	∟	43	+	58	:
14	♫	29	↔	44	,	59	;

Reprinted by permission of Microsoft, Inc.

LETTER CODES

Code	Character	Code	Character	Code	Character	Code	Character
60	‹	90	Z	120	x	150	û
61	=	91	[	121	y	151	ù
62	›	92	\	122	z	152	ÿ
63	?	93	]	123	{	153	ö
64	@	94	^	124	¦	154	ü
65	A	95	_	125	}	155	¢
66	B	96	`	126	~	156	£
67	C	97	a	127	Δ	157	¥
68	D	98	b	128	ç	158	₧
69	E	99	c	129	ü	159	ƒ
70	F	100	d	130	é	160	á
71	G	101	e	131	â	161	í
72	H	102	f	132	ä	162	ó
73	I	103	g	133	à	163	ú
74	J	104	h	134	å	164	ñ
75	K	105	i	135	ç	165	Ñ
76	L	106	j	136	ê	166	ª
77	M	107	k	137	ë	167	º
78	N	108	l	138	è	168	¿
79	O	109	м	139	ï	169	⌐
80	P	110	n	140	î	170	¬
81	Q	111	o	141	ì	171	½
82	R	112	p	142	Ä	172	¼
83	S	113	q	143	Å	173	¡
84	T	114	r	144	É	174	«
85	U	115	s	145	æ	175	»
86	V	116	t	146	Æ		
87	W	117	u	147	ô		
88	X	118	v	148	ö		
89	Y	119	w	149	ò		

GRAPHICS

Code	Character	Code	Character	Code	Character	Code	Character
176	░	188	╝	200	╚	212	╘
177	▒	189	╜	201	╔	213	╒
178	▓	190	╛	202	╩	214	╓
179	│	191	┐	203	╦	215	╫
180	┤	192	└	204	╠	216	╪
181	╡	193	┴	205	═	217	┘
182	╢	194	┬	206	╬	218	┌
183	╖	195	├	207	╧	219	█
184	╕	196	─	208	╨	220	▄
185	╣	197	┼	209	╤	221	▌
186	║	198	╞	210	╥	222	▐
187	╗	199	╟	211	╙	223	▀

MATHEMATICAL SYMBOLS

224	α	232	Φ	240	≡	248	°
225	β	233	Θ	241	±	249	·
226	Γ	234	Ω	242	≥	250	.
227	π	235	δ	243	≤	251	√
228	Σ	236	∞	244	⌠	252	^{n}
229	σ	237	φ	245	⌡	253	^{2}
230	μ	238	ε	246	÷	254	■
231	τ	239	∩	247	≈	255	(reserved)

KEYBOARD COMMANDS

Keyboard by Actions

For	Press
New paragraph	ENTER
New line	SHIFT-ENTER
New page	Ctrl-SHIFT-ENTER
New division	Ctrl-ENTER
Optional hyphen	Ctrl-–
Nonbreaking hyphen	Ctrl-SHIFT-–
Nonbreaking space	Ctrl-spacebar

To select	Press
Up	↑
Down	↓
Left	←
Right	→
Beginning of line	Home
End of line	End
Top of window	Ctrl-Home

Reprinted by permission of Microsoft, Inc.

Bottom of window	Ctrl-End
Next window	F1
Previous window	SHIFT-F1
Extend selection key on/off	F6
Column selection on/off	SHIFT-F6
Word left	F7
Previous sentence	SHIFT-F7
Word right	F8
Next sentence	SHIFT-F8
Sentence	F9
Line	SHIFT-F9
Next paragraph	F10
Whole document	SHIFT-F10

To scroll	Press
Up in document	PgUp
Down in document	PgDn
Start of document	Ctrl-PgUp
End of document	Ctrl-PgDn
Left	Ctrl- ←
Right	Ctrl- →
Up one line	Turn on Scroll Lock, then press ↑
Down one line	Turn on Scroll Lock, then press ↓
Left 1/3 of window	Turn on Scroll Lock, then press ←
Right 1/3 of window	Turn on Scroll Lock, then press →

To	Press
Erase to the left	BACKSPACE
Erase selection to scrap	Del
Erase selection, not to scrap	SHIFT-Del

Insert scrap directly before highlight	Ins
Insert scrap to replace selection	SHIFT-Ins
Calculate	F2
Turn outline view on/off	SHIFT-F2
Expand glossary name	F3
Turn overtype on/off	F5

To choose commands	Press
Move right in a menu	spacebar
Move left in a menu	BACKSPACE
Move to next field	TAB
Move to previous field	SHIFT-TAB
Repeat last edit action	F4
Repeat Search command	SHIFT-F4
Carry out command	ENTER
Cancel command	Esc
Help	Alt-h

To edit responses	Press
Word left	F7
Word right	F8
Character left	F9
Character right	F10
Erase to the left	BACKSPACE
Erase highlighted part of response	Del

To format character	Press with Alt (after Alt-x if style sheet)
Bold	b
Double underline	d
Hidden text	e

Italic	i
Small caps	k
Strikethrough	s
Underline	u
Superscript	+ or =
Subscript	—
Standard character	spacebar

To format paragraph	Press with Alt (after Alt-x if style sheet)
Centered	c
Indent first line 1/2″	f
Justified	j
Left aligned	l
Reduce left indent 1/2″	m
Widen left indent 1/2″	n
Open paragraph spacing	o
Standard paragraph	p
Right aligned	r
Widen hanging indent 1/2″ + tab	t
Double space lines	2

Outline view: text edit and outline edit	Press
Switch between outline view and document view	SHIFT-F2
Switch between outline edit and text edit (after switching to outline view)	SHIFT-F5
Lower heading level	Alt-0 (zero)
Raise heading level	Alt-9
Collapse headings	− (on keypad)
Expand headings	+ (on keypad)
Expand all headings	* (on keypad)
Collapse body text	SHIFT-− (minus on keypad)
Expand body text	SHIFT-+ (plus on keypad)

Outline view: outline edit only	Press
Select previous heading at same level	↑
Select next heading at same level	↓
Select previous heading regardless of level	←
Select next heading regardless of level	→
Select nearest heading at next higher level	Home
Select last heading at next lower level	End

Keyboard by Keys

Key	Action
↑	Select character one line up
↑ (with Scroll Lock on)	Scroll up one line
↓	Select character one line down
↓ (with Scroll Lock on)	Scroll down one line
←	Select character to the left
← (with Ctrl)	Scroll left one windowful
← (with Scroll Lock on)	Scroll left 1/3 of window
→	Select character to the right
→ (with Ctrl)	Scroll right one windowful
→ (with Scroll Lock on)	Scroll right 1/3 of window
↑ (outline edit)	Select previous heading at same level
↓ (outline edit)	Select next heading at same level
← (outline edit)	Select previous heading regardless of level
→ (outline edit)	Select next heading regardless of level
– (with Ctrl)	Optional hyphen
– (with Ctrl-SHIFT)	Nonbreaking hyphen
– on keypad (outline view)	Collapse heading

Key	Action
+ on keypad (outline view)	Expand heading
SHIFT-− (keypad) (outline view)	Collapse body text
SHIFT-+ (keypad) (outline view)	Expand body text
* (on keypad) (outline view)	Expand all headings
Alt-−	Subscript
Alt-+ or Alt-=	Superscript
Alt-b	Bold
Alt-c	Centered
Alt-d	Double underline
Alt-e	Hidden text
Alt-f	Indent first line 1/2″
Alt-h	Help
Alt-i	Italic
Alt-j	Justified
Alt-k	Small caps
Alt-l	Left align
Alt-m	Reduce left indent 1/2″
Alt-n	Widen left indent 1/2″
Alt-o	Open paragraph spacing
Alt-p	Standard paragraph format
Alt-r	Right align
Alt-s	Strikethrough
Alt-spacebar	Standard character format
Alt-t	Widen hanging indent 1/2″ + tab
Alt-u	Underline
Alt-x	Precedes format keys if style sheet
Alt-2	Double space lines
Alt-9 (outline view)	Raise heading one level
Alt-0 (outline view)	Lower heading one level

Key	Action
b (with Alt)	Bold
BACKSPACE	Erase to the left
BACKSPACE	Erase to the left (in responses)
BACKSPACE	Move left in a menu
c (with Alt)	Centered
Ctrl-←	Scroll left one windowful
Ctrl-→	Scroll right one windowful
Ctrl-—	Optional hyphen
Ctrl-SHIFT-—	Nonbreaking hyphen
Ctrl-End	Bottom of window
Ctrl-ENTER	New division
Ctrl-Home	Top of window
Ctrl-PgDn	End of document
Ctrl-PgUp	Start of document
Ctrl-SHIFT-ENTER	New page
Ctrl-spacebar	Nonbreaking space
d (with Alt)	Double underline
Del	Erase to scrap
Del	Erase highlighted part of response
Del (with SHIFT)	Erase, not to scrap
e (with Alt)	Hidden text
End	End of line
End (outline edit)	Select last heading on next lower level
End (with Ctrl)	Bottom of window
ENTER	New paragraph
ENTER	Carry out command
ENTER (with Ctrl)	New division
ENTER (with Ctrl-SHIFT)	New page
ENTER (with SHIFT)	New line
Esc	Cancel command
f (with Alt)	Indent first line 1/2"
F1	Next window

Key	Action
F1 (with SHIFT)	Previous window
F2	Calculate
F2 (with SHIFT)	Outline view on/off
F3	Expand glossary name
F4	Repeat last edit action
F4 (with SHIFT)	Repeat Search command
F5	Overtype on/off
F5 (with SHIFT)	Outline edit on/off
F6	Extend selection on/off
F6 (with SHIFT)	Column selection on/off
F7	Select word left
F7	Word left (in responses)
F7 (with SHIFT)	Select previous sentence
F8	Select word right
F8	Word right (in responses)
F8 (with SHIFT)	Select next sentence
F9	Select sentence
F9	Character left (in responses)
F9 (with SHIFT)	Select line
F10	Select next paragraph
F10	Character right (in responses)
F10 (with SHIFT)	Select whole document
h (with Alt)	Help
Home	Beginning of line
Home (outline edit)	Select nearest heading one level higher
Home (with Ctrl)	Top of window
i (with Alt)	Italic
Ins	Insert scrap
Ins (with SHIFT)	Insert scrap to replace selection
j (with Alt)	Justified
k (with Alt)	Small caps
l (with Alt)	Left align
m (with Alt)	Reduce left indent 1/2″

Key	Action
n (with Alt)	Widen left indent 1/2″
o (with Alt)	Open paragraph spacing
p (with Alt)	Standard paragraph format
PgDn	Scroll down in document one windowful
PgDn (with Ctrl)	End of document
PgUp	Scroll up in document one windowful
PgUp (with Ctrl)	Start of document
r (with Alt)	Right align
s (with Alt)	Strikethrough
(Scroll Lock on) ↑	Scroll up one line
(Scroll Lock on) ↓	Scroll down one line
(Scroll Lock on) ←	Scroll left 1/3 of window
(Scroll Lock on) →	Scroll right 1/3 of window
SHIFT-Del	Erase, not to scrap
SHIFT-ENTER	New line
SHIFT-ENTER (with Ctrl)	New page
SHIFT-F1	Previous window
SHIFT-F2	Outline view on/off
SHIFT-F4	Repeat Search command
SHIFT-F5	Outline edit on/off
SHIFT-F6	Column selection on/off
SHIFT-F7	Select previous sentence
SHIFT-F8	Select next sentence
SHIFT-F9	Select line
SHIFT-F10	Select whole document
SHIFT-Ins	Insert scrap to replace selection
SHIFT-TAB	Move to previous field
SHIFT-− (with Ctrl)	Nonbreaking hyphen
SHIFT-− (keypad) (outline view)	Collapse body text
SHIFT-+ (keypad) (outline view)	Expand body text
spacebar	Insert regular space

Key	Action
spacebar	Move right in a menu
spacebar (with Alt)	Standard character
spacebar (with Ctrl)	Nonbreaking space
t (with Alt)	Widen hanging indent 1/2″ + tab
TAB	Insert tab character
TAB	Move to next field
TAB (with SHIFT)	Move to previous field
u (with Alt)	Underline
x (with Alt)	Precedes format keys if style sheet
2 (with Alt)	Double space lines
9 (with Alt) (outline view)	Raise heading one level
0 (with Alt) (outline view)	Lower heading one level

INPUT DEVICES AND UTILITY PROGRAMS

If you've been using Microsoft Word for very long, you may also use a Microsoft Mouse. This device has gone through a number of changes and improvements through the years. For example, the newest models are far more sensitive than their predecessors. This is useful, since you no longer have to drag the mouse as far as you used to when you want to highlight text or move from one place on the screen to another.

The mouse has always been available in two versions: a bus mouse and a serial mouse. The basic differences between the two were that the bus mouse was attached directly to a circuit board included with the mouse, may have been slightly faster than the serial mouse, and didn't use up a serial port in your computer. The serial mouse easily attached to the serial port and didn't require that an extra card be installed in your computer. Thus, the question of which mouse to use related to which was needed more, an extra serial port or an extra card slot.

A new bus mouse is included with Microsoft's Mach10 board — a circuit board that speeds up the operation of Microsoft Windows and other programs. This mouse is probably the best one yet offered by Microsoft. However, the basic design of the Microsoft Mouse has some minor drawbacks. Since the mouse is actually a box with some sensors that sense the movement of a ball (and, thus, a mechanical device), the space between the ball and the housing may tend to pick up dirt and dust and, after a while, may end up getting clogged and requiring cleaning. Additionally, since this mouse is mechanical, there are parts that could possibly wear out with enough use. Also, you need to have enough clear space on your desk to make moving the mouse easy and effective.

POINTING DEVICES

The Microsoft Mouse is not the only mouse that can be used to run Word. For example, the optical mouse from Mouse Systems is often used with Word and many graphics programs. This device uses a light source, light sensors, and a special, ruled reflective pad to detect motion of the mouse. The only moving parts are the button switches on top of the mouse. Mouse Systems claims that this mouse can greatly outlast a mechanical mouse. Perhaps the greatest drawbacks to this type of mouse are that (1) it is only available as a serial device; (2) it must be plugged into a power source; and (3) the reflective pad is small, sometimes necessitating a few passes over the pad to accomplish much cursor movement.

Although other mice are available from other manufacturers and vendors, not all are compatible with Microsoft Word. If you can, try the mouse at the store, in conjunction with Word, before you purchase either product (Word or the mouse).

A variation on the mouse is the trackball. A trackball is basically a mouse turned on its back. The ball is located on top of the device. Moving the ball with your hand moves the cursor on the screen. Buttons placed near the ball are used to send the same signals that similarly placed buttons do on a mouse. One such device is MicroLynx, from Honeywell. This device plugs into the keyboard connector for your computer (instead of using a bus or serial port). The main advantage of using this product is that you don't have to clear nearly as much desk space to use it. Simply locating it near the keyboard and leaving it there is all you need to do to have it available to move the cursor. Since a sample was not available at the time of this writing, it is unclear whether the buttons actually perform the same function as mouse buttons. Since the signal goes through the keyboard, instead of through a serial or bus connection, it is possible that the key functions may not operate properly.

Finally, light pens are currently increasing in popularity. With a light pen you point at the place on the screen where you want to make a move or change and press a button. However, with Word, you often have to press and hold one of two (or both) buttons. Therefore, light pens are probably not compatible with Microsoft Word.

KEYPORT 60 AND KEYPORT 300

KEYPORT products from Polytel Computer Products Corporation are interesting input devices. The KEYPORT 300 is a touch-sensitive tablet with 300 sensitive surfaces. Each surface can be encoded to generate any desired string of characters. Similarly, the KEYPORT 60 has sixty touch-sensitive surfaces. The KEYPORT hooks into your computer's game port and interacts with your computer through that game port.

The KEYPORT has two basic uses with Microsoft Word. The first important one is as an alternate input device. For example, arrows on the tablet can move the cursor as if you were sliding the mouse in the desired direction (or pressing the appropriate cursor movement keys). You can also design the key overlays to automatically bring you into any of the command menus. Thus, if you wanted to perform a Transfer Load, you would only have to touch one area, and you would quickly go to the Transfer Load Menu. (When you pressed the key, the KEYPORT operating system would send the codes for ESC-T-L.) Having the functions conveniently placed on dedicated keys can speed the operation and learning of Word.

The second use may be more important. Each of the KEYPORT's 300 (or 60) surfaces can be defined to contain any text that you desire. Thus, you may be able to load your entire glossary onto the KEYPORT. Pressing a button can then insert boilerplate, commands, or any other desired text directly into your document.

The surfaces on both the KEYPORT 60 and KEYPORT 300 can be redefined whenever necessary. In addition, special KEYPORT files and overlays can be created and saved. Thus, you may develop a billing overlay, a legal overlay, and a personnel overlay that you load before writing a document.

THE CAUZIN STRIPREADER

The newest input device applicable to Microsoft Word is the Cauzin Softstrip reader from Cauzin Systems. The stripreader, a cylindrical tube about 15 inches long, reads a highly compressed bar code strip and enters the data through your system's serial port. Although applications are still being developed for the stripreader and the number of prerecorded strips available is still very limited, this device has potential in a number of areas relevant to Microsoft Word.

The greatest potential is as a medium for document exchange. The fastest way to send a document from one computer to another is through a communications program and a modem. Lacking these products, however, you normally have to resort to using a printout of a document or a copy of the document on a floppy disk. Transporting the disk is somewhat risky, because the disk is prone to damage during shipment. Using a special program, your documents can be printed in the form of strips that can be photocopied and mailed or expressed virtually anywhere. The strips are less expensive and more sturdy than floppy disks. In addition, they may also be copy protected, so that your files cannot be freely distributed.

This medium is ideal in a company where price lists or other input-intensive materials must be distributed to many users. Updates of Word, as well as printer drivers, can be converted to Word and distributed throughout an installation (so long as no copyright or license is violated). The cost to the organization is for photocopies (usually pennies a copy), as compared to the cost of floppy disk duplication and distribution (from 30 cents up). Although the technology is proven, its acceptance is just beginning at the time of this writing. With proper internal planning, use of software strips and readers can become widespread and worthwhile to the organization.

UTILITIES AND ENHANCEMENT PROGRAMS

Microsoft Word is an excellent word processing program. However, once you are in this program, it is difficult to do anything other than word processing. Although it is possible to do a Library Run for access to another program, it may be more convenient to be able to quickly check a calendar, time a phone call, or take notes without opening a new window.

A wide variety of memory-resident programs can be used to assist you in making Word more functional. Popular Programs' Pop-Ups, Borland's SideKick, and many other programs can provide special functions while running Word. You should be careful to try the programs on a system that uses Word to make sure they are compatible with Word. Some programs interrupt the screen drivers or do other things that may affect the display of Word text, make it difficult to jump back into Word, and, at worst, cause Word to lock up. Therefore, it is important to make certain that any resident program does work with Microsoft Word. The Microsoft product support technicians often maintain a list of memory-resident programs and a list of compatibility problems.

The Word Finder Thesaurus

Microsoft Word provides you with a very powerful spelling checker, a word counter, and other useful verbal utilities. One that it lacks is a thesaurus. Although many people go through life without using a thesaurus, it is a useful reference for finding synonyms for potentially overused words. One of the most popular, Word Finder, is a memory-resident utility that can be called up to check a word whenever you need it. The package has been well received by reviewers. However, at the time of this writing, its compatibility with Word hasn't been verified.

Font Programs

With the increasing number of laser printers, the need for font variety will also increase. A number of font vendors and programs specific to laser printers were discussed in Chapter 16. In addition to the laser font programs, other programs can provide additional fonts using other printers. For instance, Fancy Word, from SoftCraft, provides the Word user with the ability to print fonts that are very near letter quality, in addition to other decorative fonts not included with the printer.

A number of public domain utilities are also available to improve the look of dot matrix text. These programs are inexpensive (some are free), and the most popular line of printers these programs have been developed for is the Epson. Finally, a special formatting program designed exclusively for screenwriters is Scriptor, from Screenplay Systems. This package takes a screenplay prepared with Word and puts it into standard format for screenplays. Although many of the necessary formatting functions can be done by an experienced Word user using Word alone, many professional writers consider Scriptor to be an essential tool of the trade.

THESAURUS FOR MICROSOFT WORD VERSION 3.1 AND LATER

A thesaurus can be very useful. Using a thesaurus, you can look up a word you have used too often and find other words that can be used as approximate substitutes. Beginning with version 3.1, Microsoft Word incorporated a thesaurus into the word processing package. This new feature is very simple to use.

Move the cursor to the beginning of the word that you want to look up in the thesaurus and

Type: CTRL-F6

If you are running Microsoft Word on a hard-disk system, the word you want the system to check will appear on the screen along with a number of other words that can be substituted for it. If you are using a floppy-disk system, you will be prompted to insert your Thesaurus disk. After searching the word lists it contains for the word you want, you will see the screen described above.

Using your mouse or arrow keys, select the word that you want to use as a substitute for your original word. Press the RETURN key to accept the word, and it will replace the original word where the cursor was positioned in your document.

Of course, many words have a variety of usages or meanings. The thesaurus included with this package cannot tell which usage you intend. Therefore, your choices will often be labeled with information about what part of speech they can properly replace.

While it is not good style to use the same word over and over, overuse of the thesaurus can also be bad, since you may sacrifice clarity by using obscure words just to avoid repetition. Also, words that have similar meanings may have nuances that make interchanging them inappropriate. For example, if you look up the word *angry* you will probably come up with substitute words that cover a range of negative emotions, some of which may not always apply. Obviously, not all words that the thesaurus brings up as *possible* replacements will be *suitable* replacements.

At the time of this writing the thesaurus has not yet been released. Two additional features will probably be included in the final product. It is likely that you will be able to use the mouse to highlight a desired word, and that using the right mouse button will cause the system to make the word replacement. It is also likely that, if you choose not to make a replacement, pressing ESC or simultaneously pressing both mouse buttons will get you out of the Thesaurus screen and return you to your original document.

Check your operator's manual for more information on these features.

TRADEMARKS

The following names are trademarked products of the corresponding companies.

Cordata LP300 ™	Cordata
DisplayWrite™	International Business Machines Corporation
DisplayWrite 2™	International Business Machines Corporation
DisplayWrite 3™	International Business Machines Corporation
Fancy Font®	SoftCraft, Inc.
Fancy Word™	SoftCraft, Inc.
Hercules™	Hercules Computer
Hewlett-Packard®	Hewlett-Packard Company
Inset™	American Programmers Guild
KEYPORT 60™	Polytel Computer Products Corporation
KEYPORT 300™	Polytel Computer Products Corporation
LaserJet PLUS™	Hewlett-Packard Company
LaserJet 500™	Hewlett-Packard Company
MicroLynx™	Honeywell Corporation
Microsoft®	Microsoft Corporation
Microsoft Mouse™	Microsoft Corporation
Mouse Systems™	Mouse Systems Corporation
MultiMate®	MultiMate International Corporation, an Ashton Tate company
Pagemaker™	Aldus Corporation
Pop-Ups™	Popular Programs, Inc.

PostScript™	Adobe Systems, Inc.
Procomm™	PIL Software Systems
Qume LaserTen™	Qume Corporation
Qume LaserTen Plus™	Qume Corporation
QumeII™	Qume Corporation
Ready!™	Living Videotext, Inc.
Scriptor™	Screenplay Systems
SideKick®	Borland International, Inc.
Softstrip®	Cauzin Systems, Inc.
WORD®	Microsoft Corporation
Word Count™	Software Heaven, Inc.
WordPerfect™	Satellite Software International
WordStar®	MicroPro, Inc.

INDEX

The manuscript for this book was prepared and submitted to Osborne/McGraw-Hill in electronic form.

The acquisitions editor for this project was Jean Stein. The technical reviewer was Stephen Cobb of Applied Computer Consulting, Oakland, California. Lyn Cordell was the project editor.

Text design is by Pamela Webster using Baskerville for both text and display.

All figures in this book were produced using a Cordata LP300 Laser Printer.

Cover art is by Bay Graphics Design Associates. Cover supplier is Phoenix Color Corporation. This book was printed and bound by R. R. Donnelley & Sons Company, Crawfordsville, Indiana.

Related Osborne/McGraw-Hill titles include:

Desktop Publishing From A to Z
by Bill Grout, Irene Athanasopoulos, and Rebecca Kutlin

As a desktop publisher, you can use your microcomputer to create your own newsletters, catalogs, conference brochures, news releases, and more. *Desktop Publishing From A to Z* helps you choose the software, equipment, and procedures you need to achieve professional results. Grout discusses software packages and hardware that are available for desktop publishing, from project-management programs to page makeup programs, from the Macintosh™ and the IBM®PC to the LaserWriter™ printer. You'll find out how to establish a publishing plan, control costs and profits, handle printing and binding, promotion, and distribution.

$17.95p
0-07-881212-7, 225 pp., 7⅜ x 9¼

Using dBASE III® PLUS™
by Edward Jones

Osborne's top-selling title, *Using dBASE III,*® by Edward Jones, has now been updated to include Ashton-Tate's new upgrade, dBASE III®PLUS™ With Jones' expertise you'll be in full command of all the new features of this powerful database software. Learn to design, create, and display a dBASE III PLUS database, devise entry forms with the dBASE III PLUS screen painter, generate reports, use Query files, and plug into dBASE III PLUS networking. In addition, you'll find out how to install dBASE III PLUS on a hard disk, conduct data searches, and manipulate assistant pull-down menus. *Using dBASE III® PLUS™* is a thorough and practical handbook for both beginning and experienced dBASE III users.

$18.95
0-07-881252-6, 350 pp., 7⅜ x 9¼

The Osborne/McGraw-Hill Guide to Using Lotus™ 1-2-3,™ Second Edition, Covers Release 2
by Edward M. Baras

Your investment in Lotus™1-2-3™ can yield the most productive returns possible with the tips and practical information in *The Osborne/McGraw-Hill Guide to Using Lotus™ 1-2-3.™* Now the second edition of this acclaimed bestseller helps you take full advantage of Lotus' new 1-2-3 upgrade, Release 2. This comprehensive guide offers a thorough presentation of the worksheet, database, and graphics functions. In addition, the revised text shows you how to create and use macros, string functions, and many other sophisticated 1-2-3 features. Step by step, you'll learn to implement 1-2-3 techniques as you follow application models for financial forecasting, stock portfolio tracking, and forms-oriented database management. For both beginners and experienced users, this tutorial quickly progresses from fundamental procedures to advanced applications.

$18.95p
0-07-881230-5, 432 pp., 7⅜ x 9¼

Financial Modeling Using Lotus™ 1-2-3,™ Covers Release 2
by Charles W. Kyd

Readers of Kyd's monthly "Accounting" column in *Lotus™* magazine already know how helpful his 1-2-3™ tips can be. Now his *Financial Modeling Using Lotus™1-2-3™* shows experienced users how to set up a data bank that can be used by everyone in the office to make more effective use of numerous financial applications. Kyd provides models for managing the balance sheet, controlling growth, handling income statements and management accounting, using Z scores for business forecasts, and more. Each model features a summary of 1-2-3 techniques, including helpful information for using the new Release 2, and explains the financial theories behind the application. You'll also find out how data for many of these financial models can be shared in the office data bank, creating an even greater resource for business productivity.

$16.95p
0-07-881213-5, 225 pp., 7⅜ x 9¼

The Advanced Guide to Lotus™ 1-2-3™
by Edward M. Baras

Edward Baras, Lotus expert and author of *The Symphony™ Book, Symphony™ Master,* and *The Jazz™ Book,* now has a sequel to his bestselling *Osborne/McGraw-Hill Guide to Using Lotus™ 1-2-3.™* For experienced users, *The Advanced Guide to Lotus 1-2-3* delves into more powerful and complex techniques using the newest software upgrade, Release 2. Added enhancements to 1-2-3's macro language, as well as many new functions and commands, are described and thoroughly illustrated in business applications. Baras shows you how to take advantage of Release 2's macro capabilities by programming 1-2-3 to simulate Symphony's keystroke-recording features and by processing ASCII files automatically. You'll also learn to set up your own command menus; use depreciation functions, matric manipulation, and regression analysis; and convert text files to the 1-2-3 worksheet format.

$18.95p
0-07-881237-2, 325 pp., 7⅜ x 9¼

PC Secrets: Tips for Power Performance
by James E. Kelley

Power performance is at your command with these secrets for mastering the PC. This collection of shortcuts and solutions to frustrating and frequently encountered problems gives users of the IBM® PC and PC compatibles the inside edge. James Kelley, author of numerous books on the IBM PC, discloses his secrets for controlling hardware, peripherals, DOS, and applications software. You'll learn tips for keyboard harmonics, display enhancements, controlling fixed disks, managing the printer, and manipulating DOS routines that include batch files, directories and subdirectories, as well as system menus. You'll also find programs that help you use WordStar® and Lotus™ 1-2-3™ to greater advantage. With *PC Secrets*, you don't need to be a technical expert to become a PC power user.

$16.95 p
0-07-881210-0, 224 pp., 7³⁄₈ x 9¹⁄₄

PC-DOS Tips & Traps
by Dick Andersen, Janice M. Gessin, Fred Warren, and Jack Rodgers

Solve immediate problems and quickly perform specific business tasks on your IBM® PC or PC-compatible with *PC-DOS Tips & Traps*. Written for everyone using PC-DOS 2.1 or MS-DOS 2.11, Andersen provides an array of tips and discusses frequently encountered traps with their solutions. You'll find a broad range of helpful information from initializing your system and formatting disks, to controlling peripherals, and managing the DOS environment. Throughout the book Andersen shows you how to use the DOS Batch files to design your own commands and automate certain tasks. Tips for using DOS utilities including EDLIN for text editing and DEBUG for programming are also discussed. You'll save time and minimize the chance for error with Andersen's insights on the PC- and MS-DOS® operating systems.

$16.95 p
0-07-881194-5, 250 pp., 7³⁄₈ x 9¹⁄₄

Project Management Using Microcomputers
by Harvey A. Levine

Business professionals in all fields can make informed decisions about the best project management software available for their specific needs with the essential information in this guide. Levine discusses state-of-the-art project management techniques that can be applied to every business and to most computer systems. Beginning with an overview of project management, Levine considers the role of the microcomputer in this application. Various capabilities of project management software are then discussed: resource and cost planning, reporting and graphing, scheduling, and tracking. To give you a better idea of how project management software can be used, Levine divides applications into elementary, intermediate, custom designed, and mass-market categories. Every category offers project management examples, each contributed by an industry expert who discusses the reasons and methods behind the application.

$18.95 p
0-07-881221-6, 350 pp., 7³⁄₈ x 9¹⁄₄

Available at fine bookstores and computer stores everywhere.

For a complimentary catalog of all our current publications contact: Osborne/McGraw-Hill, 2600 Tenth Street, Berkeley, CA 94710.

Phone inquiries may be made using our toll-free number. Call 800-227-0900 or 800-772-2531 (in California). TWX 910-366-7277.

Prices subject to change without notice.